TEN COMMANDMENTS FOR CHURCH REFORM

Ten Commandments for Church Reform

Memoirs of a Catholic Priest

John Wijngaards, DD, LSS

Acadian House
PUBLISHING
Lafayette, Louisiana, USA

Library of Congress Control Number: 2021940982

ISBN 10: 1-7352641-5-6
ISBN 13: 978-1-7352641-5-8

♦ Published by Acadian House Publishing, Lafayette, Louisiana
  (Edited by Trent Angers; editorial assistance and research by Madison Louviere)
♦ Design and pre-press production by Allison Nassans
♦ Printed by Sheridan Books, Chelsea, Michigan

I dedicate this book to Jackie Clackson,
my dear friend, partner in mission,
and loving wife.

Prologue

On a summer's day in 1994 I stepped through the opening doors of a small restaurant in Louvain, Belgium, to meet up with a few people I had gotten to know while doing mission work in India. They were two priests and three religious sisters, all taking courses at the local Catholic University. The five of them hailed from the Indian state of Andhra Pradesh, where I had lived and worked as a Mill Hill Missionary priest for many years.

One of the sisters I did not recognise. She was in her twenties, wore long black hair that, unusually for a religious sister, cascaded down her saffron-coloured sari. She looked at me with sparkling brown eyes and introduced herself. I will call her "Preeti Gunta" to preserve her anonymity.

When I asked her where exactly she was from, she dropped a bombshell.

"I am from Gôpuram, a little village in the Diocese of Warangal," she replied.

I was more than surprised to hear that because I had been in her village nearly 20 years earlier and may very well have been the one who baptized her and gave her First Communion when she was a child.

As we sat down to talk, my mind was flooded with dramatic memories.

I vividly remembered the day in January of 1976 when I had visited her village. I went there with a local parish priest, Father Govindu Joji, who happened to be one of my former students.

We had left by jeep early in the morning, making our way along narrow sandy tracks through cotton fields, crossing the shallow, muddy waters of a monsoon-starved river, till we reached the tiny hamlet. Children came running out of their mud-and-palm leaf huts to greet us. I was told later that this was the first time a car had been seen in the village, though local priests had come previously on motorbikes.

The occasion we had come for was momentous indeed. We were to baptise the first Christians in the village: 350 catechumens who for two years had been instructed on Christian faith by a resident part-time lay catechist. He would call them together after their work on local farms, in tanneries and weaveries. Fr. Joji and a team of religious sisters had also visited the village on a regular basis.

Now, all of the catechumens, including Preeti, were "outcasts," that is, they belonged to the Mala and Madiga Dalit castes, 120 families in total. Although the Indian constitution acknowledges all Indian citizens as equal, and governments have tried to put protections in place, the Malas and Madigas were still treated with contempt by many members of the "higher" castes. In many villages they were routinely beaten up or even killed when they tried to draw water from a well that was traditionally reserved to higher castes.

After the exhausting 3-hour ceremony – which included a Mass and Holy Communion for all – I visited the home of one of our new Christian families. It was a dilapidated hut, not much better than a lean-to shack. Mud walls, palm leaves on the roof. A tiny fireplace in one corner, producing smoke that could escape through a hole in the roof. Mats on the floor on which family members would sleep at night. A beam running from opposite walls on which a sari hung to dry. A small trunk that held the family treasures.

And this was the place Sister Preeti Gunta came from. I realised she was a child years earlier when I assisted at the Baptism, one of those wild, scantily clad boys and girls with black hair who had jumped around me on that memorable day in her village.

Preeti told me that she had attended primary school at the parish headquarters, staying at a hostel for girls run by the sisters. She had then gone to high school in a nearby town. After that she had studied in college before joining a religious society.

"I'm now studying theology here at Louvain," she told me. "I will probably be appointed a lecturer in our regional juniorate."

I must tell you, I was moved to see how far she had come. What a transformation! What a success story! What progress!

I felt a glow of satisfaction that I had, in a small way, been able to contribute to giving her a better life, to releasing her full potential as a human being. I felt proud of belonging to the Catholic Church which, in this way, restores human dignity to millions of men and women around the globe.

And then Preeti dropped a second bombshell:

"I read your book, *Did Christ Rule Out Women Priests?*," she said. "Well, I have not told many people... I don't know how to put this... but I myself actually feel called to be a priest. Do you think it will happen? The Pope seems to be against it."

"Yes," I stammered. "Women will be ordained priests in the Catholic Church. But with Rome refusing to budge, this will take a longer time to come about."

My dismay arose from the fact that just a few months earlier Pope John Paul II had published his apostolic letter *Ordinatio Sacerdotalis*. In it, he had laid down that reserving Holy Orders to men was a "definitive" teaching that should be held by all the faithful. The Pope blamed Jesus for the exclusion of women from the priesthood – totally ignoring the evidence that proves the exclusion was due to social prejudice. Moreover, Pope John Paul II had a few years earlier, in his 1988 encyclical *Mulieris Dignitatem*, rooted the exclusion of women even deeper.

He stated that God the Father had planned from the beginning that his Son should not just become human, but that he should be male, a man. Thereby, the Pope reasoned, men were empowered for spiritual leadership in the Church, whilst women were relegated to a supportive, maternal, nurturing role.

As Preeti and I talked, disappointment boiled up in me. Even anger.

True, the Church had helped liberate her from a life of illiterate servitude and poverty. But now the same Church was denying Preeti her full dignity as a child of God, created in his image, sharing in Jesus' priesthood and royal status through the Baptism she had received.

"The Pope has got it dreadfully wrong," I told the group sitting around the table. "It is now up to us as leaders in the Church to put this right."

"Maybe," one of the young priests objected. "Perhaps we shouldn't worry too much. Those changes will come by themselves. Think of the mustard seed which sprouts and grows so large, in due time, that the birds of the air rest on its branches, as the Gospel teaches. Yes, we may disagree with the Pope, but if we say so in public we may lose our job, as one of our professors has warned us."

"Nonsense," I told him. "Changes will not come by themselves. Of course, they take time, but we have to work the field before we can harvest. We have to fight if we want changes to come about."

"Ah," he retorted. "You know the old saying: 'A sheep doesn't argue with his shepherd.'"

"And that's the trouble," Preeti remarked. "The Church treats us like children."

Reduced to being children? This thought stayed with me. That evening in my hotel room before falling asleep I recalled what my grandfather had taught me. I had gotten to know him, my father's father, in the Netherlands when I was ten years old, just after World War II. He had been a cavalry officer in the Dutch army. I remember him as a short and well-built man. His blue eyes would look into mine inquisitively, his bristly brown moustache trembling as he asked me searching questions. His left hand would rest on top of his walking stick, his right hand fiddling with his watch-chain.

Grandad rarely lectured me, but when he did, he would throw in a maxim, some words of wisdom such as "Eye on the target, finger on the trigger, my boy!" or "Never lick anyone's boots, not even those of your commanding officer!"

His poignant advice, coupled with the independent thinking I would learn from my mother, would have a major impact on the way I saw the world – and the Church – in the years ahead.

Preface

For most of my adult life, I've worked for the Church and its people. While on this decades-long journey, much of it as a Mill Hill missionary, I've seen and experienced the tremendous good that the Church has done. We've built schools and churches and prayer huts, administered the sacraments, brought tens of thousands into the fold of Christianity. We've fed the hungry, sheltered the homeless, counselled the doubtful, comforted the sorrowful, and brought hope to the hopeless.

And while going through life as a student, teacher, theologian, and priest, I have observed a number of areas in the universal Church that are sorely in need of reform. These needs manifested themselves one at a time over many years. For example, I see a need for the appointment of open-minded, pastoral bishops, not hard-line traditionalists. I see a need, as clear as day, to allow women into the ranks of the Catholic diaconate and priesthood. And I see a glaring need for the Church just to listen – to the people, to the scholars, the pastoral councils, and experienced pastors.

In all, I've identified ten specific areas of needed reform that would make the Church more effective, more inclusive, more Christ-like. And I call these my "Ten Commandments for Church Reform."

These "commandments" flow not only from my intimate dealings with the Church as a priest, but from my love and concern for the Church and the people it is intended to serve. I have always had the Church's best interests at heart, as you will see on the following pages.

Rather than telling the story of my life in strict chronological order, I will narrate it in five "waves," corresponding to my shifting focus in more or less successive phases.

Part I: Learning to think for myself (1941-63)

I did not attend any primary school. Instead I spent 4½ years in Japanese prisoners-of-war camps after I turned six years old.

Paradoxically, it proved beneficial, in the sense that I learned how to survive using my own mind. After the war, first in Thailand then in the Netherlands, I had to make up for lost education in record time. Then, deciding I would study for the priesthood, I attended high schools and colleges both in the Netherlands and England. After ordination I studied at the Gregorian University and the

Pontifical Biblical Institute, both in Rome.

Those 20 years of education transformed me. Yes, I picked up quite a load of professional learning. Most of all, I gradually discovered, and then strongly affirmed, my ability to think and to make up my own mind. When God created us humans, he crafted us "in his own image." He did so in part by giving us the power of reason. As such, we can examine and understand our own world and take responsibility for it. I realised soon that not all assertions and rulings by Church officials could be trusted.

To recapture just one experience, one of my theology professors in London taught us: "Don't ever believe this nonsense called 'evolution'. Some scientists... claim they can determine the age of a skeleton by just looking at a jawbone! But we know by adding up the ages of the patriarchs and kings from creation till now that the world was created in the year 4004 B.C." Do I need to say more?

Part II: On the front line (1964-82)

Having obtained my qualifications in Rome, I was then appointed to be professor of Scripture at St. John's Major Seminary in Hyderabad, India. The Catholic dioceses in that part of India witnessed phenomenal expansion at the time. They lacked essential infrastructure. It gave me the chance to be creative in a number of fields, next to my heavy duties in the college. I founded Amruthavani, a centre with departments for book production, a weekly newspaper, correspondence courses, radio and TV programmes, all through the Telugu language. I set up the Jyotirmai network, through which local dioceses could get financial support from European aid agencies for prayer huts in outstations, boardings for school children, motorbikes for priests, milk-giving buffaloes and sewing machines to give catechists another source of income. I established Jeevan Jyothi, a theological college for religious sisters. Then, in 1976, I was elected Vicar General of the Mill Hill Missionaries, which gave me a role in building up mission in all continents.

Battling on the front, I often felt like a soldier betrayed by top command at the rear. I became increasingly aware of the damage done to the Catholic community all over the world by negative policies emanating from Rome. I vividly recall a priest from Mangalore in India preaching during the celebration at which he had been ordained a new bishop: "Vatican II is the greatest disaster that has ever befallen our Church. I'll spend all my energy to eradicate its pernicious teachings from my diocese, and from the rest of the country!"

Part III: Fighting the 'anti-sex' bug in the Church (1964-86)

At the same time as all this was going on, I detected a spiritual "virus." It fatally undermined Catholic persuasions and practice. It ruined inner peace in many people's lives. It underlay mistaken church rulings such as the prohibition of all artificial contraception, the imposition of celibacy on all priests in the Latin rite, and even the exclusion of women from Holy Orders. It was the "anti-sex" bug which considers all sexuality somehow tainted by sin. On doing research, I discovered that Church father St. Augustine is largely responsible for this most unchristian form of thinking.

The operation of this bug may well be demonstrated in experiences I had with the Peace Corps, a movement of young volunteers set up by President Kennedy to help development in third-world countries. In my part of India they provided excellent professional advice to villages on how to improve their crops. But in other ways they were ill-prepared. In the coastal town of Masulipatnam I saw a group of young American women walking 'round in bikinis (!) in the middle of a steamingly hot day. It was a shock and horror to the Indian sense of modesty for women.

One of them, a young Catholic girl, came to consult me in a panic. During a lonely night she had got close to a young comrade and became pregnant. She feared that her family at home would be outraged. To minimise the damage, she persuaded her casual partner to marry her before she would return to the United States. But he was not a Catholic. The couple asked me to marry them. It would need special dispensation. A long story followed. The archbishop of Hyderabad gave me permission to bless their mixed wedding. But while corresponding with U.S. authorities for other necessary documents, I found out that the boy and the girl had already fallen out. One root cause was that she had never been properly instructed on anything related to sexuality.

Part IV: Helping Catholics become adult believers (1983-98)

In 1983 Jackie Clackson and I established Housetop Centre for adult faith formation. We counselled families caught up in the new-fangled sects and cults. We designed and produced the *Walking on Water* video courses. At the same time, I taught at the Missionary Institute of London. I conducted six-months lecture tours in India annually for ten years. Our apostolate consisted in a wide span of ministries. The target audiences ranged from priests and religious sisters to groups of lay parishioners, college students, and families at home. All of them had as their main objective "adult faith" formation.

To grasp the significance of "adult faith," consider the case of an Irish mother and her three daughters. I still see her sitting before me in front of my desk: tall and lean, wearing a dark green dress, curly brown hair encircling two anxious blue eyes. She had come to England when the girls were still teenagers, she told me. At that time they still attended Sunday Mass. But after finishing college, taking various jobs and now living on their own, they stopped practising.

"I don't know what to do!" she said. "They're not bothered."

There was very little that could be done at that moment. Intervention came quite late. Many Irish immigrants, who had been faithful churchgoers in their native communities, gave up on their religion when settling in England. They were so-called "born Catholics." Religion was taken for granted. Catechetical instructions and sermons had been part of peripheral childhood convention. In other words, faith had not been "a personal conquest of truth," to echo Cardinal Newman's writing, not one's own adult decision based on study, reflection, then conviction. But such a process requires the licence to doubt, to question, to ask for reasons, a freedom church authorities usually were not willing to grant.

Part V: The clash – and renewed resolve (1998-now)

Throughout my priestly career I had publicly expressed my disagreement with outdated decrees issued from Rome. In 1994 it came to a head. Pope John Paul II declared it to be *definitive* doctrine that Jesus had excluded women from Holy Orders for all time to come. I knew he was wrong. Then, in 1998, he attempted to insert it into the "Profession of Faith and Oath of Fidelity" that is demanded of bishops, priests, lecturers – in fact, anyone assuming an official position in the Church.

And to cap it all, Cardinal Joseph Ratzinger, Prefect of the Congregation for Doctrine, who was later to become Pope Benedict XVI, insisted that this meant that everyone who still believed women could or should be ordained was no longer in full communion with the Church. In brief: they were excommunicated!

This affected me personally, but also the millions upon millions of Catholics who like me, for good reasons, were convinced women *should* be admitted to Holy Orders. I could not, in conscience, just ignore this. It was the last straw. Subsequently, I resigned from the priestly ministry.

Throughout my story I will highlight what the Church needs to do, how it needs to change, in order to throw off its medieval cloak and update itself for our century. In the process, I will disclose what I consider to be the *Ten Commandments for Church Reform,* one at a time. Hopefully, you will see how these changes for the better will breathe new life into a Church that has been stuck in the Middle Ages for far too long.

Table of Contents

Chapter 1

What?!
Me trying to reform
the Catholic Church?

*M*y birthplace was the busy harbour town of Surabaya in Indonesia. Both my parents came from the Netherlands. As headmaster of St. Stanislaus Catholic school, my father ran both the Dutch- and Malay-speaking sections. On weekends my parents would look after an "outstation" for the parish, laying out the priest's vestments on a make-shift altar and preparing the small local congregation for the celebration of the Eucharist in one of the school's halls.

I was born on a steamy monsoon day in St. Vincent de Paul Hospital on September 30, 1935. I understand that the hospital offered little comfort to a mum of 28 about to deliver her second son at a time when sedation at childbirth was not an option.

My mother, who had been in labour all day, was finally wheeled into a small delivery room. There I saw the daylight at 7 p.m. I say "daylight" metaphorically speaking, of course, for Surabaya lies almost smack on the equator, and night falls promptly at six. At the hour I was born, the world around me lay wrapped in darkness. All I could have seen, to the extent my eyes had been geared to seeing, was an electric bulb swinging from the ceiling, faintly illuminating my mother and the religious sister who acted as midwife.

My mother remembered my birth very well. For one thing, she told me, it had been a comparatively easy birth. My older brother, Carel, had been pulled out through the narrow birth canal with the use of forceps. It deformed his skull for good, leaving his head elongated, as you see among some tribal people in Africa. The next son to be born after me, Niek, didn't breathe for ten minutes after his umbilical cord had been cut. He turned blue and purple, my mother said. He was suffocating before her eyes. A doctor saved his life by literally swinging him around like a cricket bat. So I was lucky.

When my mother had been wheeled back to the ward, she asked a religious sister to bring her Holy Communion the next day, as was her custom. My parents were devout Catholics and daily communicants whenever possible.

"Out of the question!" the sister said, refusing to put her on the list to receive Communion.

"You have not been churched!" the sister stated.

My mother and father with Carel on the right and me on the left, circa 1936.

Those were the days when "churching" was still practiced by Catholics in many countries. This atrocious custom was the outcome of ancient fears surrounding childbirth joined to medieval prejudice based on Leviticus 12,2-8. After childbirth a woman was deemed unclean. A young mum would present herself 40 days after delivery at the church door with a lighted candle in one hand and an offering in the other. Only when a priest had blessed her, thus purifying her from all menstrual stains, could she again participate in the Eucharist. It also meant that a mother was usually prevented from attending the Baptism of her newborn child, which took place in church soon after birth.

My mother, who had seen her own mum being churched many a time, had sworn she herself would never submit to the rite.

"I don't want to be churched," she asserted.

"But you're unclean. You don't want to disgrace the Blessed Sacrament, do you?"

"I've just done the most wonderful thing in my life and given birth to another child," my mother retorted. "Why would I need to be cleansed?"

The sister did not want to give in. Nor did my mother. She insisted that the parish priest be called. Father Jan Zoetmuller of Sacred Heart Parish dutifully arrived.

More words followed as he, too, tried to persuade her.

To no avail. My mother insisted that he bring her Communion as before.

Next morning, on Tuesday October 1, my mother received Holy Communion as usual. Soon afterwards the parish priest baptised me in the small chapel of the hospital. And, at her strong insistence, my mother was present.

Can the Church be reformed?

I am narrating my mother's conflict with Church authorities on the occasion of my birth with a purpose: It foreshadows the story of my life.

Think about it. My mother was a strong believer and a committed Catholic. Why else would she have bothered? She wanted to receive Holy Communion the next day, as usual. It meant a lot to her. On the other hand, she felt in her bones that "churching" was wrong. How did she know? She had never been told by anyone. She had not enjoyed any theological formation, only traditional catechism classes taught by the nuns at school. Yet she totally rejected an outdated practice defended by Church authorities. She knew she was right by her deep-seated Catholic "sense of faith" and by trusting her own intelligence.

In other words, my mother possessed the kind of critical Catholic loyalty that alone can save the Church. It has also characterised my own life. I have never downgraded the core of our Christian faith, nor the role of reliable leadership in the Christian community. At the same time, I have always challenged outdated beliefs and practices still imposed by authority.

The Church, let's be honest, faces a huge crisis. If we look at the global picture, educated Catholics are draining away every year in the millions, mainly the younger generations. Elderly clergy celebrate Sunday Masses for half-empty churches.

Church authority has lost much of its credibility. Even weekly churchgoers reject the official guidance offered by Pope, bishops and priests on several matters. More than 80 percent approve the use of artificial contraceptives in family planning, against church rules. A vast majority welcome homosexual couples in spite of official Church condemnation. There is massive support in the pews for allowing priests to marry. In the child-abuse scandal, Church leaders ignored the appeal of victims; their main concern was seen by the public as trying to protect the good name of corrupt members of the institution.

Large sections of the Church community are alienated. Women, rightly, feel offended because against all common sense and theological perception, they are excluded from Holy Orders. The often shallow and trivial homilies preached at Mass appal teenagers, who are exposed to sophisticated discussion-oriented education in high school or college.

Moreover, Church leaders fail to implement the recommendations of the Second Vatican Council. They cling to their model of a top-down hierarchy ruling the lives of a dependent laity, instead of introducing the "collegial responsibility" at all levels that the Council prescribed. They do not seem to welcome the good values of our modern world praised by the Council: honesty, a willingness to embrace progress, and accountability.

We are all part of the Church, and responsible for its well-being. I am confident that all of us together can save it. We can give the Church new life, bring about its authentic reform, its caterpillar-to-butterfly transformation. Such renovations of the Church have happened in previous centuries. We can make it happen again.

Part I

Learning to think for myself

Chapter 2

Into the gaping jaws of war

War broke out in the Pacific when I was six years old. It would force me to become an adult in record time. It all started on Sunday December 7, 1941, a day I recall with remarkable detail.

At the time, we lived in Malang, Indonesia, a hill town nestled between the slopes of mounts Kelud, Kawi and Smeru, all active volcanoes. We had attended Mass that morning, as a family, in the Cathedral Church of St. Mary of Carmel. The church lay only ten minutes' walk from our house. I had three brothers at the time: Carel, one year older than me; Niek, who was three; and Aloys, just a few months old.

While my mother was getting lunch ready, my father listened to the radio. The news was so alarming that he called all of us together.

"The Japanese have bombed Pearl Harbor!" he kept saying. "They have attacked the American fleet!" The Governor General of the Dutch East Indies broadcast the message that we, too, were now at war with Japan.

I did not understand exactly what was going on, of course, but I could see something terrible had happened. My mother cried. My father put on his military uniform and readied his khaki rucksack and rifle. All army personnel were called up immediately, including reservists, as he was. That same afternoon my father departed for his barracks after saying a fond farewell. Meanwhile the radio kept blaring out bulletins that became more distressing by the hour. The name "Pearl Harbor," which was bandied about hundreds of times during that day, engraved itself on my consciousness as a dreadful disaster.

Events now moved fast. Within weeks the Japanese closed in on Indonesia, whose rich resources were one of their prime objectives. Cities were bombed. Malang, too, was subjected to air attacks by fighter planes which strafed the streets and busy markets. I remember us huddled in a muddy make-shift air raid shelter in our back garden hearing the whining of the planes overhead and the explosions all around us. The fighters and bombers flew in from aircraft carriers stationed south of Java, as I now know from reading about it.

The first town to fall, on January 23, was Balikpapan, with all its oil refineries. "Balikpapan" is another disaster name etched on my youthful memory. I

My father, third from left, on the parade ground preparing for war, December 1941.

knew it was the writing on the wall for us. On February 27 the Japanese sank the Dutch navy in the Java Sea. Next day they invaded Java itself with overwhelming force. The Dutch East Indies government surrendered on March 9 and soon Japanese troops swarmed all over Malang. All Dutch soldiers including my father were immediately confined to prisoner-of-war camps. We saw him a final time before he disappeared from our radar.

Dutch women and children, too, had to register as enemies. We were moved into a fenced off part of Malang which became our first camp, known as the *Bergenbuurt*. We now lived with two other families crowded into one house. Ever more stringent limits were put on our freedoms. There were daily threats. Rations were tightened. However, compared to the other camps we would inhabit later, this was heaven on earth.

But before we come to that, I need to say a word about my inner life. It was during this time that I was becoming conscious of "being myself."

This may sound odd and I find it hard to describe. For instance, I still see myself, young though I was, standing all alone in the dark hallway of our house. I had just been involved in an exciting game of cops and robbers with a gang of youngsters like myself. I stood in the hallway, leaning against the wall, still panting and gasping for air. Suddenly, like a flash, a thought overwhelmed me: "I am me. I am alive." Somehow I grasped its significance and I eagerly confirmed it. Yes, I was me. And I jolly well would take control of my own life – which would prove to be easier said than done.

Being 'broken in'

My mother could be the kindest soul on earth. She also subscribed to discipline. She saw to it that as soon as we could crawl and toddle, we were potty-trained. No nonsense at table either. We were taught to eat the *nasitim*, rice porridge for infants, that was put before us. We were made to finish it till the last spoonful. We learned how to put on our own shorts and shirts. The first time each one of us tied and knotted his shoelaces by himself we were rewarded with a hug and a handful of sweets. When we played with toys, mother expected us afterwards to clear up the mess by ourselves. But control leads to clashes.

Her worst conflict with me, my mother told me later, had happened two years earlier. Every morning when she woke me she would lift me out of my cot, sit down on a chair with me on her lap, and make me say a prayer. I had to fold my hands, close my eyes and repeat a short prayerful rhyme after her. One day I refused to say my prayer. She kissed me and explained that Jesus was watching us and that I should say "good morning" to him.

"No!" I said.

My mother was taken aback and decided that she should use her parental authority. She ordered me to pray.

"No!" I said.

My mother put me back and called upon my father for support. He, too, failed to make me comply.

Then my mother told me that I would not get anything to eat or drink until I agreed to say my prayer.

"No!" I said.

She came back once or twice every hour to repeat her demand. No prayer, no food!

Tearfully but stubbornly I kept saying "No!"

It was only late in the afternoon, after eight long hours, that I gave in, my mother recalled. She was amazed I could defy her for so long. None of her other four sons had ever challenged her like that. From the way she talked, I surmised that she considered the whole episode a minor victory in her effort to tame a wild stallion.

I myself do not remember the incident for I was too young at the time, but I have often wondered whether the heavy-handed way in which my mother forced me to "surrender" did not leave a scar on my sense of autonomy. It probably shaped how I related to my mother: utter devotion hid an undercurrent of resentful rebellion. On reflection this ambiguous bond with my mother foreshadowed a similar relationship I would have with Mother Church.

During the early months of the war, my mother and I clashed again in an incident I will never forget. It happened during an afternoon siesta, as was customary in Indonesia. Carel and I shared a bed in our downstairs bedroom. Rays of the tropical sun penetrated through the drawn curtains and cast everything in a glow of shimmering light. Carel and I could not sleep, and suddenly – I do not know why – we jumped out of bed, threw off our pajamas and started to dance around stark naked. We laughed and sang and hopped around on our bare feet.

I still recall the utter exhilaration I felt, the total abandon, the excitement of being body, the thrill of complete freedom. In fact, we were getting ready to waltz as naked as we were out of the room and onto the street. However, my mother heard the commotion. She entered the room and was horrified to see the state we were in.

Later I would find out from her how in her family home in Apeldoorn, nakedness had been completely *tabu*. Every nude body was a lewd body. This called for special measures in a household of nine children, five boys and four girls, crammed into three bedrooms. Every night all lights were switched off whenever anyone was undressing. Pajamas were put on in the dark. And whenever my grandfather went on a cycling tour with some of the older children along the Apeldoorn Canal, he would cycle ahead. On seeing bare-chested men swimming in the canal, he would shout the warning: "All of you, look away!" Nakedness should not be seen. It was bad enough having to carry a naked body under your clothes!

The specter of Carel and I dancing naked filled my mother with forebodings and thoughts of future sexual debauchery. She called us to order, her face clouded over with anxiety and distress. She made us dress. She lectured us.

"Naughty, naughty boys!" she said. "You should be ashamed of yourselves!" And pointing to a picture of Jesus on the wall: "See, Jesus is crying. He feels embarrassed looking at you!"

And she explained how being naked was dirty, smutty, sinful.

Her reaction stunned me. I knew I had committed an unspeakable crime.

Three months later, as a pupil of the nursery school run by Ursuline Sisters, I was chosen to be one of the sheep in the Christmas play. I steadfastly refused to undress, ignoring the pleas of the nun in charge. I insisted on putting on the sheep's skin over all my clothes in spite of the hot weather. I would not reveal my naked body again! The repression of my sexuality had successfully been set in motion. It would reign supreme for many decades to come.

Carel and I were admitted to first Holy Communion amidst growing rumours that everyone was to be transferred to another camp. Meanwhile, we received preparatory instructions on Holy Communion. On the day before the great event, I made my first confession - which no doubt featured my antics in the nude.

The celebration of First Communion itself made a deep impression on me. We were all dressed in white, the girls among us wearing flowers in their hair.

The church had been beautifully decorated. And in the midst of it all: the magic moment itself, meeting God in an intimate encounter of prayer. Unforgettable.

Mankubumen camp

On May 25, 1943, the Japanese rounded us up. Every person was allowed to bring along only a small bag with belongings. This was a shock to my mother, who had hoped that she could rescue some of the provisions of food she had thoughtfully piled up. There were five of us: my mother and four young sons. Carel and I were considered old enough to carry a bag.

The Japs transported us in military trucks to Malang Station. There they loaded us onto trains and sent us on our way. The windows of the carriages had been boarded up so we did not know where we were going. We endured ten long hours in a searingly hot murky compartment with little to drink or eat.

Late that night we were disgorged at Surakarta, in Central Java.

Confusion at the station. My mother managed to keep us together as we were marched to our camp. She carried baby Aloys on her left arm, holding the main bag of our belongings in her right hand. Three-year-old Niek stumbled along, holding Mother by her skirt. Carel and I followed, each clutching a precious bag. Everything in the dark. Guards shouting at us and pushing us along with their rifle butts. Stumbling over obstacles, falling and crawling up again. I recall that night so well. In the middle of all the confusion I clutched the bag my mother had entrusted to me.

We entered the camp. People were assigned to barracks, first come first served. We were crowded into a ramshackle narrow shack made of bamboo with ten other families. A long, low wooden bunk along one wall served as our common bed. Space was meticulously measured out on it: 50 centimeters [approximately 1½ feet] of width per person. Finally, we could lie down in our own small home in the world. All five of us shared the same flimsy mattress and mosquito curtain which my mother had managed to bring along.

Mankubumen camp, also known as *Bhumi* camp, in the middle of Surakarta, housed 4,000 prisoners. Conditions defy description. Rats, bed bugs and termites infested the barracks. No clean water. Dirty latrines. The Japs considered us cheap labour. My mother worked on construction and paving roads. Children, too, had to work. I remember Carel and I toiling in a barren field with rows of boys of our age, preparing it for cultivation by removing stones and flattening clods of earth by hand.

But the worst by far was the lack of food.

The food was prepared in a central kitchen. We received only one meal a day in our tin bowl: a portion of boiled rice with curry, just one small ladleful for each person. Mornings and evenings we were given one tablespoonful of tapioca flour in our bowl. Hot water was poured onto the flour, producing a watery jelly

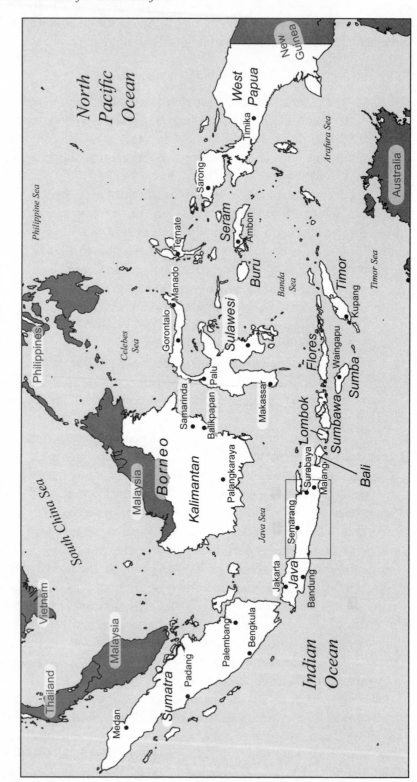

Indonesia
(Formerly known as the Dutch East Indies)

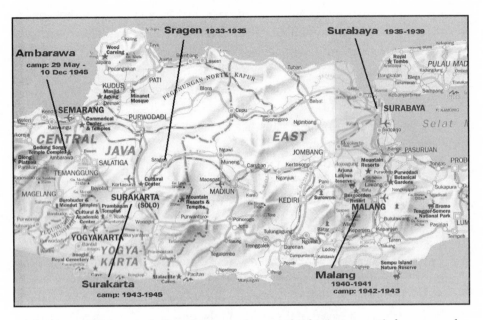

Map (corresponding to the boxed area on the map on the facing page) shows several cities in Indonesia where my family lived, as well as the POW camps where we were held captive during World War II; note the dates with the various locations.

◄ Indonesia, previously known as the Dutch East Indies (until 1949), is where I was born – Surabaya, to be exact, on September 30, 1935. My family and I lived in Indonesia until after World War II, when we were released from POW camps by the Japanese. We were finally repatriated to the Netherlands in 1946.

of no substance. Day and night we were hungry, dreaming of food.

I often went on a foraging trip to the kitchen. I'd crawl on all fours over the stinking rubbish heap at its back, looking for leaves of cabbage or peels of onion discarded during the preparation of the curry.

On one occasion a new group of prisoners arrived and I noticed how one family that evening threw out on a garbage dump the half-eaten sandwiches they had brought with them. Ignorant, inexperienced fools they were! I stealthily collected the scraps and brought them back in triumph. Later, when it was dark, the five of us huddled under our mosquito net and enjoyed the unexpected bonanza.

Our Japanese and Korean guards treated us with brutality. No surprise perhaps since a handful of them had to keep thousands of women and children in check. It was a formula that led many prisoners of war to hate the Japanese for life, each and everyone of them. I escaped that fate through a number of spiritual experiences, one of which I would like to share.

Revelation

By way of concession, a priest from a nearby men's camp was allowed to say Mass for Catholics twice a year. I had received my first Holy Communion only recently. The Eucharist meant a lot to me, as it still does today.

Imagine the large crowd of us, sitting on the dusty ground or standing barefoot in dense semi-circles under tall *tjemara* trees next to one of the camp's reeking rubbish dumps. Facing us stood the rough wooden table that served as the altar. The priest recited his prayers in Latin. Next to the altar, seated on a comfortable chair, sat Colonel Sakai, our camp commander, his *samurai* sword plainly visible as it dangled by a long chain from his belt.

A bell was rung. Consecration.

We all knelt down.

I looked at our Japanese oppressor. To my utter surprise, he rose from the chair and he, too, knelt down, his glittering sword lying flat in the dust next to him.

You will appreciate my surprise better if you know that this same man, just a few weeks earlier, had displayed all the traits of unmitigated Japanese fury. The whole camp had been summoned to stand in the noonday sun to listen to one of his harangues. The Dutch interpreter, who was standing next to him, made a mistake. Colonel Sakai slapped her across her face and she, acting on impulse, I am sure, struck back. This, of course, constituted an unforgivable offence: the male emblem of imperial authority being publicly humiliated by a female of a disgraced and defeated nation.

The scene that followed defies description. He undid his belt and beat her time and again. She sank to the ground, unconscious. He ordered a bucket of water to be poured over her. When she staggered to her feet, he belted her again until she collapsed, this time for good. She succumbed to her injuries soon after. While the beating was going on, we shouted, cried, wept as soldiers right and left pointed their guns at us. I remember how I trembled all over with fear and anger. It imprinted a hatred of bullying that has never left me.

This was the same man who knelt down with us and bowed his head at the consecration!

The event moved me deeply on a human and spiritual level in a way I find hard to put into words. The paradox of a "pious brute" perplexed me. I suddenly grasped, somehow, that the commander, too, was human, frail, groping for God as much as we were. This thought created a bond with him. Under his mask of cruelty lay a reverence for the divine that I shared with him. While remaining a dangerous oppressor, he had humbled himself before the mystery of the universe and so acknowledged himself a seeker in need of God.

I have learned much more about the Japanese since then, through personal Japanese friends and through reading. What I perceived intuitively as a child, I can now rationalise to some extent. Our guards were formed by their masculine culture, their *bushido* military indoctrination and unquestioning loyalty to the emperor. The brutes who terrorised us probably loved their wives and children tenderly. They were the victims of a tyranny of mind control, which institutions, whether social, political or religious, all too easily slide into.

Violence needs to be checked with a strong hand, as our daily experience proves. Untruth needs to be exposed. We may not tolerate bullying of any kind. But true peace and reconciliation between people can only come about by understanding individuals as they are: mixtures of evil and good. What we need is empathy, not black-and-white condemnations. The popes who burnt heretics, incredibly, believed it was God's will. Suicide bombers, though appallingly misguided and dangerous, commit themselves to a generous act of self-sacrifice.

We are walking paradoxes, all of us human beings who populate this globe. We are courageous cowards, blind teachers of partial truths, fired by misconceptions no less than by high ideals. I have often wondered if this is how Jesus Christ saw people? He ate and drank with tax collectors even though they took bribes. He praised a prostitute for "having shown much love." He invited the repentant thief to join him in paradise.

All this has had practical consequences for me. Peace, whether in society or in the Church, starts with a love of people, even a love of our adversaries, candidly commending what is good in them. I have always seen this as one implication of that seemingly unachievable challenge: "Love your enemies, do good to those who hate you, bless those who curse you, pray for those who treat you badly." (Luke 6, 27-29)

Chapter 3

From the pincers of death

While we were enjoying the luxuries of *Mankubumi* camp, my father - totally unknown to us - had been shipped to Singapore. From January to March 1943 he was in the notorious *Changi* POW camp.

After that, he was transported by train to Thailand with thousands of other Dutch, Australian and English soldiers. They had been selected to work on the railway of "Bridge over the River Kwai" fame. Five days packed together like sardines in cattle wagons. Roasting heat. Hardly any food or drink. And on arrival in Nong Pladuk came the real test: a march.

The march of his life, as he later told us: 260 kilometers through the jungle, often at night, in ten days! A death march. Those who could not walk were shot or left to die.

"It was the most grueling ordeal I ever faced," my father told me. "Many of my friends gave up. I clenched my teeth and kept going. Dusty narrow paths climbing up and down and snaking through never-ending bush. Hunger. No rest. Just stumbling on in spite of wounds and blisters. But I got there."

To speed up construction of the 415-km-long railway between Thailand and Burma, the Japanese spread the POWs over 128 work camps along the whole length of the projected railway. My father was assigned to Camp *Thamayo* 2, manned by 200 Dutch soldiers. The men had to excavate the track from the hillside, using primitive tools to hack into the rock and to remove tons of rubble. Smaller and larger bridges had to be constructed. A total of 240,000 men worked on the railway, both POWs and forced labour from Burma and Malaysia. Some 98,000 died of disease, beatings and/or starvation.

The Japanese army failed to provide the camps with regular supplies of food. Since my father was good at languages, he was sent out by the camp commander, under armed guard, to procure provisions from the local Thai villagers. Also, while in Singapore he had picked up some Japanese words so that on occasion he was summoned to serve as an interpreter.

One day, my father told me, an important colonel visited the camp and insisted on addressing the POWs. My father was called upon to translate his speech. As the man raved on, pausing from time to time to give my father a

Rare photograph shows prisoners of war being marched through the Thai jungle during World War II.

chance to interpret, my father played the part.

"I have no clue of what the chap is saying," my father kept telling his comrades in Dutch. "As far as I can see he's hopping mad. For God's sake, don't laugh! This *banzai* buff is getting terribly worked up. Pretend you are impressed!"

By just chatting on and on, he kept filling in the gaps. The Japs did not notice.

On another occasion, he was walking through the jungle with an 18-year old Korean soldier as his guard. Many Koreans served in the Japanese army. My father needed a rest and sat down. The boy soldier was afraid of the jungle and wanted to move on.

My father refused to budge.

The Korean took my father's spectacles and put them into his shirt pocket. This was really cruel. My father's eyesight was abysmal, and he could not bear to think of losing his glasses.

But he refused to give in.

The Korean now pointed his rifle at my father. Then, as he failed to make an impression, the Korean slung his rifle over his shoulder and walked away, spectacles still in his pocket.

After half an hour my father heard a wailing sound in the distance. It was the Korean who had lost the way.

"Nikkeeeh! Nikkeeeh!" he kept screaming.

"Nikki" was what the Japanese called my father, whose name in Dutch was "Niek" from "Nicholas." My father sought him out and retrieved his spectacles.

"The poor chap was crying and shaking," my father said.

"Wasn't it risky?" I asked. "Letting him walk off like that – with your specs!"

"Perhaps," he replied. "The game of survival is complex. Diplomacy is your best tool. Stay as far away as you can from real brutes. Make sure you make allies of the good guys. Fight when you need to. And at no time show any weakness!"

It was advice I could have used very well in our own camp.

Baring my knuckles

It is said that children undergo their social birth when they enter school. Parental nurture and protection recede. Peer group pressure takes over. The child struggles to survive the seduction and bullying of teachers and classmates. If that is so, my social birth happened in the camp.

Crammed with thousands of others in small, enclosed spaces, we learned how to share the little there was. Give and take. I rub your back, you rub mine. But also, as we say in Dutch: "Don't let anyone snatch the cheese from your slice of bread!"

I soon had to engage in my first real fight.

In a group of boys of my age I found myself harassed by a lad stronger and taller than I was. In the beginning I took the humiliations, to maintain peace. It led to more humiliations. I suddenly realized I could not let this happen. A ferocious anger, as I had never felt before, took hold of me. I remember it like it was yesterday. I decided to enter the arena, for better or worse.

We came to blows. I got a beating but I kicked and punched in return, refusing to surrender. We rolled on the dusty ground holding each other. My heart pounded. I felt tears welling up in my eyes. My body trembled. But I did not let go. A beast had been unleashed in me. I scratched his face. I sank my teeth into his arm. He was equally vicious to me. When a woman finally tore us apart we were both bleeding. He growled. So did I. After that, he never bothered me again.

On May 29, 1945, we were transported to our last camp. I now know why. The Germans had surrendered in Europe. The Americans had conquered the Philippines and had begun to occupy the Japanese island of Okinawa. A possible next target was Indonesia. The Japs expected an invasion in East Java. All prisoners of war were promptly clustered together in central locations, away from the coast. Ten POW camps sprung up around the hill towns of Ambarawa and Banjubiru. We were destined to spend the final months of the war in notorious *Ambarawa 6*.

It so happened that when we were suddenly hauled out of *Mankubumi* camp to board a train, I had sprained my ankle. So, I was carried by a friend to the railway coach. Trouble broke out upon our arrival in *Ambarawa*.

The others were taken to lorries outside the station for further transport to various camps. I had been carried out and laid down on the platform. My mother and brothers stood nearby, hanging on to our few belongings. A Jap-

A scene from a POW camp soon after the war ended... Only then did our situation improve greatly as restrictions on our movements were eased and our food allocation was increased.

anese officer returned to the platform to see why we were dragging our feet. When he saw me lying on the floor, he ordered a soldier to heave me back onto the train. At that moment my mother intervened.

She placed herself firmly in front of the door of the railway carriage and refused to see me carried back on.

The officer yelled.

My mother yelled back.

The soldier tried to push my mother aside.

She did not budge.

Still shouting with anger, the officer gave in. I was dropped back onto the floor of the platform. And then – my heart still stops when I think of it! – the train pulled out of the station.

If my mother had not stood up for me, I might well have been separated from my family forever. Believe me, it happened to quite a few children at the time.

I am still wondering why the officer ordered me back on the train. Maybe he presumed that I would eventually land up in the boys' camp. Boys over ten years old were routinely rounded up and consigned to such a camp. Or maybe he saw an opportunity of "adopting" me into his own family. Japanese fathers were at times looking for substitutes to take the place of their own lost sons. Just the thought of it! I could have grown up eating *sushi* and *sashimi* delicacies – and telling a different tale!

Whatever his intention may have been, I owed my life and well-being for the second time to the care and courage of my intrepid mother.

I cried with joy that evening as we were all huddled again under our mosquito net, this time crammed with 72 other families in danky barrack No. 10, right at the end of crowded *Ambarawa 6*.

The end game

I do not want to bore you with endless tales of the misery that awaited us. People died like flies. I myself had contracted permanent dysentery and, because of the lack of proper food or medicines, the prospects looked bleak. Our camp doctor later told my mother that he had already written me off. If the war had lasted another month, I would not have survived, he said.

Meanwhile, girls in our camp were picked up for "exclusive operations." After the war we learned that they had served as "comfort women" in the Japanese army brothels of Semarang. My good-looking but 30-year-old mother escaped this fate. She was considered too old.

We noticed that our guards were getting frantic. In spite of tight military censorship, rumors were trickling in that battles had been lost. A group of Korean soldiers went on a rampage and took over part of our camp. Regular Japanese troops moved in and suppressed the mutiny with ruthless efficiency. The rebels were shot.

This scene from a neighbouring camp, Banjubiru 9, was photographed just after the war ended.

On August 15 our Japanese camp commander flew into a rage. He went around brandishing his sword and smashing everything in sight. With hindsight, we know the reason. Emperor Hirohito had addressed the Japanese nation in an Asia-wide radio broadcast announcing Japan's defeat. He ordered all Japanese forces anywhere in the world to lay down their arms.

From the frying pan into the fire

It took days before we were informed about the victory of the Allies. But immediate improvements began to happen. Our meal ration was substantially increased. Instead of one meal, we now got food in the mornings and the evenings. The women were even allowed to leave the camp to shop in the local market. My mother promptly did so and returned with a bag full of eggs, which she bought with rupiahs she had hidden in the seams of our clothes.

We ate boiled eggs till we were all sick. My mother herself ate 15 eggs, she told me later. It is amazing what hunger can make you do, and in those days we never knew if tomorrow would offer the same opportunity.

The Japanese had lost the war, but another war had begun. For years Indonesian freedom fighters had prepared for their own rule. With the Japanese out of the way, they declared independence on August 17. They decided to take control of Indonesia before the Dutch army could move back in.

Unknown to us, it came to violent clashes in Surabaia. The British had promised to secure Indonesia for the Netherlands. They landed troops in Surabaia. The *permuda* youth brigades resisted. Hastily a truce was arranged. When the British officer in charge, Brigadier Anthony Mallaby, was killed on October 30, the British retaliated. They counter-attacked on November 10 with two full brigades. Planes were sent in to bomb Surabaia. Tanks confronted tens of thousands of freedom fighters who had converged on Surabaia. Not all were fully armed. It is estimated that 6,000 of them were killed before Surabaia was firmly in British hands.

All this had instant repercussions for us. Remember that in our area, ten camps with Dutch POWs lay isolated in the middle of mountainous Java. Freedom fighters surrounded us on all sides. They broke into a neighboring camp, herding people together and firing on them with machine guns. We escaped that ordeal. The British dropped a platoon of *Gurkhas* and a set of heavy guns near our camp.

Two anxious months of a siege followed. From the adjacent mountaintops, the Indonesians bombarded our camp with heavy shells from which there was no running away. We were sitting ducks. Casualties were buried within the camp itself just hours after their deaths. There were days we had no food or even water as supplies were cut off from outside. From time to time, food parcels were dropped from the air. For the time being, our handful of brave *Gurkhas* kept thousands of freedom fighters at a safe distance.

Finally, British military convoys from the coast began to fight their way through to our camp. It was only on December 5, nearly four months after the victory over Japan, that such a convoy brought me and my family out of *Ambar-awa* to the relative safety of harbor town Semarang.

Chapter 4

Rescuing my self-respect

*A*few days after arriving in Semarang's *Halmahera* Camp it was Sunday. We learned Mass would be celebrated for Catholics in a meeting hall. We attended.

While queuing up to receive Communion, I suddenly remembered that I had woken up during the night and, because of the sweltering heat in our hut, had drunk some water from a bottle. I did not remember the exact time, but during the instructions I had received before my First Communion it had been drummed into us that eating or drinking anything after midnight before going to Communion was a serious sin indeed.

I did not know what to do. During our camp years we had been allowed to go to Mass only a few times, and Communion was such a precious experience. Moreover, I did not remember the exact time I had drunk the water, but I decided to take the risk. I received Holy Communion.

Then doubt and fear overwhelmed me. After Mass I approached the celebrant, an old Dutch priest. He bent low to hear me whisper.

"Father, I have committed a mortal sin," I said.

"Oh," he said. "I can hear your confession."

He took me to a corner of the hall, sat down on a chair, drew a purple stole from his coat pocket which he put on, and had me kneel in front of him. Then I confessed what I had done.

"Don't worry, Jesus understands. You meant well," he said, then gave me absolution.

We stayed in Semarang for only one week. Because a few days later, early in the morning a jeep crossed the camp. Its loudspeaker blared out a message:

"American troop ship in harbour. Going to Bangkok. Women wanting to meet their husbands in Thailand should report at the main gate within one hour."

Within one hour! It came as a shock, and a thrill. For it offered the chance to meet up with my father, who had been working on the infamous railway line over there. My mother immediately responded. Without ado, we grabbed our meagre belongings and dragged ourselves to the gate. There we were loaded on trucks and driven to the harbour.

Now, Semarang did not have a proper harbour. Ocean ships lay at anchor quite some distance away from the quays. We were let down into small dinghies that would transfer us to the ship. The sea was choppy. In our small boats we hopped around on the waves. And then the shock when we approached the ship. No steps leading up to the deck. Instead, a wide net of rope had been thrown down from one side of the huge ship. As we heaved up and down in our dinghy we were expected to jump onto the net and climb up to the railing.

My heart stopped with fear. I was only ten years old, seriously underfed and totally unprepared for physical stunts. My mother had her hands full coping with my two youngest brothers. Carel and I had to make our way up by ourselves. I froze in terror as I looked up the 25 feet of steel wall I would have to climb up.

"Come on. Jump!" my mother cried.

Carel jumped. Then I jumped, too. I managed to catch the rungs of the net and hang on to them. The waves banged and bounced against the side of the ship below me. Trembling all over, I clutched my teeth and tried to clamber up. Then, fortunately, some sailors climbed down the net. One took me under his arm and carried me up. Eventually all of us got safely on board. I collapsed, sobbing with relief.

Those moments of utter dread and horror have never left me. I still have nightmares re-living the scene.

Meeting my father

Four days later, our American ship, after negotiating its way through mine-fields we were told, delivered us safely in Bangkok. We were put up for a week in an old army camp.

Then the next stage. With other Dutch families we boarded a train to go up north. It proved a long journey because, after a few hours, we had to leave the train. A railway bridge had been bombed during the war. So, carrying our bags we were led down a slope to the river bank. There a flagstone walkway had been constructed over which we could cross to the opposite bank. We heaved our bags up another slope. Finally, we reached the railway on the other side, where another train was waiting to carry us on.

Late that night we arrived at the small station of Tah Muang, the town that housed my father's garrison. It was pitch dark, but a group of soldiers had lit up the platform with flashlights. My father was among them. As the train came to a stop, he ran alongside of the train cars – and when he came to ours he rec-ognised us through the open window. My mother leaned out and handed him my youngest brother, Aloys. Then the rest of us made our way out.

It was a happy, happy reunion!

Later that night, after we had eaten in the canteen we retired to the tiny house on stilts where we were billeted as a family. My father kissed each of us goodnight as we lay on our bunks.

"Thank you for looking so well after mother!" he whispered in my ear. It was the sweetest compliment he could have given me.

Plans for the future

During our stay in Thailand, we got to know an Italian missionary who visited our camp from time to time to celebrate Mass for us. My older brother, Carel, and I volunteered to be Mass servers. Learning the Latin prayers for the responses was a real challenge for me, but I managed. Talking to the priest was extremely difficult though he was a nice person. On one occasion he took a whole group of Catholics for an outing to his parish headquarters out in the jungle.

It became a memorable day. The army had promised to lend us a truck, but when that did not turn up, the priest marched us to a main road. There he waited for a public bus. He stopped the bus and talked to the driver and passengers, explaining that he required the use of the bus to take his guests to his mission station. To our surprise, the driver and all his passengers agreed. Cheerfully, men and women, still carrying shopping bags, chickens and bundles of clothes vacated the bus. In the village itself, we were shown round the houses built on stilts, the floors inside looking impeccably clean and polished. Youngsters like Carel and me played with the village children in the nearby river, wrestling and splashing each other without being able to speak the same language.

Even before the war Carel had dreamed of becoming a priest. I saw myself as a future surgeon. The experience in Thailand confirmed Carel in his ambition.

View of Tah Muang prison camp in Thailand, where my father's garrison had been detained...

A doubt about my intelligence

A make-shift primary school of bamboo huts had been erected, in our reha-bilitation camp at Tah Muang, to make up for what children had missed in the Japanese camps. For teaching had been forbidden all those years. Carel and I had learned how to read and write on scraps of wrapping paper. No textbooks. The only formal education we had received was from my mother and some of her friends talking to us about history, or the geography of Indonesia.

One evening I overheard my father talking to the teacher who had taken charge of ten-year-olds like me. They were sitting in wicker chairs outside our temporary home drinking a glass of Mekong beer. I was sitting some distance away on the wooden planks of our veranda, my feet dangling over the dusty ground below. The two men did not know I could hear them.

"I'm afraid I've bad news," the teacher told my father. "Hans over there... Well, I don't know."

"What do you mean?" my father asked.

"Well, this will disappoint you since you're a teacher yourself. How shall I put it? Hans will have problems."

"Why?"

"To put it bluntly: He's not very gifted. He's willing enough but slow in the uptake. Hasn't got it upstairs. Not cut out for study, I'd say. Sorry, old chap."

This damning assessment put a dent in my self-confidence that would remain for a long time. Again and again I had to prove to myself that my critic was wrong. The first opportunity came a few months later when I joined a village primary school in Baarn, in the Netherlands. After some hesitation I had been put into the fifth form, in spite of my lack of proper schooling. A math teacher made us do multiplication exercises. I completed them faster and better than most others.

"Did you do this yourself?" the teacher inquired suspiciously. She insisted she wanted to watch me while I was doing the next exercises. She was surprised to see how accurately and quickly I finished the job.

A few months later again, Carel and I were admitted to the top form of a slick city primary school in Utrecht. We were expected to fill in weekly tests based on lecture material and homework. I scored excellent marks. When I joined the missionary high school in Hoorn, I soon ranked among the top students. In Haelen, I was selected with three others of my class to attempt the Dutch State's entrance exam for university studies.

The challenge was formidable. Exams in six languages: Dutch, Greek and Latin (each requiring two written and one oral exam); French, German and English (each requiring one written exam); history, geography, algebra and geometry (each requiring a written and oral exam). Since these were public tests, the exams were conducted in central locations by independent teachers and scholars.

In Baarn, the Netherlands, 1947: My mother
with (left to right) Carel, Niek, my father, Aloys and me.

Our next level of training followed a grammar school programme that was heavily weighted in favour of languages. Math therefore posed the challenge. Imagine my surprise – and delight – when I was particularly successful in algebra. During the oral interview the two examiners wanted me to explain graphs.

"How can you make a graph of graphs?" It was a question with which I had never been confronted.

"Ah, you need to make a three-dimensional graph," I replied.

They kept pressing me with ever more demanding questions. At the end of the exam one of the examiners told me that they were astounded at my grasp of graph theory. And right at the end of the week-long ordeal when each applicant had to face a four-member board of the examination committee, I was handed my certificate with a special recommendation.

"Though you also excel in languages," the chairman of the board told me, "we recommend that in your higher studies you switch to mathematics, for which you got full marks. That is quite rare. You have a natural gift for figures and mental calculations."

I report all this because it was only this ringing endorsement by an official panel of teachers that laid to rest the lingering doubts I had had about my intelligence. I did not know that the real test of my intelligence was still to come.

Chapter 5

Pledging utter dedication

When we were finally repatriated to the Netherlands in May of 1946, we found a country largely in ruins and recovering from the disastrous famine of the last year of the war.

For some time, my grandparents on my mother's side gave us shelter in a village called Baarn. When my father secured a job in Utrecht, we were accommodated in a small flat in de Bemuurde Weerd. The apartment was a pigeon hole situated over a busy dairy shop and opposite the place where the river Vecht leaves the canal system of Utrecht to flow north. The sluice gates made a racket day and night, but once we got used to the noise it did not rob us of our sleep.

It was during this time – Carel was 12 and I was 11 – that the two of us decided to study for the priesthood in a high school for missionaries, which was known as a minor seminary. To people today it may seem incredible, but at that time it was normal for children leaving primary school to decide on their future careers. We chose to serve God. It still puzzles me to fully explain how this came about.

From even before the war Carel had expressed the wish to become a priest. I always said I wanted to be a medical doctor. Rather than joining one of the Dutch dioceses, Carel chose to go out to the missions. He examined the various missionary orders and finally settled on the Mill Hill Missionaries, a society founded in England that recruited half its workforce from the Netherlands.

When Carel decided to sign up as a student in the minor seminary at Hoorn, I did not know what to do. Until that time we had always been bosom friends who shared everything. Now our paths would diverge. Also, it upset me to think that Carel was choosing a nobler option than I was: He was going to serve God while I would be pursuing a "selfish" career. In the end, I surprised everyone by declaring that I, too, wanted to become a missionary. It caused a lot of consternation all around. However, as good Catholic parents, my father and mother did not want to stand in the way of our priestly vocations, even though my mother kept protesting – quite rightly – that it was cruel that the two of us would have to leave home so young, after having missed a normal family life during the previous five years.

In spite of all that, both of us travelled by train to Hoorn, accompanied by our mother, and entered the St. Boniface Missionary College on a wet September day in 1947. I was 11 years old at the time. When my mother left to go home late that afternoon, I cried as I had never cried before. It took Carel and me weeks to get over the separation from our family.

Our college functioned as a boarding school. All our teachers were priests. Our daily routine reflected the spiritual goals that inspired us.

With hindsight, I realize that the priestly vocation Carel and I felt was greatly influenced by the traumas we had experienced during the war. The German psychologist Eugen Drewermann counseled many priests and religious who had chosen their spiritual careers as young boys or girls soon after the war. In his books, he documents the unconscious motivations that drove many of them and their parents: guilt for having been spared while others died, fear of God's punishing hand if his invitation was ignored, feeling personally responsible for having to set the world right.

"The war did produce many zealous priests and religious," he writes, "but not without unrecognized psychological distress."

My training for the priesthood took 12 years, moving to ever higher colleges. I spent four years in Hoorn, two in Haelen, two in Roosendaal and the final four in Mill Hill, in northwest London. It is not my intention to bore you with the many smaller incidents and adventures that occurred in those various colleges. But I do want to highlight some major changes that affected me.

The first one concerns my commitment to God.

Whatever the human origin of my vocation may have been, a real conversion took place in me. The famous Bishop Nico Stam, pioneer in East Africa, lived in our college at that time. He told us wonderful stories of the challenges that faced him during the early 1900s. On one occasion he left with a train of 70 carriers to visit an unexplored area in present-day Kakamega, in Kenya. He found village after village devastated by *trypanosomiasis*, popularly known as sleeping sickness. He nursed the sick and comforted survivors. Some of his carriers, too, caught the virus and died. The rest fled. In the end Bishop Stam came back to his head station all alone. His example inspired me.

And so did that of the Belgian missionary Damien de Veuster, who volunteered in 1873 to look after a leprosy colony on the Hawiian island of Moloka'i. He died 16 years later after having contracted leprosy himself.

The fervent sermons of Jaap Zuijdervliet, who was Rector at the time, also fired me with enthusiasm. He quoted God saying: "Since you are lukewarm and neither hot nor cold, I am going to spit you out of my mouth!" (Revelation 3,16.) It made me think. As a result, I solemnly decided to commit myself 100 percent, unreservedly, utterly and wholeheartedly to lifelong service as a Catholic priest and missionary. I confided to my spiritual director, Father Bruins:

"I want to be radical in my commitment to God. Absolutely radical."

The staff of Hoorn seminary turned out for a picture in 1948, when Carel and I were confirmed by Bishop Nico Stam. That's Bishop Stam in the front row with the prominent white beard. Next to him are my mother, my father, Carel and me.

I did not realize, of course, that a radical is often a person with both feet planted firmly in the air. My commitment though was serious enough.

Total commitment

To my intense sorrow, Carel, my dear brother and best friend, died suddenly. Cancer of the lungs and bones. He wasted away in a couple of months. We had always shared our deepest secrets, and as intimately as ever during the three years while we shared our priestly training. His loss shook me. I threw myself with even more determination into preparing myself for a life of selfless service.

I have been wondering whether I should write about what happened next, or pass over it in silence. In the end, I decided to be brutally honest so that others may benefit from my experience – not only individuals intent on selfless ministry as I was, but also educators, spiritual directors, religious superiors.

A period of intense spiritual reflection and deepening followed after Carel's death. I became engrossed in a mystical exploration. I wanted to discover the dimension of God, immerse myself in it, plunge myself into its mysterious universe of light and darkness. Parallel to my studies, I devoted most of my time to prayer and to reading spiritual classics such as *The Interior Castle* by Teresa of Avila and the *Ascent of Mount Carmel* by John of the Cross. I tried to rigorously put into practice the demanding steps of inner and outer asceticism they prescribed.

It is difficult to describe the intensity of this inner search that carried me through the final years of my priestly formation. Rigorous self-examinations. Regular retreats. Long periods of meditating on my knees in my room. Hours and hours of "presenting myself to God" in churches that were dimly lit and smelling of incense. Much of this has remained with me as a lasting awareness of the reality of the divine in our baffling and astounding universe.

But, looking back to that time, I now recognize an element of *unreality* in my obsessive devotion.

It is difficult to express the nature of that devotion accurately. The closest I can come to the truth is to say that I had fallen in love with a *phantom* Jesus.

Jesus of Nazareth, I believe, revealed to us that God is Love. He is the Word God spoke to us, the Image of the invisible reality we call God. But fastening my affections on him as if he were a human person in the here and now was unreal. I considered my "love" for him the gift of myself, and I placed myself totally at his service. To get the gist of what I am trying to say, listen to this extract from my spiritual diary dated May 1, 1956.

"My dearest, dearest Jesus! The aim of my life is to love you as passionately as possible. All I possess, my talents and gifts, my whole body and everything I own, I entrust totally to you. Show me, your humble friend, how to speak only words pleasing to you, how to focus my thoughts on no one else but you, how

As I appeared in 1953, when I began the study of philosophy...

to ensure that all my actions start with you and are completed in you. Grant that I may spend each moment of the day for you, so that I will think, say or do nothing that does not spring from my love."

I suppose that offering myself in absolute service to Jesus, I was in a way trying to express my love for God the creator and ultimate meaning of all that exists.

Sex to be avoided at all costs

I never was given a proper sex education, either by my parents nor by superiors in the various seminaries I attended, in spite of me asking for it once or twice. I had no access to adult novels, romantic films or the kind of pornographic literature that helped teenagers discover sex in our time.

In the final college I attended, in Mill Hill, I joined a small group of art enthusiasts. For one of our discussions we used a book of classic paintings but Father Duyvestein, our master of discipline, had first solicitously covered all of Rembrandt's nudes with sticky paper.

We were also constantly told to avoid any social contact with women. I was considered fortunate because I had no sisters, and the female friends of one's sisters were marked as posing a special risk to future priests. We were, after all, trained to become celibates. Friendship or intimacy with any woman was firmly discouraged. Here are the points I noted after a coaching session I received in 1956:

"Be wary of women. Respect all — at a distance. Always hands off. Never fondle or kiss any woman.... Don't call adult women by their Christian name. Be aware of the risks involved in visiting a woman at home, in corresponding with a woman or talking to her privately. Avoid being alone with a woman anywhere. Be short and business-like in any dealings!"

My training as a celibate was put to the test one day in a particularly memorable incident. I had gone on a short holiday to Paris with my father. We visited the *Musée de l'Art Moderne*. In a department of 19th century French paintings I suddenly came face to face with a frontal nude.

It was a large canvass. A life-size young woman boldly stared at me. I took in her tall slender figure, her two taut breasts, the navel on her slightly bulging stomach.... I found her breathtakingly beautiful. But there was more than the thrust of her naked body. I recognized in her face a femininity, a tenderness, an invitation to intimacy that was utterly new to me.

My father walked back from another room and saw me looking at the painting.

"If it's too much for you, just move on," he said.

His remark reminded me of the fact that I was wearing a black clerical suit, including a Roman collar, and others were watching me. So I did move on. But inside I still reeled from the impact of meeting that young, naked, vulnerable woman.

In fact, the encounter came to nothing. I duly reported it to my confessor as a temptation. I was, after all, quite caught up in the brainwashing that accompanied my priestly training.

The Apostle Paul had a point when he wrote:

"An unmarried man can devote himself to the Lord's affairs, all he need worry about is pleasing the Lord; but a married man has to bother about the world's affairs and devote himself to pleasing his wife." (1 Corinthians 7,32-34).

Policemen, too, politicians and business tycoons have more time when they do not have a family. Yes, there should be room for some priests and religious who leave everything "for the sake of the Kingdom." But Christian ascetic tradition has infused an unhealthy ingredient into this way of thinking. It frequently has presented God (or Jesus Christ) as a rival to an ordinary human partner. This, of course, is a false dichotomy. Enlightened Christian understanding will help us discover the extra depth of God's love in and through a human partner.

It would take me a long time and a tortuous journey to come to that realization.

Chapter 6

Learning to think independently

*M*y two-year philosophy studies in Roosendaal College (1953-54) did not overtax either my capability or my interest. So I began to look for a worthwhile hobby that could absorb my excess energy. I found it in the study of Arabic.

My father, who was a keen linguist, had begun learning Arabic at the time and it struck me that knowing Arabic would be extremely useful in my future dealings with Muslims. Hilaire Belloc, the far-sighted historian, had correctly prophesied that Islam would pose the greatest challenge to Christian mission in years to come. In most territories entrusted to Mill Hill missionaries, such as India, Pakistan, Malaysia and East Africa, this was indeed the case. So I fixed my gaze on dialogue with Islam and on Arabic as a tool in that process.

My father donated to me the best Arabic course books available at the time, written by a Jew, Jochanan Kapliwatzky. I bought a number of other classic commentaries on Islam. And when I discussed my programme with Arnulf Camps, professor of missiology at the Catholic University of Nijmegen, he urged me to start reading the Qur'an in Arabic with the help of commentaries and translations.

"Knowledge of the Qur'an will open many doors to you in Muslim society," he said.

His advice would prove right during my work in India. The fact that I could read the Qur'an and other Muslim literature in Arabic would prove a valuable asset in my frequent contacts with Muslims. However, there was a problem. The Qur'an had been placed on the *Index*, the list of forbidden books, by the Vatican authorities in Rome.

When book printing spread in Europe, both civil and religious authorities became aware of the opportunities it presented to rebels and heretics. Various governments, notably those of France and England, declared some books to be forbidden. The Roman *Index* was first published in 1559 under Pope Paul IV. From 1571 to 1917 it stood under the care of the Vatican Congregation of the Index, which kept updating it. And whereas civil authorities by and large relaxed their bans in the course of time, the Roman *Index* firmly remained in place till 1966.

In its final edition, the *Index* listed 4,000 titles. These included works by some of the greatest European thinkers: Johannes Kepler, Galileo Galilei, René Descartes, Francis Bacon, John Milton, Blaise Pascal, David Hume, Erasmus, John Scotus Eriugena and many others continuing to our day. Also novels were listed such as *The Three Musketeers* by Alexander Dumas, and *Les Misérables* as well as *The Hunchback of Notre Dame* by Victor Hugo.

The *Index* affected me because the Qur'an featured prominently on it. I would be allowed to read it only if I were given a dispensation, Professor Camps told me. It was at times given to scholars for research purposes. Camps wrote a letter of recommendation that I presented to Father Padberg, Rector of Roosendaal College, who in turn approached the local bishop.

As a result, I got a two-year dispensation. I bought an Arab copy of the Qur'an as well as two English translations by well-known Muslim scholars. So far so good.

Two years later, when I had started my theological studies at Mill Hill College in England, I noticed that the dispensation had expired. Conscientiously, I approached Father J. P. Martin, the Rector of the College, with the request to apply to the Archbishop of Westminster, our local bishop, for an extension of the dispensation. Imagine my surprise when a few days later Father Daan Duivesteyn, the Master of Discipline, visited my room.

"We have had a staff meeting," he said curtly. "We consider it totally inappropriate for an inexperienced theologian like yourself to be dispensed from the *Index* of forbidden books."

"But that's ridiculous!" I protested. "The Qur'an does not pose any risk to my faith. Moreover, if it *were* to be dangerous, the damage has been done already. I have been reading the Qur'an for two years!"

"Don't argue!" he said.

With that, he initiated a thorough search of my room. All my copies of the Qur'an were confiscated. So were a couple of other books, like those by Voltaire and Emmanuel Kant, which I did not even know were listed in the *Index*.

The whole affair left a bitter taste in my mouth. Why did the authorities not trust me? And even if the *Index* was supposed to protect uneducated people, why was it imposed on theologians?

Was the whole purpose of studying theology not to examine issues critically, considering arguments for and against?

I began to look more carefully at the way we were taught theology.

On all crucial questions the opinions of so-called "opponents" were reported in short summaries. But were we ever exposed to what these "opponents" really said? The answer is no, not even regarding key questions! We were never given the original texts to read.

The spiritual interpretations of the early Gnostics, and the criticism of the

Me (in the back) with my family on holiday in 1965. The others are (left to right) my father, Niek, my mother, Aloys and Guus, who was born after the war.

Roman interpretation of Christianity by Luther, Calvin, John Knox or Erasmus, were simply withheld. It dawned on me that we were expected to swallow the orthodox view wholesale — without being allowed a critical evaluation of the true thinking of people labelled as "opponents."

We were being *brainwashed*, not allowed to form our own mature appreciation of the issues involved and the reasons why the Catholic position made sense.

I entered a note in my spiritual diary that I would practice absolute honesty and openness in my theology. I made up my mind that no one would stop me from studying "the other side" of any issue and this in the actual words of so-called "opponents."

Since that time I have regularly bought the classic writings of such "opponents." The collection has swollen to hundreds of volumes and now forms a sizeable part of my library.

Creation in 4000 B.C.?

It was my misfortune to have Father Daan Duivesteyn as our main theological lecturer in Mill Hill College. It soon became clear to me that I could not agree to his overly conservative stand on many issues. At the centenary of Darwin's publication of *The Evolution of Species*, Duivesteyn poured scorn on the whole idea of evolution and rejected it totally as far as human beings are concerned.

By that time I had picked up many outstanding works on evolution that reported extensively on the scientific research that underpinned evolution. I found the arguments in favour of evolution incontrovertible. Nowadays we know that humans and apes share 98 percent of their genetic code. A study by Ralph von Koenigswald on hominids and apes convinced me that a common ancestor was undeniable.

"Of 1,065 anatomical features, human beings share 396 with chimpanzees, 385 with gorillas and 354 with orangutans" (*Evolutie*, Spectrum 1959, pp. 142-165). So much more evidence has come in since then, of course. The point I want to make is that at that time there already was sufficient proof to establish that humans evolved like all other animals.

Duivesteyn saw this as a threat to the special status of the human soul. He quoted at us Pope Pius XII's encyclical *Humani Generis* (1950):

"The Teaching Authority of the Church does not forbid that, in conformity with the present state of human sciences and sacred theology, research and discussions, on the part of men experienced in both fields, take place with regard to the doctrine of evolution, in as far as it inquires into the origin of the human body as coming from pre-existent and living matter — for the Catholic faith obliges us to hold that souls are immediately created by God.... Some, however, rashly transgress this liberty of discussion, when they act as if the origin of the human body from pre-existing and living matter were already completely certain and proved by the facts which have been discovered up to now and by reasoning on those facts, and as if there were nothing in the sources of divine revelation which demands the greatest moderation and caution in this question."

Also, it did not help that in 1953 the "Piltdown Man," a supposed fossil of an ancient human skull, was exposed as a forgery.

"The whole exercise is utterly preposterous!" Duivesteyn exclaimed. "Palae-ontologists look at a jawbone and tell us how tall he was, what he ate for lunch, how long he had lived and so re-construct a whole human ancestor from a fragment of bone!"

Duivesteyn rejected the fundamentalist claim that the world had been created in the year 4004 B.C. But he explained the seven-day creation narrated in *Genesis* as creation in seven lengthy periods.

Anyway, I disagreed with Duivesteyn's rejection of human evolution, noting the origin of the human soul as something that still needed to be resolved. And this prompted me again to make another resolution. I refused to simply swallow what lecturers, authors or even church authorities would present to me. As a theologian, I myself would be responsible for my own conclusions and convictions, based on the arguments of my own intelligence. I also decided to take scientific research very seriously. I noted in my spiritual diary:

"I will have great respect for the positive sciences. In fringe questions that affect both science and theology, I will not accept anything that is not justified also from a scientific point of view. Without the support of the positive sciences where possible, theology, and therefore our faith, lacks a solid foundation."

The sciences are, after all, based on the use of human reason. I knew I had good grounds for asserting my support for reason. The First Vatican Council had solemnly declared in 1870:

"Even though faith is above reason, there can never be any real disagreement between faith and reason, since it is the same God who reveals the mysteries and infuses faith, and who has endowed the human mind with the light of reason. God cannot deny himself, nor can truth ever be in opposition to truth."

The methodical use of reason, as is pursued by the modern sciences, should teach theology a thing or two: the need of a rigorous examination of fact, of the freedom of expression, of methodical doubt, of lateral thinking, of debate and willingness to test unusual ideas.

Thus, I discovered the first commandment of Church reform: **Allow theologians and other scholars unrestricted freedom of research.**

Chapter 7

What kind of priest?

*T*he last four years of my training for the priesthood took place in Mill Hill, in northwest London. Our theological college on a hill overlooked beautiful grounds. The building itself was composed of an old section and a new one. To the 19th century monastic cloister, chapel and tower had been joined a postwar businesslike wing that contained floor above floor of student accommodation.

This mixture of old and new curiously ran parallel to the ancient and modern strands in our formation programme.

In the Middle Ages, hierarchy and monastic scholarship had sculpted an image of the Catholic priest based on a temple cult. A priest was a *sacerdos*, a consecrated functionary handling sacred objects and mediating at sacred events. A good priest was the person who could radiate God's "otherness" to people entrusted to his flock. His duties consisted mainly in presiding over the Eucharist, preaching at Mass, administering Baptism, hearing confessions and blessing marriages. However much a priest might wander from the parish church to visit families in their homes, he would always gravitate back to the hallowed spaces of the sanctuary, the confessional, the sacristy. Peak moments in his daily life included recital of the prayers found in his breviary, his visit to the Blessed Sacrament, his punctual daily examination of conscience.

Some of our college staff still held out such a medieval ideal of the priesthood. For them, the priest was anointed, pure, set apart. Texts were quoted at us from Cardinal Herbert Vaughan's *The Young Priest* and from Cardinal James Gibbons' *Faith of Our Fathers*:

"To the carnal eye, a priest appears like another mortal. To the eye of faith, he is exalted above the angels."

Presenting heavenly values to earthly people as a priest does, he should dress in black and stay out of pubs, workshops and picket lines.

But times were changing.

A more dynamic ideal of the priesthood appealed to us students. And it had a biblical foundation.

What else had been in Jesus' mind when he sent apostles to proclaim the Good News? Had he set them apart to offer sacrifices to a worship-loving God as mere ministers of ceremonies? Or did he not rather commission them to gather stray sheep and assemble a community that could usher in the new kingdom?

Where should their hearts be: in the crowded, turbulent homes of people – or in the sanctuary?

I knew I had been called to be "a priest for others." For me, the priest had to be, as Jesus had been, someone who mixed with publicans and sinners, someone vulnerable enough to need the support of friends, someone finding encouragement in the way the Father reveals himself to ordinary men and women. I was set to live out a people-oriented priesthood, focussing on people's problems and speaking their language.

My priestly heroes

A priest who spoke to my heart was **Rupert Mayer**. He had acquired lasting fame as one of the earliest and most outspoken opponents of Hitler. He spent nine years in prison for his damning of Nazism.

"No Catholic may ever be a Nazi!" he kept saying.

But that was not the main reason why thousands of Germans kept visiting his shrine in the crypt of St. Michael's Church at Munich. He was a priest who won people's hearts because he went to meet them where they were.

As chaplain to the Eighth Bavarian Division during World War I, he could have opted for safety, well behind the lines. Instead, he stayed in the trenches, crawling from one outpost to the other, heartening the living and comforting the dying. We can imagine what that means when we learn that his division was decimated in 1916 during the battle of the Somme. The particular battalion he served was reduced from 900 troops to 220 in eight days. Of the new 770 troops with which the battalion was hastily reinforced, 650 became casualties in the next week. The official dispatch reads:

"Throughout these devastating attacks from 20 July to 13 August, one man stayed put in the front line: Padre Mayer. Under withering artillery fire he saved many lives by giving first aid and by carrying the wounded to safety."

Having earned three military distinctions and the Iron Cross in two years of service, he lost his left leg when shrapnel shredded his knee.

The collapse of Germany after the war was almost as dreadful an experience as the war itself: disruption of families, unemployment, poverty, political confusion everywhere. Rupert Mayer, now the limping parish priest of St. Michael's in Munich, proved once more his closeness to the people. He visited the sick and the poor, organized the men in a strong Marian sodality, and joined political rallies in the tumultuous *Bierhallen*.

It was here that he challenged first the Communists, then Hitler and his associates. Repeatedly he was shouted down. On one occasion a bully kicked against his wooden leg and sent him sprawling to the ground. But, whether

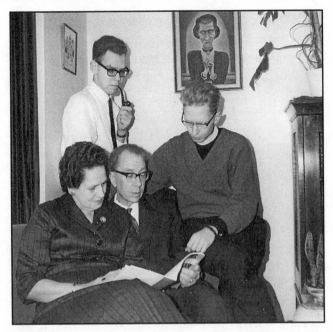

That's me on the right, one year before priestly ordination, with my father, mother and brother, Aloys.

friend or foe, people knew that here was a priest who spoke their language and cared for them.

Then there was **Teilhard de Chardin**, who had also served in the First World War. Teilhard was French. As a stretcher-bearer in the 8th Moroccan Rifles, he was constantly in the midst of enemy fire comforting and rescuing the wounded. For his courage he was awarded the *Médaille militaire* and the *Legion d'Honneur*.

Teilhard became a Jesuit scholar who combined expert knowledge of paleontology with profound present-day mysticism. His name as a scientist was secured when during one of his many geological expeditions to China, he was involved in the excavations at the so-called *Peking Man* site of Zhoukoudian, near Beijing. Teilhard helped establish that Peking Man belonged to the species of hominids called *Homo Erectus* and dated more than half a million years ago.

Next to his long and fruitful academic work, Teilhard also developed a revolutionary approach to understanding the evolution of human beings. In the seminary, I was thrilled reading his books such as *The Phenomenon of Man, The Divine Milieu* and *Hymn of the Universe*. Teilhard was a different kind of priest than Rupert Mayer and yet he too was a hands-on spiritual leader, not a sanctuary-hugging, thurible-swinging cult man.

And this is what I liked about *real* priests, as I called them. They could not be put into a narrow mould. They responded to the needs of the Catholic community in exciting, unexpected ways.

Mayer had been persecuted by the Nazis. Teilhard faced other enemies: conservative theologians in the Vatican. His writings were censured. He was forbidden to publish some of his best work during his lifetime. Fortunately, friends published them for him after his death. It prepared me for the opposition that a dedicated priest might face even from within his own Catholic community. And as I am writing these lines, the warnings against Teilhard's thinking are still not fully lifted by the Congregation for the Doctrine of the Faith.

Priests for people

The academic courses we studied at Mill Hill College - theology, sacred scripture, liturgy - were woefully substandard. Fr. Daan Duivesteyn ("Duivy," in students' parlance) entertained us with lengthy lectures on angels: Do they have wings? Are cherubim different from seraphim? Do they rank higher than human beings?

Only *moral theology* and *church law* stood out under the instruction of Fr. Serafino Masarei. We were not aiming at becoming scholars, however. We wanted to set the world ablaze with the revolutionary vision brought by Christ. So a number of us looked around to supplement our formation with other energetic teachers.

One such person was **Father Bernard Basset, S.J.**, who had been a chaplain to the Royal Air Force. He dreamt of transforming a passive laity into vigorous apostolic teams. So he founded the Cell Movement, which consisted of a wide network of laypeople connected mainly through the telephone. The network could trigger national campaigns, such as having hundreds write to newspapers to support Christian values when moral issues were debated. The network also initiated the push to "Put Christ Back into Christmas" and helped Britain focus on fairness to the Third World.

I read a number of Fr. Basset's books - *Priest in the Piazza, Seven Deadly Virtues* - and attended his courses in the centre of London. In one talk to seminarians he spoke these memorable words:

"Whatever you become as a priest, don't be a wimp. Christ's cause is not served by weak and spineless cowards. Stand with both legs firmly on today's ground and be prepared to wade through the muck and mud of real life."

I also admired the Flemish priest **Josef Cardijn.** Hailing from a working-class family himself, he was moved by the struggles of the men and women who toiled in Brussels' sprawling industrial estates. He saw that these workers needed to liberate themselves from their degrading circumstances through their own action. The trade unions usually failed because they did not address the root problems and ignored Christian principles. So he founded the Young Christian Workers (YCW).

Bringing groups of workers together, he taught them the method of "see, judge and act." *Seeing* required becoming aware of the facts. The group had to *judge* these facts according to Christian principles of justice for all. They then had to decide on a concerted plan of *action.* The YCW soon grew out into a vast and influential movement that formed generations of Christian leaders.

As Cardijn told priests in 1951:

"It isn't enough to preach to laypeople. The priest must go further; he must awaken in the laity a desire for the apostolate. He must help, encourage and guide them.... The priest must develop a profound sense of this responsibility, as well as the qualities which are needed to put it into action: human capabilities, fraternal love, a vision of the world and of the Church, boldness, courage, perseverance."

A small group of us set up a "task force" among the students in Mill Hill College with the explicit objective of seeing to it that the apostolate of the laity would be introduced to all the missionary areas to which we might be sent. We studied the training programmes conducted by the YCW in London. We followed with interest the reports of "extension workers" sent by the YCW to Third World countries to start the movement there.

On one occasion one such extension worker, on return from East Africa, held an important briefing session in the middle of London. We knew it would be crucial for us to attend that meeting. So, in spite of a clash with our strict college rules and without the necessary permissions, I and another student travelled to London and shared in the event. We returned back to Mill Hill College without our absence having been spotted by the authorities. If they had found out, it could have led to our expulsion from the College. We were serious indeed.

When Cardinal William Godfrey, Archbishop of Westminster, laid hands on me and 27 of my classmates on a sweltering day in June of 1959, he may not have realised what "troublesome priests" some of us might become.

I for one did not intend to be an institutional priest irrevocably chained to medieval structures, a member of a male mandarin caste. I sought to be a *priest for people*. I wanted as a leader to further the unusual dimensions of God's kingdom: love without profit; seeking peace instead of securing power; conquering fear by hope; reaching out to endless horizons in prayer. I wanted to help people see with new eyes; I wanted to spell out and evoke the deeper, spiritual meaning of reality. I wanted to interpret mystical realities and transform them into real life, to heal, dispense God's Spirit, celebrate God's presence.

I was set to defy convention, and to be a priest for people.

In my long ministry as a priest that was to follow, I often had to combat the ingrained idea that the first duty of bishops and priests is to defend the institution of the Church. Hence, my second commandment: **The first priority of pastoral leaders is caring for people, not upholding ecclesiastical institutions.**

Chapter 8

Training for 'academic war' at university

On the day I was ordained a priest I was given my first assignment. I was appointed to do higher studies in Rome in order to obtain a doctorate in dogmatic theology and a licentiate (a Master's) in Sacred Scripture.

So in September of 1959 I reported for duty in central Rome, to the lodge for Mill Hill university students.

There were eight of us studying various branches of theology. The frugal Fr. Martin Fleischmann, Procurator General of the Mill Hill Society, was our rector. Our house was actually an old villa that was surrounded on all sides by a lush garden. Its location could not have been better. In theory, we could travel to the centre of town by bus.

But boarding a crowded Roman bus turned out to invariably involve elbowing one's way in. Italians do not wait in polite queues, for that runs counter to Italian impetuosity, I was told. Impatient hordes would cluster round each bus terminal, all intent on boarding the next bus before anyone else. It proved a nightmare. I often stood, defeated, with one bus after the other carrying off triumphant Romans leaving me and some other stragglers behind. So I decided to find independent transport through Rome – which became possible when a Christmas gift from my parents enabled me to buy a bicycle.

Anyway, let me go back to the beginning. On arrival, Fleischmann directed me to register the next day at the Gregorian University in the *Piazza Pilotta*. My first aim was to acquire the licentiate of theology within one year, bypassing the normal course of four years. This was in consideration of the fact that I had already studied four years of theology in Mill Hill College. Gregorian authorities agreed but on the condition that I pass a one-hour oral theological entrance exam – *in Latin*! Latin was the official language of the Gregorian at the time.

I was in shock. I had studied a fair amount of Latin in my high school days, it is true, and in Mill Hill College we had used Latin textbooks for theology though lectures had always been given in English. Never had I been lectured to in Latin nor had I ever myself *spoken* Latin.

On the appointed day I found that the hour consisted of four 15-minute oral exams given by four different professors, each testing my knowledge of a different aspect of theology. I spluttered, I stumbled, I often groped for the right Latin words. But to my immense relief, I passed.

Thinking back on this gives me even greater satisfaction since I came to know that the talented Karol Wojtyla, who later became Pope John Paul II, failed a similar entrance exam at the Gregorian in 1946. This, in essence, re-routed him to join the nearby Angelicum University instead.

On reflection, this change of course may have proved his downfall as a theologian. For he missed the more modern and critical approach to theology taught by the Jesuits of the Gregorian in exchange for the antiquated Thomist approach still favoured by the Dominicans of the Angelicum. If he had studied at the Gregorian, he might have been less stuck in medieval thought – which led to huge setbacks to the universal Church.

God's people in Rome

I was determined not to lose myself totally in dusty academic libraries. I knew I was a priest, and priests are ordained for people. After a few months I had picked up enough Italian to start looking for priestly work in Rome on evenings and during weekends.

The situation of the Catholic Church in Rome was actually shocking. The population of the Roman suburbs had already slid into the mood of secularist indifference that now holds the whole of Europe in its grip. I scouted around and accepted a job as part-time assistant priest in the parish of Saints Francis and Catherine in Monteverde Nuovo. The church was popularly known as the *Due Patroni*, in view of the fact that Francis of Assisi and Catherine of Siena are the two patron saints of Italy.

Our parish was entrusted with the spiritual care of well over 20,000 people, 90 percent of whom were supposed to be Catholic. In fact, you would get a standard answer if you asked anyone, as I did a strikingly handsome young man who cut my hair in the local hairdressers:

"Are you a Catholic?"

"*Si, Padre. Cattolicissimo!*" (Yes, Father. I'm very Catholic!)

Such a reply did not necessarily mean he had visited church since his First Communion. Of our hordes of nominal Catholics, hardly 1,500 visited our church on Sundays, even though missing Sunday Mass was still officially listed as a mortal sin. The state of alienation from the Church may also be judged from the circumstance that hardly one in a hundred persons who died would receive the last sacraments. Rather than calling a priest to help a dying person make peace with God, they would wait for him or her to die, then pay two nuns to spend a night in prayer at the deceased person's bedside, as a superstitious remedy. For superstition flourished.

Our parish priest found a man on his knees before the statue of Our Lady.

I'm wearing typical student's clothing while sitting in the Forum Romanum *in Rome. The round black hat, known as the "tondo," was prescribed for clerical students.*

He had lit seven candles and was saying the rosary seven times, he told the priest. And he had started punctually at seven in the morning. He was convinced this would secure his passage to heaven. When the man had left, the parish priest realized that day was the seventh of July — therefore, the seventh day of the seventh month.

My main job consisted in celebrating Mass for the congregation at 10 o'clock, and hearing confessions during the 8, 9, 11 and 12 o'clock Masses. Every hour another Mass with a new congregation. And, since this was before the liturgical reforms, some of these Masses were for weddings, others for funerals, as the moment demanded. The changeover from one kind of Mass to another was stage-managed by a team of efficient sacristans.

I vividly remember an occasion when the 11 o'clock Mass had been a funeral. The altar had been draped in inky silk ribbons. Black banners were slung from the columns behind the altar. The deceased lay in her open coffin, flanked by tall, dark candlesticks and bouquets of white lilies. Because the funeral cortege had arrived late, the Mass ran overtime. The priest, predictably wearing a pitch black chasuble, was still incensing the body and praying the final commendation when, suddenly, a wedding procession stood at the main door to enter for the noontime Mass. I held my breath.

Brilliant Italian improvisation sprang into action. The coffin was quickly sealed and, along with the principal mourners, it was deftly conducted out of sight via a side door. The black decorations everywhere came down as if by magic. The soot-coloured mat down the main aisle was folded up, and a crimson carpet was quickly rolled out. Vases with explosions of red, yellow and pink flowers appeared as if from nowhere. In five minutes flat, a scene of somber mourning had been transformed into the flamboyant setting for a wedding.

During Easter time, all priests of the parish were expected to take part in the traditional blessing of homes. I, too, took part. I got a Mass server assigned to me who carried a small bucket with holy water. I was dressed in cassock and a white cotta, holding a sprinkler in my hand. We walked to the apartment buildings, the *palazzi*, as people called them.

In each building we would take the lift to the sixth or seventh floor and then work our way down. Four apartments opened out on each floor. The server would ring each doorbell and most people would invite us in, anxious to have the Easter blessing. But while I sprinkled room after room with holy water, they would simply continue doing what they had been doing before. I might as well have been a window cleaner. Only a few might kneel down and make the sign of the cross as I passed. In spite of the midday hour some were still in bed. I recall sprinkling a bedroom with a young couple wriggling and giggling naked under their bed sheets.

Now back to my studies.

Scriptural carnage

In today's Catholic Church, ancient and modern ideas clash, turning the study of theology into a battlefield. And the interpretation of Sacred Scripture stands right at the centre of the conflict.

When I began my spell in Rome's universities in 1959, the scriptural battle, which had already gone on for centuries, was coming to a head. And Scripture was the main focus of my own studies. So I found myself in the midst of the raging conflict on how Scripture should be understood.

What was at stake? Please, allow me here to digress into what may seem to be a slightly technical discussion. I assure you it is something every educated Christian should thoroughly grasp. And it was, and still is to some extent, a major battleground between blind tradition and openminded reform.

In the sixteenth century, the astronomer Copernicus had begun to show that it is not the sun that moves around the earth, but the earth that circles the sun. Theologians rejected this finding as heretical because, they said, "It goes against the inspired Scriptures." Matthew 5,45 was one text quoted to prove this claim. For Jesus says: "The Father makes the sun rise over good and bad alike." Therefore, it is the sun that moves and not the earth, they said. Moreover, Joshua 10,12-15 relates a miraculous event in which "the sun stood still." When Galileo Galilei proved that Copernicus had been right, the Holy Office ordered him in 1633 to retract his belief that the earth circles around the sun, and condemned him to house arrest till the end of his life.

Other conflicts developed during the 19th century. The Gospels were shown to be full of internal contradictions. Take the accounts of cursing the fig tree. According to Mark 11,12-25, Jesus cursed the tree on the way to the Temple. Then, "*next morning* as they passed by they saw the fig tree was withered to its roots" (vs. 20). Matthew 21,18-22 tells the same story but states that the fig tree withered instantly. "Jesus said: 'May you never bear fruit again!' and *at that instant* the fig tree withered (vs. 19)." Since this refers to one single, specific occasion, which of the two is right?

And what about such fantastic stories as the devil hauling Jesus up onto the pinnacles of the temple, or Peter catching a fish with a shekel in its mouth? Which of the Gospel stories are simply myths? Friedrich Strauss, writing in *The Life of Jesus* (1835), maintained that most of them are.

And it did not stop there.

Analysis of geological layers established beyond doubt that the earth must be millions of years old. Biologists such as Charles Darwin in 1859 postulated a gradual evolution of species. But this seemed to contradict texts such as Genesis 1,1-31 and Exodus 20,11 which assert that "*In six days Yahweh created the heavens and the earth and the sea and all that they hold.*"

The reaction of Christians is well known. Many refused to accept the findings of science. Others looked for harmonizing explanations. The creation in six days, for example, was explained as a creation in six *periods*. Desperate efforts were made to fit various scientific discoveries into the appropriate "period" of creation. The approach is still popular among creationists today.

The Jesuit scholar George Tyrrell (1861-1909) stood out among the theologians who attempted to solve the conflict between traditional faith and modern science. He sponsored a scientific method of examining Christian sources. Catholics should be "more open" to modern science, he urged. He argued that the Church's response to the religious problems of the modern age could not be simply to reiterate Christian dogmas that had been formulated in the thirteenth century. He held that the externals of the Church, like its laws and customs, needed to be trimmed to fit the religious culture of modern times and that Scripture, too, needed to be interpreted in a new way.

"Each age has the right to adjust the historico-philosophical expression of Christianity to contemporary certainties, and thus to put an end to this utterly needless conflict between faith and science which is a mere theological bogey" (*External Religion: Its Use and Abuse*, 1899).

We now know that Tyrrell was right in many ways. To interpret Scripture correctly, we first have to understand it accurately as human literature.

Scholars began to look at Scripture with new eyes. How should its texts be read? Galileo Galilei had already pointed the way with the observation

My parents toured St. Peter's Square in Rome in 1963, on the occasion of my promotion to the doctorate in theology.

that scriptural *teaching* is limited to what it says about God and salvation. In *presentation*, it adapts itself to how people popularly see things.

"With regard to the standing still or the movement of the sun and earth, the inspired Scriptures must obviously adapt themselves to the understanding of the people and this is what they achieve through the chosen expression, as experience shows. Even today the ordinary people, though they are no longer so uneducated, still have the same idea that it is the sun that moves." (*Letter to Duchess Christina of Lotheringia, 1615*)

But this was not the full explanation. After many false attempts, the liberating insight proved to be quite simple: Sacred Scripture is written language, is *literature*, and should be read as any other literature. And literature is governed by *literary forms*.

You cannot read a newspaper properly, for example, without distinguishing its literary forms. You know that the headline on the front page, "Beauty Queen bares her pitch black skin," reports a *fact*. An article somewhere more central in the paper bears the caption: "How to save the nation from skin cancer." You realise it expresses an *opinion*. Down the page a smiling girl declares, "Cranbury Cream cleared my face of pimples!" You recognise it to be an *advertisement*. You dismiss a strip story showing an alien putting on a human skin as *pure fiction*.

Understanding each of these scraps of text, we simply need to know their "literary form": News item? Ad? Editorial? And so on. The same applies to Sacred Scripture.

I began to realise that Scripture study consists not only of *exegesis*, which means drawing the right meaning from the original text, but it also needs *hermeneutics*, that is, an interpretation that makes sense to the ordinary people for whom Scripture was written.

All of this is to prepare you for the enormous battle in which I would soon be involved. For on the eve of the Second Vatican Council, when I was still in Rome, the Congregation for Doctrine suddenly suspended two most prominent scholars of the Biblical Institute from their teaching posts: Stanislas Lyonnet and Maximilian Zerwick. The Congregation also manipulated to have an arch-conservative document submitted to the members of the Vatican Council. It denied the validity of literary forms. It declared it to be Catholic doctrine that every single word spoken by Jesus in the Gospel was *literally* spoken by him.

This amounted to a declaration of war.

After obtaining my licentiate in theology in 1960, I attended the Pontifical Biblical Institute for two years, which resulted in my acquiring the licentiate in Scripture. Then I returned to the Gregorian University to obtain a theological doctorate with a dissertation based on Scripture.

Part II

On the Front Line

Chapter 9

Subversive tactics
at the heart of the Church

*T*he Second Vatican Council was probably the most important event
for the Catholic Church in the twentieth century. By a stroke of good
fortune for me, its preparations and opening happened during the time I was
studying in Rome.

It provided me with a unique insight into the inner tensions within the international Church community, notably between dyed-in-the-wool conservatives
on the one hand and open-minded reformists on the other. It also created in
me, for the first time, a feeling of deep anger at the abuse of authority by traditionalist Church leaders.

To understand the importance of the events of the time, it should be remembered that in the Western part of the Church, Latin was still the official language of the liturgy and of theological study. This had worldwide effects for
mission areas in Asia, Africa and South America, for these had been evangelised
by missionaries from the West. Missionaries had introduced Latin everywhere.
For all practical purposes, Latin had become the Church's official *lingua franca*
over much of the globe.

This, of course, made no sense. In Indonesia, for instance, where I was born,
no one had the slightest connection with Latin. The ordinary people spoke
Malay or various local Javanese dialects.

I was delighted, therefore, when an international study week on Mission and
Liturgy at Nijmegen in 1959 recommended that the liturgy in each country
should, as far as possible, adopt the language of the area. In fact, a year later
bishops and priests began to introduce the vernacular in some liturgical contexts
in the Netherlands. I myself eagerly adhered to this policy.

During one of my summer breaks from Rome, an uncle of mine, Karel van
Hoesel, who was parish priest of Buuren and Geldermalsen, had asked me to
take over his parish for a month so that he could go on a holiday. So for a month
I was an acting parish priest. At the time, priests in Holland had begun to read
the liturgical readings from Scripture in Dutch, but the rule prescribed that one
should first read the text in Latin before reading the Dutch translation. Most
priests would quickly rattle off the Latin in a muffled mutter and then read the
text once more in Dutch, this time audibly and understandably.

Following the example of some others, I boldly decided to omit the useless reading of the Latin before reading the Dutch. A more difficult decision arose when one of the older parishioners was at the point of dying. Again, the official regulations prescribed that the last rites should be performed in Latin. This made absolutely no sense since the dying person did not understand a word of Latin, neither she herself nor her family. But I was worried about any consequences of conducting the whole ceremony in Dutch.

I quickly consulted a theologian at Nijmegen University.

"Will the anointing of the sick be valid in Dutch?" I asked him. "Will it still be a sacrament?"

"Yes, it will be a valid sacrament. The language of the prayers does not belong to the essence of what you are doing," he assured me.

Fine. So I conducted the whole service in Dutch. This seemed all the more important to me because most of the members of the family in question were no regular churchgoers and mumbo jumbo in an ancient language would only make matters worse for them. I anointed the woman using the Dutch translation of the sacramental formula.

When my uncle returned from his holiday, he heard from me what I had done. And – to my relief! – he wholeheartedly applauded. He told me I had been right. He himself would do the same from now on.

Now to come back to Rome and the preparations for the Ecumenical Council. Various commissions had been set up, one of them dealing with liturgical reform. It so happened that I got to know one of the members of the liturgical committee, a certain Bishop Theo Valemberg, who was a retired missionary bishop from Borneo, Indonesia. He was a short man, a Capuchin monk, then in his seventies, with a white beard and long white hair and sparkling blue eyes.

During a visit to our Mill Hill community in Rome, he told us that certain conservative members of the commission were systematically suppressing demands from missionary countries that the liturgy should be adapted to the vernacular. It was a first indication of what was to come.

"How can they get away with such a thing?!" I asked with indignation.

"Easy enough," he said. "The Roman Curia controls the commission. They occupy all leadership positions. Also, the administration is totally in their hands. The secretaries and correspondents report to the Curia."

This made me feel uneasy. Rightly so, as it turned out.

◀ *A bishop serving on a preparatory commission for Vatican II visits our Mill Hill community, circa 1962. I don't recall the bishop's name or diocese. I am third from left.*

Thunderbolt from a clear sky

On a particular weekday in 1962, all the students at Rome's theological universities were invited to attend a special gathering in the *Gesù*, an ancient Church in the middle of Rome. I felt quite excited about this because we were going to be addressed by Pope John XXIII, whom I had come to like. He had a very human touch. During his weekly Sunday address from the balcony of his rooms overlooking St. Peter's Square and during general audiences, I had seen how he could really speak to the hearts of ordinary people, just bubbling away in colloquial Italian whenever he could. So I was wondering with pleasant anticipation what this special meeting was going to be about.

Imagine my surprise when, at the beginning of the ceremony, before the Pope even began to speak, it was announced that the Pope would be signing an important decree. It turned out that this decree, which was read out to us, imposed Latin on the whole Church with a new, formerly unknown ferocity. Latin was to continue throughout all liturgies. Latin was also to remain the central language for all theological studies. Candidates for the priesthood had to be tested specifically for their ability to learn and speak Latin. The decree stated:

"Any applicants for the priesthood who have no aptitude for learning or speaking Latin should not be admitted to ordination, whatever other good qualities they may possess."

The decree was read to us by Cardinal Antonio Bacci, an expert in Latin, who had been the head of the obscure Vatican office called "Secretariat of Briefs to Princes" for the previous 30 years. It was the office entrusted with translating all official Church documents into Latin, since Latin was considered the official language of the Church. Now, Bacci was an archconservative, a close associate of Cardinal Alfredo Ottaviani, the head of the Holy Office and the leader of opposition to reforms in the Church. At once it was clear to me that this decree, just a few months before the opening of the international Council, was a master stroke by traditionalists to try to close any doors to introducing the use of the vernacular.

I find it hard to describe how angry I was.

I refused to even listen to what the Pope said afterwards. I was just hopping mad at the thought that this scheming plan by a few Cardinals in the Roman Curia might block some of the necessary reforms that the Vatican Council was going to discuss.

After all, at the time I still considered the Pope as the person to look up to for real leadership. And now his authority was being abused in order to keep the Church firmly chained to its medieval dungeon!

After the student gathering in the *Gesù* was finished, I cycled around Rome in a state of fury. I travelled around to various ancient sites: the Coliseum, the busy streets of a market in Trastevere, the *Piazza Argentina* with its hundreds of wild cats climbing over ancient ruins of buildings that had been left exposed in the middle of the square, the old *Forum Romanum*, and several other places. I ended up in the park on top of the Gianicolo Hill with its magnificent views over the city of Rome.

Here had stood the temple of Janus, the god of ancient Roman mythology whose head possessed two faces: one turned eastward, the other westward. Janus was said to be able to forecast the future for anxious worshipers. I got off my bike and sat down on a patch of grass. I looked down on Vatican City, the dome of St. Peter's Basilica towering in its middle.

The long history of Rome oppressed me. I called to mind the abuses of the papacy in century after century from the Middle Ages on. I felt the Church needed to free itself from this unnecessary burden, not so much the burden of central leadership, which an international community needs, but of a central bureaucracy that was stifling the growth and development of authentic Catholic communities all over the world.

Again, dark and ominous anger welled up in me. The image of Moses came to my mind. He climbed down from Mount Sinai cradling the precious tablets of the covenant in his arms and then saw how down in the valley the people of God were dancing 'round a golden calf! In a fit of sacred fury he had smashed the tablets to smithereens on a rock, before rushing down to unleash his wrath on Aaron.

What was I going to do?

I could hardly claim to be another Moses. The visions I carried of a dynamic, open Church were not tablets of the covenant written on by God's own finger. But I refused to dismiss my dream of a vibrant Church as insignificant. In my own small way, I too was responsible for the health of the Church, like Moses had been for the relationship of his people to God.

It is hard, especially after such a long time, to re-live the storms raging in my mind and the prayers welling up from my heart. It all resulted in a firm resolution on my part not to let the traditionalist forces get away with their underhanded tactics.

Somehow or other the anti-reform movement had to be frustrated in its aims. I had no idea how that could be achieved, considering the power wielded by such a small group of determined Cardinals. But, acknowledging myself to be a fighter, I made up my mind that I would contribute in some way to making the dream of a relevant, vigorous and open Church come true.

From this experience, I formulated the third commandment for Church reform: **Select perceptive administrators in the Roman Curia, not narrow-minded bureaucrats intent on blocking Church reform.**

Chapter 10

Joining the battle at Vatican Council II

*I*n late September of 1962, the 2,200 Catholic bishops who were to take part in the Second Vatican Council converged on Rome. They were lodged in seminaries, colleges, tourist hotels, monasteries and convents. Our Mill Hill house provided accommodation to ten of our own bishops who worked in eight different countries. Sparks of excitement hung in the air.

Talking to one of our bishops from North Borneo, I found out that the traditionalists had been at work in preparation for the opening of the Council. When the bishop heard that I was studying at the Pontifical Biblical Institute, he inquired about two of our professors: Stanislas Lyonnet and Maximilian Zerwick. I told him that they were both brilliant New Testament lecturers – Lyonnet, an expert on St. Paul's letters, and Zerwick, an authority on Biblical Greek and on St. Luke's Gospel.

The bishop then told me in confidence that just before travelling to Rome, he and other bishops had received a letter to tell them that these two professors of the Biblical Institute had been suspended by the Holy Office because they were supposedly teaching suspect methods of interpreting Scripture. The letter further asserted that the whole Biblical Institute could not be trusted.

"The letter told us to keep this information secret," he said.

Sure enough, I soon found out that the Holy Office had suspended the two Jesuits from all teaching. I realised that this was another ploy by Cardinal Ottaviani in order to intimidate the bishops before the discussion on Sacred Scripture that would take place during the Council. By sending their warning to all bishops of the world in advance, they were trying to discredit the real scriptural experts even before these could be consulted by the bishops.

A joke soon made the rounds in Rome. A bishop from New Guinea had arrived at the local airport and had taken a taxi to go to his hotel near St. Peter's Square. However, the taxi driver got lost, could not find the right location. The driver excused himself saying, "Sorry! I'm new at this job. I used to teach at the Biblical Institute."

Meanwhile, it became clear that the more progressive leaders in the church had not been sitting still either. Before the Council started, some of the key cardinals in Europe with their close advisers had met in Bonn, Germany. There they had been fully informed about the machinations of the Curia. So when the bishops started arriving in Rome, the European leaders began to divulge the information they possessed. It is not widely realised how big an influence, for instance, Dutch bishops played at this time. Although only five residential bishops had dioceses in the Netherlands, there were another 70 Dutch bishops working in more than 50 missionary countries.

I was asked to drive our own six Dutch Mill Hill bishops in a minibus to a gathering in Nemi, just outside Rome. There Cardinal Alfrink had invited all 75 Dutch bishops to a complete briefing on the situation in the Vatican. Of course, I myself was not present at that meeting, but I received a lot of information from one or two of the bishops who were friendly to me.

When we had returned home late that night, I discovered that the Dutch bishops carried copious documentation with them to meetings of the bishops' conferences belonging to countries in Asia, Africa and South America in which they had dioceses. In that way, in a short time most of the bishops coming to the Council were given advance information on the objectionable tactics being employed by the Vatican offices.

At the same time a series of articles on the Curia was published in the *New Yorker* by someone with the pseudonym Xavier Rynne. It was obvious that the articles had been written with the help of insider information. These articles documented the many ways in which conservative Vatican officials had been trying to manipulate the process of preparation for the Council.

The first big conflict within the Council itself came to a head during its opening business session. Cardinal Ottaviani presented to the members of the Council ready-made lists of participants for the ten major conciliar commissions that would have control over the key areas of discussion. Ottaviani and his allies had stacked the proposed commissions with bishops whom they knew to be conservative. Ottaviani brazenly told the general assembly of the Council that it would be nonsense to expect bishops from far-flung countries to assess the expertise of bishops residing elsewhere. Candidates for the commissions had to be selected centrally, he asserted.

However, now the European counter-plan swung into action. Cardinal Liénard of France rejected Ottaviani's proposal and suggested instead that the Council should adjourn for two weeks to give the bishops a chance to suggest other names for the ten commissions. Cardinal Frings of Germany seconded. The assembly embraced the European proposal.

Frantic negotiations now began between the many bishops' conferences. The conference of each country was asked to prepare a list of the candidates from their own area whom they wanted to see appointed to particular commissions. These lists were then traded between countries, one country agreeing to adopt another country's experts, in exchange for that country accepting their own. It was a true democratic process with everyone having a say.

And so the miracle happened.

In spite of the huge number of bishops involved, new candidate lists for the various commissions were drawn up that carried the support of the majority of the 2,200 assembly members. So two weeks later, when the Council met again, these new lists were adopted rather than the stitched-up lists that had been cunningly engineered by the Curia.

I heaved a sigh of relief when I heard about this happy development. But my joy was short-lived. The first draft of a Council document submitted to the general assembly concerned Sacred Scripture. It was entitled "*De Fontibus Revelationis,*" which means "On the Sources of Revelation." Again, the Council members were told that this document was for personal use only. Fortunately, most Council members had enough sense to realise that they needed expert advice to assess the value of the document. One of our Mill Hill bishops, Cees de Wit, the Bishop of Antique in the Philippines, who also happened to be the youngest bishop at the Second Vatican Council, was one of my friends. He showed me the Latin document at the end of that day.

When I read the text, my heart sank. It obviously was a frontal attack on modern Scripture studies. As I perused paragraph after paragraph, I discovered at least 11 major errors. Though it was already late in the evening, I decided it was important enough to clearly flag these errors and provide a good translation of the text and an explanation of what was wrong in it.

To give just one example, the draft document stated something like this:

"This sacred Council solemnly declares it to be a matter of faith that the Catholic Church has always held, taught and believed that every single word spoken by Jesus as recorded in the Gospels was literally spoken by him in that form."

It is obvious that this cannot be true. For instance, the eucharistic words spoken by Jesus at the Last Supper are recorded in different forms by Mark, Matthew, Luke and John. Matthew 26,28 reads, "This is my blood of the covenant," whereas Luke 22,20 reports that Jesus said, "This cup is the new covenant in my blood." Both phrases express the same reality of course, but their formulation is different.

Though the evangelists faithfully recorded the *substance* of what Jesus said, they often interpreted his words according to their own theological themes and according to the needs of the audiences to which they addressed their Gospels. It is legitimate to ask, therefore, did Jesus himself speak of a *new* covenant? Or was the word *new* added in Luke 22,20 and 1 Corinthians 11,25 as a theological pointer to the "new covenant" announced in Jeremiah 31,13-34?

While the "Our Father" in Matthew 6,9-15 follows a Hebrew formulation because Matthew wrote for Jewish converts, the "Our Father" in Luke 11,2-4 has been adapted to a way of speaking familiar to Hellenistic audiences. Matthew still has "Forgive us our debts" (which well may have been the actual words spoken by Jesus), and Luke translates the phrase as "Forgive us our *sins*," which would be understandable to his Greek readership.

The enormity of the definition in the draft prepared by the Vatican is apparent. The Council was asked to define it as *a truth of faith* that every single word of Jesus as found in each gospel was *the actual word* spoken by him. It was obviously a mistaken proposition. But the implications lay deeper. For the pronouncement would have denied the whole process of gradual interpretation and elaboration of Jesus' message by his followers during the first generation of believers.

As I reflected on the state of the draft, I felt despondent. I was painfully aware of the fact that of the 2,200 bishops taking part in the Council very few had enjoyed the academic training needed to be aware of the true issues involved in that document. I thought of our own Mill Hill bishops, in Malaysia, Kenya, Pakistan, and the Philippines. Would they be a match against the wily, persuasive and overpowering pressure of the Vatican moguls?

I suddenly saw, as in a nightmare, that it would be so easy for even a large body of ill-informed men to be steamrolled by the heavy-handed leadership of a small group of determined Cardinals. I must admit that I began to almost despair, wondering if the Church would be able to escape this disaster.

After spending the whole night at finalizing my critical assessment of the draft and writing everything down, I handed it next day to my friend Bishop Cees de Wit with the request for him to make copies of it and hand it out to as many bishops as possible. He promised to do as I asked.

At the Biblical Institute later that day, I was informed that the draft on Revelation had been crafted by Cardinal Ottaviani himself with the help of Cardinal Rufini of Sicily and conservatives such as Professor Salvatore Spadafora of the Lateran University. Before the preparatory commission concluded its proceedings, they had invited two representatives from the Biblical Institute to attend. This included its Rector, Professor Vogt. This was done so that it could later be claimed that experts from the Biblical Institute had been involved in the production of the draft.

But when, on seeing the draft, the two experts from the Biblical Institute had voiced their strong objections, their intervention was rejected as coming too late in the process. Of course, Professor Vogt had seen to it that the European bishops' consortium was informed of what had taken place. Vogt was a German and had the ear of Cardinal Frings.

I also learnt from American Professor Moran that the suspension of Zerwick and Lyonnet had a happy side effect. They were being invited by many

A cartoon in a Dutch diocesan weekly of the time depicts confusion among Vatican monsignori.

gatherings of bishops who wanted professional guidance, and their suspension had freed them from lecture duties. So they could accept invitations round the clock. The Frenchman Lyonnet addressed French-speaking bishops of France, Belgium, Switzerland, Gabon, the Ivory Coast, the Cameroons, the Congo and Zaire. Zerwick explained the situation of Scripture studies to the German-speaking bishops of Germany itself, Austria and Switzerland.

Determined as I was to put my oar in, I prepared an article defending Zerwick and Lyonnet for the Gregorian University students' magazine *Vita Nostra*. The suspension of these two professors was totally unjustified, I wrote, because they were both deeply committed Christians and highly competent scholars. As a member of the editorial committee, I expected it would be relatively easy to get the article placed. Instead, I was summoned by Father Joseph Fuchs, a well-known German moral theologian who was the spiritual guide of *Vita Nostra*.

"I agree with every word you say in your article," he told me. "But, please, withdraw it."

"Why?" I asked.

"It's wiser to avoid confrontation."

"Should we not speak up when the Holy Office is wrong?"

"Look here," he said. "I understand your indignation. You are right. The Holy Office *is* wrong. But here at the university we are in a vulnerable position. We know that Cardinal Ottaviani has spies in all our lecture halls. Everything we say is monitored and reported on. Various of our professors have been called in for questioning in recent years. All our Jesuit institutions in Rome are under such scrutiny. Please, don't tell others about it."

"But that is ridiculous!" I protested. "They are bullying you. Should you just take that lying down?"

"Open conflict will harm us," he replied. "For your own sake and that of the Gregorian, please, withdraw your article. I am requesting you to do this as a favour."

I withdrew the article. I did not want to upset a good man like Joseph Fuchs, but to this day I am not sure that he was not too timid. Abuse of authority can only be cured when it is exposed.

The discussion on the Scripture document started in the Council hall on November 14, 1962, and lasted for six days. There was significant opposition to it, both because of its dismissal of modern scholarship and its separation of Scripture and tradition. When the German Cardinal Bea, head of the Secretariat for Ecumenism, and Cardinal de Smedt of Belgium demanded that the whole draft be rewritten, Cardinal Ottaviani retorted that the draft could not be rejected because it had been *approved* by the Pope.

This was not true, of course. The Pope had approved its being the *basis for discussion*. He had not approved its contents. Moreover, article 33.1 of the Council's rules clearly stated that drafts could be discussed, amended *or rejected*.

It came to a vote on November 19, and the draft was rejected, but by a small margin only. This caused a stalemate for outright rejection required a two-thirds majority. Next day, the Pope intervened. The draft *was* rejected, and another commission was appointed to produce a new draft.

Again, a moment of immense relief for me, as well as the realization that I had underestimated the intelligence of the bishops no less than the power of the Holy Spirit. The Council had shown it was capable of steering the Church to reform.

The document on the Liturgy sailed through stormy waters and was the first Council document to be formally ratified a year later. Full participation by the faithful was stated to be the main aim of liturgical reform. Translations of liturgical texts into vernacular languages was permitted.

This was a huge victory, the significance of which I was to see with my own eyes in India.

Chapter 11

Teaching future priests in India

*I*n the mid-1960s, I was appointed professor of Sacred Scripture at what was then known as St. John's Major Seminary in Hyderabad. A major seminary is a college in which future priests, called "seminarians," study philosophy and theology before their ordination.

Few people in India understood the term "seminary." We often got letters addressed to St. John's Cementary, St. John's Censustry, or even St. John's Cemetry! In this book I will refer to it as St. John's Theological College, or simply St. John's College. It was run by a fully qualified academic staff.

Hyderabad was at the time the capital of Andhra Pradesh, an Indian state that encompassed present-day Andhra Pradesh and Telangana. It was the fifth most populous state in India. In 1964 the state counted seven Catholic dioceses with a total of 460,000 baptised members.

Andhra Pradesh was at that time one of the regions of India in which many people felt attracted to Christianity, in marked contrast to the hostility or indifference displayed almost anywhere else in India. Look at the facts. The *Catholic Directory* of 1875 registered only 24,173 Catholics in Andhra; by 1964, these had grown out to 500,000! Fr. J.F. McGlinchey, who visited Vijayawada in 1922 on behalf of the Propagation of the Faith, made this observation:

"The mission of Bezwada [Vijayawada] is one of the most promising in India. Outside of the city, people would stream into the church in large numbers if only more missionaries could be found. Whole villages are ready to undergo instruction and embrace the faith, if the bishop could only supply the necessary personnel to go among them. The number of catechumens might easily be ten times larger with more men."

The need of fostering local vocations and training suitable candidates to become priests was obvious. After some earlier attempts, a major seminary for all of the Telugu-speaking area was established in Nellore in 1926 by the Mill Hill Missionaries. This institution was transferred to Hyderabad in 1963/1964, at exactly the time when I arrived in India to take up my teaching post there.

Staff and student body

Upon my arrival the academic year was already in full swing. The staff was comprised of ten men, most of them colleagues of mine, Mill Hill missionaries, and a few Indian professors. The students, in a two-year philosophy and four-year theology programme, soon numbered 180.

My principal task was to teach Sacred Scripture. As Dr. Gali Bali and I were the only Scripture professors, it proved a real challenge. The college library collection was very small, and preparing lecture material on topics ranging from the Old Testament prophets to the Johannine letters taxed a lot of my energy. Moreover, we were short of good handbooks, and effective teaching requires more than just oral instruction, as I soon learned.

When lecturing on Genesis, for example, I discovered that among the younger students, in spite of my presentation on "literary forms," many students tenaciously clung to the literal six-day creation concept. Small wonder, when I found out that in Kerala the standard catechism for high schools still carried this entry:

"In how many days did God create the world?"

"God created the world in six days."

Another issue I had to deal with was that it was nearly impossible for students to take accurate notes of my lectures. A student called "Balaswamy" came to see me one evening with some frank critical comments.

"What you say may make sense," he told me, "but it is all too complex! We can't be expected to write all that down. And how will we remember it afterwards? You have to provide us with notes, printed notes."

I knew he was right. So I decided to prepare printed notes for each lecture. It proved an enormous job. I had to type the text with a typewriter onto stencils, which were then copied on paper with the help of a Gestetner stencilling machine. With at least three lectures a day on different parts of scripture, it was a huge job. But it worked.

In a two-year lecture programme for the philosophy section and a four-year programme for the theologians, I had to cover all crucial parts of the Old and New Testaments. In the course of many years I produced hundreds upon hundreds of stencilled pages on a wide variety of courses.

I should also report that, on account of the lack of local resources, more than once I made the 10-hour voyage by train to Pune to do research in the library of the theological college run by the Jesuits. The SVD Missionaries would give me accommodation for a couple of days. Fr. Schlegel, SJ, librarian of the college, would give me a key to the library so that I had access day and night while I was in Pune. Remember that we had no photocopying facilities in those days. From commentaries and encyclopedia I had to laboriously write down on paper what I needed for my Scripture courses.

I loved my students. With few exceptions, they turned out to be keen learners, but also wonderful friends. They shared my ideal of a priesthood aimed at being of real service to people. This was confirmed when, with a local study group, I conducted a survey on vocations to the priesthood in Andhra Pradesh. It showed that Catholic boys in Andhra had great respect for the priestly ministry. Asked which professions or states in life they esteemed most, 247 college students established this order of importance: priest, teaching brother, teacher, doctor, engineer, soldier, farmer, lawyer.

I was fascinated in my study to note the difference between virtues stressed by the high school students (ages 10-16) and those recommended by the college students (ages 17-22). The former insisted more on the personal sanctity required ("purity of heart," "holiness of life," "devotion to God"). The latter emphasized the readiness to serve that should radiate from priests, brothers and sisters ("kindness," "patience," "love for people"). I wondered whether this difference indicated a maturing of judgment. Whatever the explanation, priests were expected to live up to high expectations. The students preparing themselves for ministry were very much aware of this.

The apostolic academy

Next to my teaching task, I was also entrusted with looking after the apostolic formation programmes that took place outside of class. These concerned skills such as public speaking, singing, youth ministry, adult faith formation and much more. Students would join small groups that focused on these areas. Once a month, in a full session of the academy, groups would report. Sometimes all would listen to an outside speaker.

Because our college well would dry up during the height of the dry season, our students would have an 8-weeks' break around that time. Visiting their families was important, of course, yet – with little work in the villages – it also amounted to a waste of valuable time. So to fill the gap, I created what I called the "holiday training projects." This meant that students were encouraged to attend events in other parts of India that provided opportunities for learning.

Organising productive training programmes for up to 150 students was a real challenge. Some students I sent to conferences or training sessions of the young Christian workers, Catholic family encounter, writers' courses, out-station building projects, charismatic prayer sessions, etc. Gifted individuals were given the chance of specialized training in playing traditional Indian instruments such as the *veena*, learning classical Indian vocal *ragas*, professional drawing, woodcarving, and so on. At the end of the holidays, each group would report to me and to the whole academy in a special session.

Travel and accommodation were rather inexpensive at the time. But with so many students, even small amounts would add up to considerable sums of money. And the money needed to be approved by each bishop for the candidates applying for the programmes in his diocese.

Fortunately, the annual bishops' conference for our State took place just

That's me on my motorbike surrounded by a group of students.

before the beginning of the dry season. So, with the help of my students I would prepare lists of the "holiday training projects" for the candidates of each diocese with a calculation of the expected costs. At archbishop's house in Secunderabad, where the Andhra Pradesh bishops' conference would take place, I would arrange to meet each bishop in person, submitting the list and asking him to sanction the amount budgeted.

In the beginning I faced stiff opposition from some bishops. Not only were they tight-fisted where money was concerned, but they also objected to students being offered special "holidays!" So in subsequent years I learned to re-name the whole exercise from "holiday training projects" to "summer training projects" – STPs for short.

A last chore remained. During the final days of the academic term, I would visit with each student individually. With each I would discuss the purpose of the STP for which he had applied. I would then hand over an envelope containing the exact amount in rupees needed for the event.

The language

I also made a great effort to learn the local language, Telugu. I speak six European languages and can read texts in Latin, Greek, Hebrew and Arabic.

But Telugu really is difficult. For instance, the language has four "t" sounds of which the most important are the soft "t" and the hard "ṭ." Pronunciation proved a challenge. To us who speak English, "pita," "p(h)ita," "pitta," "p(h) itta," "piṭa," "p(h)iṭa," "piṭṭa" and "p(h)iṭṭa" sound identical. Telugus hear the difference, and attach different meanings to them. In the beginning, when I tried to say "pitā putra pavitrâtma nâmamuna" – "In the name of the Father, the Son and the Holy Spirit" my students in Hyderabad would giggle. They told me I said "In the name of *the Bird*, the Son and the Holy Spirit."

Telugu script also comes with plenty of surprises. The vowels are attached to

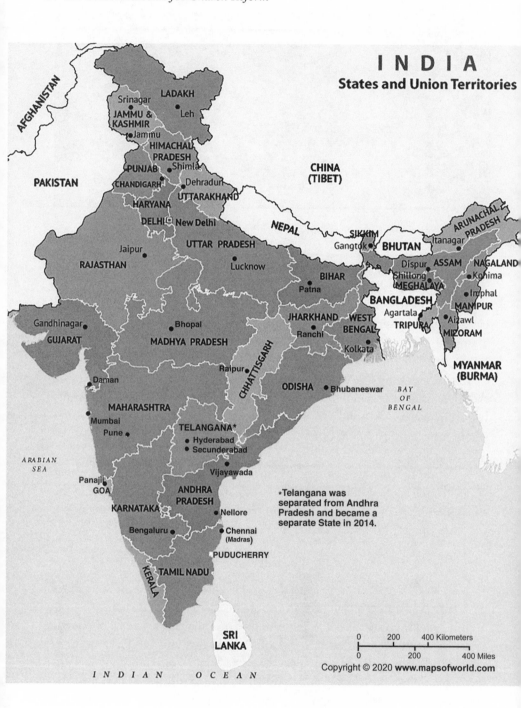

the letter so that there are separate signs for "ta" – "tâ" – "ti" – "tî" – "to" – "tô" – "tu" – "tû" – "tau," etc. If an "r" is added, as in "tra," "tro," "tru," etc., the sign changes again. Small wonder that Telugu printing presses at the time needed 600-plus separate blocks, to deal with each combination of the 48 consonants and 16 vowels the language possesses.

Throughout the 14 years I stayed at St. John's College, I continued to learn Telugu. Apart from employing a Brahmin teacher who gave me a weekly class in classic Telugu grammar, I was instructed by groups of students four evenings a week. Some tutored me in reading classic Telugu literature, some engaged with me in everyday dialogue. I also used to invite a crowd of Telugu children into my classroom after Sunday Mass so that I could tell them stories while they corrected me under, at times, fits of laughter.

And I frequently went to local cinemas to watch Telugu movies and learn from their dialogue. I recall in particular some wonderful films such as *Manushulu Mârâli* (People need to change), *Kôdalu Kâpâdina Kâpuramu* (A Family saved by the daughter-in-law), *Shrîkrishnâvâtâramu* (The Incarnation of Shri Krishna) and *Mêghadhûta* (The cloud with a message).

Although I could never speak the language fluently, I can say that I could understand and read almost anything in Telugu.

In line with new policies of the Mill Hill Missionary Society at the time, we were sent on short home leaves every second year during the dry season. On the alternating years I used the hot months to visit the homes of my students. One

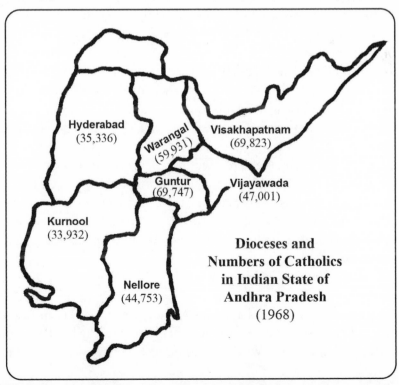

Hyderabad
(35,336)

Warangal
(59,931)

Visakhapatnam
(69,823)

Guntur
(69,747)

Vijayawada
(47,001)

Kurnool
(33,932)

Nellore
(44,753)

**Dioceses and
Numbers of Catholics
in Indian State of
Andhra Pradesh**
(1968)

year I would systematically travel throughout Andhra Pradesh to the villages from which my students hailed. Two years later I would do the same for students from Kerala.

The trips were long and exhausting. I would travel one day, say, by bus from Hyderabad to Mattampally. I'd stay in that village the next day, going to the homes of students, talking to their parents, seeing the local institutions, and joining in events. Next day I might travel, by bullock cart from Mattampally in Nalgonda Diocese to Dondapadu, home village of another student.

Getting to know the background situation of my students proved extremely useful. I really discovered people's lives and what mattered to them. Everywhere I was made to feel welcome. I made friends for life.

Once or twice the challenges almost proved too arduous for me. When, in Eluru diocese, a train full of passengers stood for hours on end in the midday sun outside a railway station, I felt a heatstroke coming on. A Hindu fellow passenger may have saved my life by offering me a drink.

Shadow of the Roman Inquisition

I cannot close this chapter without recounting a funny incident that happened in the college. In 1966, the "Dutch Catechism" was published with support from the Dutch Bishops' Conference. Its full name was *The New Catechism: Catholic Faith for Adults*. The 510-page book presented Catholic faith in a more up-to-date format. It acknowledged, for instance, that traditional formulation of doctrine needed to be revised, such as the medieval term "trans-substantiation," which is used in connection with the Eucharist.

It was an immediate mega-hit, with the original Dutch edition selling 400,000 copies in a short time. The English, French, and Spanish editions sold millions.

However, the Roman Curia was alarmed. They noted a list of "errors," among them the Catechism raising questions about the existence of angels, and when discussing evolution, its omitting to stress that human souls are "directly created by God."

Anyway, in 1968 the book also reached India. Our college bookshop ordered a good number of copies, but few of the students showed any interest in it – in spite of my recommending it. Then, one evening, the archbishop's car unexpectedly drove into the college compound. Archbishop Mark Gopu stepped out of the car and demanded an immediate emergency meeting for all the students in our conference hall.

When all the students had been assembled, the archbishop explained the reason of his visit.

"The papal *nuncio* has issued a serious warning," he stated. "There is a serious menace to Catholic faith. A catechism has been published in the Netherlands that is full of heresies. We should be on high alert! No one should read the book or distribute it! It destroys orthodoxy. I just came to make you all aware of the danger."

Obviously, conservative forces in the Vatican had been at work.

After a few other short remarks, the archbishop ended the conference and headed home.

And then the fun started.

Within half an hour all the copies in the bookshop had been bought up by the students, and many more were ordered. It confirmed my trust in the good judgment of my students.

Chapter 12

Establishing a Catholic
Information Centre

*A*lthough my work at St. John's kept me quite busy, I was soon drawn into the wider apostolate. In 1965, we received a crucial letter from Fr. Anthony Arulappa, director of the Catholic Centre in Chennai.

Fr. Arulappa, who later would be elected Archbishop of Madras-Mylapore, wrote:

"Until now we have run from here, in Tamilnadu, a correspondence course on Christ in Telugu. But Telugu is the state-language of Andhra Pradesh. Most of our enquirers come from Andhra. I feel it would be more appropriate for the course to be sent out from Hyderabad. Can you take over? I will send you all the printed copies of the lessons we still have."

The letter landed on my desk since I was in charge of the apostolic academy of the college.

After reflection, I agreed with Fr. Arulappa. Telugu was only a secondary language in Tamilnadu but the principal language of Andhra Pradesh. Moreover, when I surveyed how little the Catholic Church in Andhra Pradesh was doing in the field of the media, I was shocked. There were some small printing presses, one local Telugu Catholic weekly, and two ragged monthlies. But a concerted effort to communicate through the modern media - the printed word, radio, TV, film, etc. - were totally lacking. Something needed to be done.

I replied to Fr. Arulappa asking him to send us the material he had - which he did. In the college I recruited a team of volunteers to take up the challenge of the correspondence course. I studied how the course worked.

Correspondence courses were actually highly effective at the time. More than 80 percent of the population lived in villages and their literacy rate was improving through better education. Bookshops were found only in towns. A trickle of copies of Telugu newspapers would reach a village. Few could afford to subscribe to them, but visitors to a local town might bring a copy home - which would then be passed on to friends and neighbours. The lessons of a correspondence course, which were sent out through the postal service, could reach almost anyone.

The system consisted in advertising a free Christian leaflet in the Telugu dailies. Leaflets dealt with topics such as "Why I believe in one God," "The Voice of Conscience," "Your real beauty lies inside you" and "The Parable of the Lost Son." When a person ordered a leaflet, he or she would receive it with an invitation for him or her to join our information course on Christ. Our experience was that one of every four persons asking for a leaflet would enroll in the course.

I ran the course for a year with the help of my volunteer students. We sent out thousands of copies of lessons every month. I realised that while the potential was huge our amateurish attempt to run it from the college would not meet the task. So I took it to the Bishops' Conference of Andhra Pradesh.

Giving birth to the new centre

The seven bishops showed little interest in setting up a new structure. They were more interested in the day-to-day survival of their 219 parishes with the 3,230 outlying mission stations served by these parishes.

But fortunately, Mark Gopu, the Archbishop of Hyderabad, listened to me. He was willing to support the new venture – even though part of his mind still hovered in the Middle Ages. For instance, he did not want a telephone installed in Archbishop's House, which caused many unnecessary personal visits by priests, religious and lay leaders where a simple phone call would have solved a problem. Eventually, a telephone *was* installed in his office, without his knowledge, by his Vicar General, when he was away on vacation.

Anyway, Archbishop Gopu helped me acquire provisional premises for the new centre, to be called Catholic Information Centre, in the middle of Secunderabad. It consisted of one classroom released free of cost for this purpose by St. Patrick's School. Now I needed to find staff, especially a competent person who could run it full-time with the help of volunteers. That person, I reasoned, should preferably be a religious sister or brother, therefore someone committed to the apostolate and well trained.

I had by then been made moderator of the Conference of Religious, known as the CRI, in Andhra Pradesh. That gave me access to the superiors of the eight religious congregations working in the archdiocese.

Believe it or not, it took me five months to achieve my purpose. I met many superiors face to face and explained the need. I pleaded at general meetings of the CRI. The standard answer I received was that all the sisters (or brothers) had been trained to teach in schools or be nurses in hospitals and clinics. Mass media communication, and certainly just organising a correspondence course, was well beyond their reach.

"Religious orders can't afford to waste a person," I was told.

Meanwhile, the new centre limped on with the part-time help of some college students and primary-school teachers. I came close to despair.

This valiant group of volunteers helped a lot in our first office for our Catholic Information Centre. Left to right: Sr. Barbara, Gloria, Cecilia, Mrs. Braganza, Victoria, and two others whose names I don't recall.

The breakthrough came when one of the more conservative congregations, the Sisters of Charity, presented a candidate for the job: Sr. Attilia Saldanha, a trained librarian who had asked to be given a more apostolic task. She proved to be a godsend. Her training provided the skills needed to set up a really professional administration. She was intelligent, so I was able to plan with her the design of new leaflets and the expansion of our range of courses, like the ten-lesson "Meet Christ" course for beginners and the 40-lesson "Know Christ" course for advanced enquirers. Attilia also got on well with her helpers, the volunteers. And most of all, she was utterly committed to the task as a ministry, keen to help the enquirers who were looking for guidance in their life.

While the correspondence courses were now beginning to flourish, I knew we were not tackling the other media that should be employed. It was time to express my concerns in public.

Rallying cry

I found a compelling thought in the writings of Thomas Jefferson, one of the founding fathers of the USA:

"Even when few are convinced of a certain mode of action, if among them there is one who sees a new light and has the courage to speak, if he speaks loudly and convincingly with good reasons, then though he be laughed at and ridiculed in the beginning, slowly there will be more to think like himself and all will come to see the new light."

Good advice indeed!

So in 1971 I published a 16-page booklet with illustrations entitled, "New Priorities in Andhra: Communications." In it I described the various means of mass communications, their potential for India, and what involvement would mean for the Church. And I passionately implored those responsible in whatever institution not to ignore this challenge.

"I feel it my duty to call the attention of all engaged in the apostolate to a number of indisputable facts, to a vision of new possibilities, to a few crying needs which should no longer be overlooked. In Christianity we are very much involved in the work of communication. We are communicating to people a new message, the Word of God, and we are communicating to them the grace, the forgiveness of our lord Jesus Christ....

"It is practically impossible to overestimate the important role which the means of mass communication are playing and will play in the future for the building up of Indian society. Literacy rates are steadily improving. Radio has successfully conquered the hearts and minds of many in the nation. Films have already begun to mould the ideals and aspirations of Indian communities. India is now the largest film-producing country in the world. Likewise, the greatest potential force of the future is television.... The task that lies before the church in this field is enormous."

To my delight, the Catholics of Andhra Pradesh began to respond. For example, Bishop Ignatius Mummadi of Guntur Diocese released Fr. Yeruva George to start a department for producing Telugu books. Then, I got scholarships for Mr. Thumma George and Fr. Marneni Julian to study communication courses in Manila, with a view of opening a radio department. Also, the JMJ Congregation released a Telugu sister to write personal letters in Telugu to enquirers who had asked questions.

Our Centre in St. Patrick's school was expanded by one more room. But it soon became clear that much better premises would be needed.

Planning a new home

In 1971 Archbishop Mark Gopu died suddenly. His successor, Samineni Arulappa, showed even more interest in the communication apostolate. When I went to discuss my vision of establishing a new permanent base for the Information Centre, he promised full cooperation.

In fact, he showed me a plot of land right in the centre of Secunderabad, owned by the archdiocese, which he was willing to give for the project. An old, decrepit house stood in the middle of the plot. It was known as "the widows' home." Recent monsoon rains had penetrated deeply into the roof and walls of the building. The house was literally crumbling.

"I can find alternative accommodation for the women who live there," the archbishop stated. "You can build your new centre here."

I was delighted. But for the project to succeed I needed money. I drew a rough sketch of a small two-story building which, I thought, would do. Then I

Sr. Attilia (left), a member of the Sisters of Charity, helped to set up a truly professional administration that proved effective in launching our new Catholic Information Centre.

dashed off on a lightning trip to Europe to dig up finances. Three encounters would prove crucial to my eventual success.

Dr. Joseph Eilers, SVD, at the Catholic Media Council in Aachen looked scornfully at my drawing. He told me that experience in other countries had shown that I should "think big" and not start with tiny structures that would prove inadequate in just a short time. He also advised me to design the Centre in two halves: a rear end for offices used by the Centre, but also a front half for offices that could be rented out to outsiders to create income.

His ideas struck me as brilliant. I immediately revised my plan as he suggested. The building now encompassed a larger area and was to be four stories tall.

With the new plan and a recommendation by Dr. Eilers, I visited *Missio*, also in Aachen, and submitted an application. Then I travelled to the Hague in the Netherlands to meet with the organisers of a new Dutch initiative called *Kom Over De Brug* (KOB), a one-off campaign to support major projects in mission countries. I was lucky. The secretary-general of KOB assured me that my application was just the kind of project they were looking for.

The crisis

I could not believe my good fortune when soon afterwards, in 1973, I got the news that my applications had been accepted by *Missio* and KOB. I received the money needed for constructing the new building. Fantastic! I got an architect to draw up detailed plans.

Knowing that I had no experience at all in the construction business and would not have the time to oversee the actual building process, I got lucky again. I managed to secure the services of Brother Hubert de By, MHM, who until then had been working at St. Joseph's Technical School.

So far so good. In September, at the end of the second mini-monsoon, when a regular flow of water for cement mixing was assured, I told the contractor to go ahead and start the work. The Archbishop of Hyderabad laid the foundation stone and said a prayer. Since the building firm had a Hindu workforce, a coconut was then broken in front of a statue of the Hindu god, Ganesh. Drinks and cakes were served. The digging of the foundations started under Brother Hubert's competent guidance.

Then, a big problem. A government inspector visited the site, looked at the plans and declared them unfit. However, he would allow us to go ahead, he said, if we gave him an enormous bribe. Building works were halted.

I was just on the way to Bangalore to give a four-day course on Scripture at the National Biblical Catechetic Liturgical Centre when I got the bad news. What could I do? Our budget was tight, but any delay would cost us money as we had to keep paying the contractor. Moreover, after some days the dependable flow of water might stop, thereby seriously hampering construction. The blackmailing inspector was well aware of this.

While at the Centre in Bangalore, I met a well-known moral theologian, Fr. Finbar O'Connolly. He was a good man and I had a lot of confidence in him. I told him of my dilemma.

"I feel I will have to give the bribe," I said.

"I advise you strongly against it," he replied. "You may not do so with a clear conscience. Yes, it may be robbery but by giving the bribe you condone all the corruption that is constantly going on in Indian society. Don't do it."

On the plane on the way back to Hyderabad I carefully weighed his argument. Obviously, I did not want to condone corruption. But if it was robbery, as was clear in this case, how far did we need to go in opposing it? If a thief were to assault me and demand my money on pain of harm or death, I would gladly hand over my money.

So as soon as I arrived back in Hyderabad, I gave orders to pay the bribe, and the building work resumed.

I had hardly recovered from this upset and from my moral torment, when a second, even heavier blow, struck. Just two weeks later, in October, the first global oil crisis happened. Arab countries withheld oil supplies, and the price of oil skyrocketed. In a short time the cost of a barrel of oil quadrupled, from $3 to $12. This impacted the cost of building supplies such as cement and bricks. The whole world reeled under the financial turmoil, and it hit India in a very big way.

I saw that the increased cost of building material would cause an enormous shortfall in our budget. The building work was going on, and I could not stop it.

I immediately began seeking a loan from all church authorities I knew. Everyone refused – the archbishop and all the other bishops, religious superiors and heads of Indian charities. I knew that some of them had the capital to help me out on a short-term basis. But in spite of all my pleas, they threw responsibility back at me:

"This is your pet project, your baby. Sort it out yourself!"

It is difficult to describe the agony I went through. Big action was called for.

I travelled back to Europe and visited *Missio* again. KOB had wound up its campaign. I explained to the new Secretary General of *Missio* what had happened, but he dismissed me, saying that *Missio* could not give loans and that I had to complete the project within the budget I had submitted in my application.

"The world oil crisis is no valid excuse!" I was told.

Fortunately, I had gotten to know about the Swiss Lenten Fund. Ferdinand Luthiger, the project manager for Asia, and a commercial expert, Dr. Willi Dober, were due to visit India soon. I met them and persuaded them to use the

Presiding at an Indian-style Mass for the Catholic Information Centre staff are (left to right) Fr. A.C. Jesurajan, Fr. Christopher Coelho, Fr. Y. George, Fr. Raymond, me, Fr. Mariadas, and Fr. P.D. Varkey.

occasion to judge the situation for themselves.

This eventually saved the day. Mr. Luthiger and Dr. Dober visited the building site and declared that the sudden financial upset was not due to mismanagement on my part. Catholic Media Council agreed. Finally, just in time for us to complete the building, various Catholic agencies, including *Missio*, God bless them, released a further grant to cover the debt.

It is a miracle that I survived that crisis in one piece!

Phenomenal growth

At the advice of Mr. G.S. Reddy, a Catholic member of the Indian Parliament in New Delhi, we chose a truly Indian and Telugu name for the Centre. From about 100 options that wide consultation had produced, we chose *Amruthavani*. "*Vani*" means "voice, sound." "*Amrutha*," from Sanskrit for "immortal," stands for the sweet nectar the gods and goddesses drink in paradise. *Amruthavani* expresses "the good message'" in a truly Indian metaphor.

I commissioned Dr. A.C. Jesurajan, SJ, who had just completed doctorate studies in Manila, to take a close look at *Amruthavani* and what its priorities should be in the Andhra Pradesh of the time. His excellent report produced reliable guidelines on the printed word, radio, film, TV and traditional folk media.

While the structure was rising, I had also started concentrating on attracting more competent staff. I knew that my full-time teaching job in St. John's College would prevent me from giving the Centre the 24-hour leadership it would need. So I used my nationwide travels, giving courses and attending meetings, to recruit an overall director. I was determined to find the best.

After two years my search was rewarded. Fr. M.M. Balaguer, SJ, took the job of Director General. He had a good track record. For years he had held top jobs, such as being the principal of the renowned St. Xavier's College in Mumbai and being in charge of all 2,000 Jesuits undergoing training in India. Fr. Balaguer was both a saintly priest and a man of great vision.

He was soon joined by Fr. Raymond Ambrose of Hyderabad Archdiocese, who became the Executive Director of the Centre. In all my life I have not met anyone who could match his dynamic and creative style of organisation.

I retained the position of Director of Planning until I had to leave India, in 1976. By then, *Amruthavani* had 12 flourishing departments with more than 70 capable staff members, and the Centre was clearly succeeding in its mission.

Chapter 13

Funding Church projects
at the grassroots

*T*hough Christianity made little headway in other parts of India, in the State of Andhra Pradesh it received a welcoming response.

The response was so strong, in fact, that in the 1960s and '70s thousands of Telugus were applying for Baptism every year. This alone put a heavy strain on the local churches' resources. The churches were indeed experiencing growing pains and were under significant financial stress. The need for steady, reliable financial aid was obvious. I felt called to help, and so I went to work to try to find a solution to this widespread financial problem.

The scope of the problem came into clear focus in 1967 during a follow-up meeting to Vatican II.

Delegates from the seven dioceses which the State possessed at the time had come together in Kurnool, in Anantapur district. After spending the night lying on our mattresses in a boys' boarding school, we gathered in a classroom where seats and desks had been arranged in a circle. The topic of the meeting was evangelisation. The chairman was the stocky, irritable and unpredictable Bishop of Kurnool Joseph Rajappa.

The priests who were present reported on the steady stream of catechumens who were entering the church. But they expressed dissatisfaction, if not frustration, at the manner in which aid agencies in the West were supporting their apostolate. Common complaints were:

- "My neighbour gets enough money to build a cathedral; I can't even afford a motorcycle."
- "For every small request, you have to fill in endless forms or wait for months before it is approved, and for some months more before the money actually arrives. Meanwhile, you may have been transferred to another parish."
- "One only gets aid if one follows the policies of the grant-giving agency. I find it easier to apply for a pigsty than for a prayer hut to instruct catechumens."
- "How can people in Europe decide on what is needed most in India?"

Heated discussions followed. Some suggested that we should apply for pigsties, which some agencies supported, but then use the money to build prayer huts in catechumen villages. Others wanted the bishops to complain to the Pope.

It was obvious that something was terribly wrong.

On the one hand, I understood the general mood in the West, which was in favour of giving priority to relieving poverty. On the other hand, I was convinced that the aid agencies, if properly advised, would try to help the local church in their genuine needs. So I addressed the meeting and made a promise:

"If I will be allowed to represent the bishops of Andhra Pradesh, I will talk to the aid agencies and see if something can be organised."

The other side of the picture

The bishops authorised me to represent them. So in 1968 when I was granted a short home leave during summer holidays at the seminary, I visited the headquarters of various aid agencies.

First, I went to the *Katholische Jungschar* in Vienna. I was well received by Mrs. Helga Schriffl, who was in charge of the mission department at the time. She was very sympathetic to what I had to say. And she made me understand that the aid agencies had problems of their own. This was confirmed in meetings I had with other aid directors.

The project desks of a typical European aid office were flooded with applications. The staff responsible for screening and approving them had little factual information to go by. When I visited the offices of MIVA in Breda, the Netherlands, for example, I could see the problem firsthand. MIVA dealt with applications related to vehicles for missionaries and development workers. They showed me a list of 15 applications for jeeps and motorbikes by priests in Andhra Pradesh. They asked me:

"Can you let us know which of these are the most deserving cases?"

"I can't," I said. "Andhra Pradesh is so large that it is impossible to know the situation in all dioceses, even less in each of the 219 parishes with their 3,230 out-stations. It is only the local people who would be able to tell you which of these applications is more urgent than others."

I also found that the sheer volume of the work reduced the time available for evaluation. The project director for India in *Missio Aachen* told me he could allow no more than 20 minutes' assessment time per application. Skillful writers who presented projects well had a better chance of receiving aid than, perhaps more deserving, local leaders who were fluent only in their own vernacular. Moreover, the European staff would be more inclined to sanction bigger projects which might look more worthwhile than smaller ones which they found it difficult to assess. So one particular parish might be given Rupees 100,000

◀ *Fr. Boon of the Diocese of Kurnool instructs catechumens in front of their prayer hut.*

(£6,000 at the time) to build an oversized church while the same amount could have been utilised to finance dozens of smaller projects:
- 2 one-day instruction camps for 100 persons each
- 2 motorcycles for parish priests
- 10 prayer huts for catechumen villages
- 2 one-year scholarships for children in a village boarding school
- Grants to 10 catechists of a pushbike, a buffalo, and an annual salary each

Giving birth to the 'new baby'

It was clear that the solution required more than superficial adjustments. It needed a radical re-think. Not only much of the administration of aid application, also a large share of the decision-making should be in the hands of local churches. But how?

It was while visiting the headquarters of Swiss Catholic Lenten Fund in Luzern, Switzerland, that I began to see new possibilities. What impressed me most of all was the structure of the Swiss setup. They made a clear distinction between three bodies with specific and separate responsibilities:

1. Data gathering about the projects and their administration were handled by the "central office."

2. An "advisory committee" of independent experts met from time to time to decide on principles of priority and to select the specific projects that deserved to be funded.

3. "The bishops conference" retained ultimate responsibility by appointing the officials in the central office and the members of the advisory committee.

I concluded that we should adopt this same model for Andhra Pradesh.

The difficulty was not only setting up the actual organization in India but especially to sell this new approach to our bishops who were anxious to keep as much control over their dioceses as they could. Would they accept the decisions of a statewide advisory committee? And what about the aid agencies? Would they agree to work with the dioceses of Andhra Pradesh in this manner?

Months of negotiations followed. I talked to individual bishops as well as to our bishops' conference in session. I kept in touch with the agencies. A beginning was made by the recruitment of full-time staff to our central office. The bishops appointed the first diocesan delegates to the statewide advisory committee. A first overall pastoral programme was drawn up with a budget for the whole region.

But what would we call the whole venture?

Originally we called it "Illuminare" [to illuminate]. But then I recalled the advice of Mr. G.S. Reddy, a Catholic member of the national parliament.

"Our Christian missionaries have made mistakes by giving their institutions Western names, such as Institute for the Poor, Communication Centre, etc.," he told me. "We should choose Indian names which resonate naturally in the hearts and minds of our people!"

So I enlisted the help of seminarians, college students, religious sisters, diocesan priests and prominent lay people to search for the right name. Eventually I had a list of more than 100 possible names. These were scrutinised on their merits.

In the end, a good name emerged: "*Jyotirmai.*" When the bishops accepted the name, the unique partnership between local churches and European aid agencies was born. *Jyotirmai* is Telugu for "radiant with light." And light it would shed!

Now we had to get the agencies on board. The five most interested partners proved to be AMA, the mission fund of Dutch religious congregations; the Austrian *Katholischer Jungschar*; *Missio Aachen* and *Missio Munich* in Germany; and Swiss Catholic Lenten Fund. Next, a proper agreement needed to be worked out.

At my invitation the agencies sent a delegation to Andhra Pradesh: Ferdinand Luthiger of Swiss Lenten Fund and Dr. Willi Dober, an expert on business management, who was also an advisor to Swiss Lenten Fund. They spent two weeks going round various dioceses to see the parishes in action. Then they met with the statewide *Jyotirmai* Advisory Committee and finally with the bishops' conference. Dr. Dober and I drew up an agreement that outlined the principles of the partnership. After discussion it was signed by both parties.

Seeing the baby grow up

Under the new agreement, local applications were no longer submitted to the agencies separately and judged on their own merits. Instead, every year the local needs and priorities of the dioceses were expressed in one overall statewide pastoral plan. The agencies supported the plan by providing the lion's share of the required budget.

Though the bishops' conference retained ultimate responsibility, it had entrusted the tasks of screening and planning to the *Jyotirmai* committee, which consisted of 2 bishops, 15 priests, 9 sisters, 2 brothers and 14 lay people drawn from different dioceses. I was general secretary of the committee.

The committee had true decision-making power. It laid down pastoral priorities. It allocated which portion of the budget should be spent for each type of project. It determined which specific projects could be funded in a particular year and on what conditions. It supervised the execution of the projects for which aid was given. It acted as an economic planning body, a parliament, and a ministry of finance, all wrapped into one.

After decades of successful operation, the merits of *Jyotirmai* have been unmistakable. Its impact has been proved beyond doubt. Large-scale and expensive

Gathering for a picture at a public meeting in an Indian village are (left to right) Dr. Willi Dober, the village chief, me, the local parish priest, Ferdinand Luthiger, and the village's mother superior.

building programmes were effectively stopped or at least curbed. It was the smaller projects that were favoured. Preference went to training and to helping the "underdog:" village communities, one-shirt catechists, children from far-out hamlets who could receive a good Catholic education only in parish headquarters.

The budget for 1982, for example, spent only one-third on buildings: four dormitories for village boarding schools, three moderate-size churches, 25 multi-purpose chapels/schools, seven houses for priests, three convents for nuns, and 50 thatched-roof prayer huts. The other two-thirds covered 298 instruction camps benefiting 25,000 people, 21 literature programmes, 9 motorcycles, grants to 583 catechists for one-month in-service training, and scholarship grants to 1,305 school children and 400 college students.

Without *Jyotirmai* most of these mini-projects would never have received aid. No agency in the West could have handled the screening required or guided the funds so effectively to village-level beneficiaries.

The Vatican was not pleased

You will not believe this, but nervous monsignori in the Roman Curia watched *Jyotirmai* from a distance with a measure of disapproval.

In those years Aid to the Church in Need had grown out to be one of the largest aid agencies in the Church. It had been founded by Dutch Fr. Werenfried van Straaten. He was concerned about the plight of the millions of East

Germans who fled to the West before the iron curtain came down. I knew the movement. While studying at the Gregorian university in Rome I devoted one month of my summer break each year to helping out German parishes that were straining under the influx of migrants. In the beginning Aid to the Church in Need focused exclusively on supporting dioceses under communist control in Eastern Europe. Later they extended help to missions worldwide.

So could *Jyotirmai* benefit?

I contacted Frau Willemen, Fr. Werenfried's niece, who managed the agency at the time. She welcomed me and the other *Jyotirmai* aid-giving partners to a meeting at her headquarters outside of Frankfurt, Germany. Representatives from *Katholische Jungschar*, Swiss Lenten Fund, *Missio* and AMA duly turned up. When we explained how *Jyotirmai* functioned, Frau Willemen replied that she would need to consult some experts in Rome. The reply soon came back:

"I am afraid we won't be able to join the scheme," she said. "The problem is that the *Jyotirmai* committee takes fundamental decisions which affect projects in individual dioceses. But according to Church law, each bishop should have total control over his diocese. *Jyotirmai* works on democratic principles. It runs counter to the hierarchical nature of the Church."

"But that is nonsense," I argued. "Each bishop appoints delegates to the *Jyotirmai* committee. The bishop also helps to choose the projects to be submitted to the committee for inclusion in the overall budget."

"Not enough," she replied. "The bishop has to have final control. Aid to the Church in Need will only sanction projects directly submitted by the bishop."

"Final control?!" I said. "Your agency decides whether to finance the project or not. Don't *you* exercise final control?"

I could not make her change her mind. I and others who had *Jyotirmai's* best interests at heart left that meeting in Germany with considerable frustration. We were sorely disappointed.

Chapter 14

Creative endeavors
in book and film

*W*hile trying to do justice to my lecture programme in the College I was also involved in a whirlwind of creative endeavors that were exciting, thrilling, and often exasperating.

One such effort was my writing the text for an illustrated version of the life of Christ. The highly successful booklet is part of the famous *Amar Chitra Katha* series of illustrated lives, which was popular all over India at the time.

The series was founded by a devout Hindu editor, Anant Pai. Impressed by the popularity of comic books like *Spiderman*, he realised that a picture book series on religious and political figures from India's past would help to inculcate respect for traditional Indian values. So he founded *Amar Chitra Katha* [in Hindi, "Immortal Stories in Pictures"] with the financial backing of Sindhi capitalist H.G. Mirchandani.

In 1969 the first booklet appeared: *Krishna*. Twenty years later, by 1989, 400 titles had appeared in English, Hindi and other major Indian languages, selling more than 70 million copies.

I learned about the series from the Catholic Indian artist Francis Freitas, who had gotten to know Anant Pai when both of them were working for the *Times of India*. I met Freitas at the "All-India Seminar on the Church in India Today," held in Bangalore, May 15-25, 1969. In this huge gathering, 500 delegates from all 90 Catholic dioceses in India had come together to discuss how the Second Vatican Council should be implemented in the country.

Freitas told me he wanted to get the life of Christ into the *Amar Chitra Katha* series. I agreed to help. To make a long story short, negotiations followed. I went to visit him in Bombay. I agreed to write the script for the booklet. He would make sure that the story line and illustrations would not conform to some of the mistaken notions of Christ commonly found in Hindu books.

But under what name should I write the script?

"It is not good in this context if the author of the script is recognised as a foreigner," I said to Freitas.

"You are right," he replied. "Yes, perhaps you should translate your name into Indian language."

So that is what I did. In Telugu Catholic Gospel translations, "John"

The cover of an illustrated life of Christ, which I wrote under a pseudonym for sale throughout India, was written specifically to introduce Christ to non-Christians. The book was produced by a Hindu firm and published in 10 languages.

was rendered as "Aruliah." "Wijngaards" (Dutch for "vineyard") becomes "Drakshathota" in Telugu. That is why I adopted the pseudonym *Drâkshathôta Aruliah*. I wrote the basic script, the narrative text under the illustrations, and the dialogue in the "bubbles."

The execution of the project faced many obstacles which were eventually overcome. So the coloured 98-page illustrated book on Christ did appear, in ten major Indian languages: English, Hindi, Gujarati, Kannada, Konkani, Malayalam, Marathi, Oriya, Tamil and Telugu. Within just a few years 300,000 copies had been sold, and most copies were passed on to multiple readers, as is the custom in India. By now, millions of copies will have been sold.

Film on Christ: *Karunamayudu* – the Merciful One

It began, if I recall well, in 1975. Two Hindu film producers from Chennai, then called Madras, turned up at our *Amruthavani* office. They introduced themselves as A.S. Raju and M.V. Reddy of Janatha Art Theatres. They told me that they wanted to produce a film on the life of Christ in Telugu.

"We have done research," they said. "Jesus Christ ranks high among religious leaders people love – whether they are Christian, Muslim or Hindu. But we need help. We heard that you do this kind of thing so we flew in from Madras this morning."

The help they needed was both startup capital and information on Jesus' actual life. I immediately grasped the potential. A good film on Jesus Christ

The title role for our film on the life of Christ was played by a Hindu actor.

would prove of immense value. And, if we joined in the venture as financial sponsors, we could insist on a correct portrayal of Jesus, rather than accepting only the soft-spoken miracle worker image that was popular in Hindu literature.

Now, at the time we were absolutely strapped for cash. *Amruthavani* was in the process of being built. Also, I did not have enough information about the two gentlemen. They could well be impostors, conmen. So I decided to give a positive response, while playing it safe. I needed to check things out. Moreover, I had to make sure that we would get financial backing from some of the mission agencies.

"Gentlemen," I said. "I congratulate you with your project. We, too, believe that a film on the life of Christ in Telugu would be very successful. In principle, we are happy to become your partners in this venture. But, obviously, we have to work out the terms of our working together in detail."

They agreed.

I wrote a "concept" for the film, an outline of the story. We signed a preliminary contract. I managed to get a substantial grant from Germany.

Then disaster struck. The film producers used our money on another project. Then they went bankrupt and went to prison.

Meanwhile, in 1976, I was transferred to London as the new Vicar General of the Mill Hill Society. So, our capable staff at *Amruthavani* stepped in to help with the film. Fr. Raymond Ambrose took over general management and saved the project, arranging for other producers. Fr. Christopher Coelho wrote the complete film script. Both he and Brother Hubert de By were present throughout the filming to make sure it presented the right message.

Karunamayudu, a full-length film on the life of Christ, was featured in cinemas in many states of India. When its Telugu, Tamil and Hindi versions were launched in 1978, they caused a sensation. Many dioceses acquired mobile film units so that the film could be taken round to rural areas and projected for village communities in their own village squares. Copies of the film were distributed in other Asian countries, too: Nepal, Bangladesh, Pakistan, Sri Lanka, Singapore, and Bhutan. It is difficult to estimate the millions upon millions of people who saw the production and who, by all accounts, were inspired by this life of Jesus Christ.

The production of the film included more than just a few notable ironies and light moments. For one, I found it ironic that the first producer, a devoutly *Hindu* man, was our partner in making a film on Jesus Christ. And the Hindu actor who played the part of Jesus also did a good job. But during filming sessions he would disappear. The explanation:

"Jesus has gone outside to have a smoke!"

Support in St. John's College

My involvement in the wider Church, such as through *Amruthavani, Jyotirmai* and other ventures, did not go unnoticed in our College. I am happy to report that the other staff members rallied around me. They advised, commented, and criticised but always in a positive vein. They believed, as I did, that my involvements outside the college made my teaching more relevant.

I seem to have had the full support of my students, as well. One of those students, Marampudi Joji, who would later become the Archbishop of Hyderabad, visited me in England some years later and revealed an incident that occurred when I was teaching at the College.

"One day in St. John's College," he said, "a group of students led by myself went to Father Turner, the rector at the time. 'We want to lodge a complaint about Father Wijngaards,' we told him. 'He has far too many engagements outside the College.'"

"'Tell me,' he asked us. 'Does Fr. Wijngaards neglect his lectures? Is he not there when you need him?'"

"'No, he *is* there,' we told him."

"'Then, should you not rather be happy that he is doing so much good outside the Seminary?' the rector replied."

After relating this story, Archbishop Joji told me, "We talked about it, and we knew the rector was right."

I had never heard about this discussion among the students. But even after so many years, the affirmation it implies did my heart good.

Chapter 15

Coordinating mission worldwide

*I*n September of 1976 I attended the General Chapter of the Mill Hill Missionary Society in Mill Hill, London. I was there as the representative elected by the Mill Hill members in India. To my surprise and dismay, towards the end of the chapter the delegates elected me to be Vicar General and Director for the Home Regions for the next six years.

It was a blow. At the time, I was involved in many crucial projects in India: St. John's College, *Amruthavani*, *Jyotirmai* and *Jeevan Jyoti*, to mention but a few. What was I to do? Should I accept or not?

My leaving India at that critical stage would entail setbacks to the institutions I had founded and had helped build up. But then, I asked myself, was there no local leadership that could step in and fill the gap? And did the Society's international mission work not merit priority support?

I have always liked challenges. I saw my election as another great challenge. And if I did not accept, someone else would be pulled out of an important task on the missions. So after weighing up the pros and cons, I decided to accept.

A look at Mill Hill Society

The Society was founded in 1866 by the Welsh priest Herbert Vaughan who would later become Archbishop of Westminster Diocese. Vaughan correctly saw that, with Britain having such a strong colonial grip on a large proportion of Asia and Africa, it would be very helpful to have English-speaking Catholic missionaries. They could supplement the work already being done by French, Italian and Spanish missionaries, men who often endured opposition from English officials.

The problem was that England itself at the time had few priestly vocations. Its Catholic population depended greatly on priests imported from Ireland.

Vaughan went over to the continent to recruit new members. He was successful in Tyrol, both Tyrol in Austria and northern Italy, but he found the greatest response in the Netherlands. The Catholic Church in Holland was emerging from centuries of persecution and repression. With the Netherlands, too, being a colonial power, awareness of Third World needs abounded. Learning English

Members of the Mill Hill Missionaries General Council in 1976: 1-Fr. Brendan Sullivan; 2-Fr. Louis Purcell; 3-Fr. Noel Hanrahan, General; 4-me; 5-Fr. Piet Leliveld.

posed no obstacle.

The end result was that the Dutch joined in droves. They have, from the beginning, formed the vast majority of the Society's membership. And, together with the English, they gave Mill Hill Society its characteristic stamp of efficiency. It produced no-nonsense present-day apostles, down-to-earth, totally committed, hand on the plough till the bitter end.

The collection of Mill Hill legends contains a revealing story. The Dutch were in the habit of smoking. When the first batch of Dutch students discovered that smoking was forbidden by rule in Mill Hill College, they staged a protest. They confronted the rector, Vaughan himself, with a challenge.

"Why is smoking forbidden? Does smoking stop you from being a good missionary?"

Vaughan reflected. The students were right. Mill Hill College was not aiming at producing religious monks under vows. Its training focused on forming efficient missionaries. Smoking should not be a problem.

"You have a point. Smoking will be allowed," Vaughan announced.

Between 1976 and 1982 the Society was still a formidable force. When my term of office ended, we still counted 956 members. The largest number, 550, worked in mission territories, spread over 37 dioceses in 16 countries of Africa, Asia and Latin America. Of the remaining 451 members, not counting the 11 members of the general staff, 440 fell under my immediate responsibility. They resided in our five home regions: Britain, the Netherlands, Ireland, North America, and North and South Tyrol. Our six retirement homes housed 153 of them, 144 did society work at home, 143 were "non-residents."

My initiation experience

I had hardly taken up the job when I was suddenly confronted with my first real challenge.

The rector of our retirement home in Freshfield rang to say that Bishop Billington had died. He asked the Superior General to come and be the main celebrant for Billington's funeral Mass a few days later. Billington had been bishop of our diocese of Jinja in Uganda, and because of his status in the society it seemed appropriate that a top-ranking Millhiller preside at his funeral.

At the last minute, our Superior General could not go, so he delegated me to take his place. I took an early train up to Liverpool, then to Formby and arrived in Freshfield just in time for Mass to begin. I felt under considerable pressure because I had not been to the house before.

I went to the sacristy. As I was putting on the celebrant's vestments, the door suddenly flung open and Archbishop Derek Worlock of Liverpool stepped in.

"I heard about Billington's funeral this morning," he said. "I will be the main celebrant."

"Great!" I said, with some genuine relief.

I concelebrated with the archbishop. After Mass I accompanied him in the procession to the cemetery. And after the whole service, I stayed with him as we were invited into the members' lounge for a cup of coffee. While shaking hands with others I came across, I stayed with the archbishop as much as possible and chatted with him. I felt it was my responsibility as the principal Mill Hill representative.

So far so good.

After a short while, the archbishop looked at his watch.

"I have to go," he said, signalling to his secretary that time was up. Both men made ready to go, taking leave of the rector and other Freshfield staff.

I stayed with the archbishop as he was leaving the lounge and I conducted him through a lengthy corridor to what I thought was the main entrance. There I said goodbye and opened the door for him.

The archbishop walked in - then, almost immediately, with a red face, walked out again.

It turned out that I had conducted him into a toilet!

Shock, horror!

Some of the retired men saw the incident and laughed – which, I fear, the archbishop may have seen. Anyway, I laughed myself, afterwards. At that moment it was a great embarrassment, a somewhat unusual culmination of my first official function as Vicar General.

The annual routine

As personnel manager of the 451 members in our home regions, it was my task to meet as many of them as possible every year. This meant, first of all, visiting all the society houses, of which there were 24 at the time. For instance, there were five houses in the British Region: Mill Hill itself, Freshfield near Liverpool, Burn Hall near Durham, Courtfield on the border with Wales, and our house in Glasgow.

I would meet each person living in the house, then have meetings with the various teams working in the house to review their progress. Meanwhile non-resident Millhillers working in neighbouring parishes would also be invited to come and meet me in that house. I would visit some non-residents in their own places. I would keep a detailed record of all these encounters. Finally, I would have a concluding meeting with the regional council in the region – to evaluate my findings and see what action, if any, should be taken.

Four times a year the General Council would meet. I would submit a full written report to them of my travels during the preceding three months, outlining the situation in each of the houses I had visited and the needs of individual members. Other council members would do the same with reports about Africa, Asia, and so on. This often led to personnel changes, as I will explain later.

Needless to say, my job entailed a lot of travel. Journeys did not always go smoothly. I remember the first time I flew in from the UK to Kennedy airport at New York in the USA. My flight was delayed, and on arrival I found there was no one to meet me. I decided to phone our house in Yonkers, but it was well after midnight. I discovered that I needed American dimes to operate the public phone system. I possessed no U.S. coins. Exchange offices were closed. I then persuaded a fellow traveller to give me a few dimes. I spoke to the rector at Yonkers, an Irishman. He was not pleased to hear from me so late at night. He told me to catch a commuter bus to a meeting point in the Yonkers area where he would pick me up.

On another occasion, in the Tyrolese region, Fr. Henry Palhuber was going to give me and an elderly German Millhiller named Anton Schmidt a lift to Innsbruck, Austria. We had been attending a meeting with retired members in another Austrian community. It was snowing heavily. Henry had put snow chains on his tires. But as we wound up a treacherously slippery mountain road,

Henry heard on the local news that an avalanche had blocked the road to Innsbruck.

"Wait!" he said. "There is a station not far from here. You can catch a train to Cologne."

As we entered the station dragging our luggage, an international train roared in and stopped.

"Quickly! Get in!" Henry shouted.

We climbed in without having gotten tickets first. Almost immediately the train pulled out of the station. We thought we had made it, but a ticket collector came by and told us we were on an intercity train to Vienna. The wrong direction!

"Fortunately for you," he said, "because of the snow, the train is making an emergency stop in five minutes' time. You can catch a train to Cologne from there."

The train did stop after five minutes. We got out – and found ourselves in a tiny station. Snow still drifting down around us. No one to be seen anywhere. And when we finally located the station master in his dingy office, he told us very few trains ever stopped there.

"The next train in the direction of Germany leaves after eight hours," he advised us, much to our dismay.

We found a small tavern in front of the station. Sitting close to the wood-fire hearth we ordered sauerkraut and beer and whiled away the hours exchanging stories and dozing off in our chairs.

To pass the time, I asked Anton to tell me about his pioneering work in the interior of the Cameroons. Most villages he visited, he told me, had never seen a European. And they applied for Baptism in droves.

"That was mainly because of the women," he said. "They were badly treated by their men."

And then he told me a story which still haunts me today: that in those villages, people were cannibals! I laughed, thinking it was a joke. But Anton swore he was telling the truth.

Personnel manager

In Mill Hill Society all major appointments were made centrally, that is, through the General Council. Our quarterly session gave a chance to each of us to report on our findings during visits to mission areas and home regions. Because of the needs that had emerged and taking into consideration our discussions with individual members and local councils, proposals could begin to be formulated on the transfer of personnel from one occupation to another. And each transfer involved a long and complex procedure.

Moreover, the scale of the operation was huge. To give you an idea, during

Me (right) presiding at an Indian-style Mass for Mill Hill members and friends in Los Angeles. To my right is Hans Hienkens.

my term of office (1976-1982), the General Council made 146 major appointments: 53 members were appointed from society work in the home regions to tasks in the missions; 48 members were appointed from positions in the missions to work at home; 45 members in the home regions were appointed from one task (e.g., teaching in a minor seminary) to another (e.g., fundraising).

As Vicar General and Director of the Home Regions, I often played a central role in such appointments. I was well aware that my own judgment and decision in the matter could have life-changing consequences for the particular member in question. While most transfers were routine, I do have some distressing memories. Take the case of Father Hans Hienkens.

Hans had had a short but successful career in the Philippines. He had been the first President of St. Anthony's College in San José, on the island of Antique. When I visited the USA, I found that he was acting as one of the local Mill Hill organisers in Los Angeles. His job consisted mainly in collecting the contents of mission boxes and, occasionally, preaching on mission. He also helped out in a local parish. Now Hans had a brilliant mind and my honest assessment was that his talents were seriously underused. He was wasted in the job that had been assigned to him.

Then, in 1980, the Mill Hill Society was asked to provide a staff member to the German organization *Missio*, in Aachen. This was the agency that distributed millions of dollars from German dioceses to missionary projects all over the world. I knew *Missio* intimately since I had often presented Indian projects to them. The director of *Missio* asked Mill Hill to provide a missionary who could head their Asian section. Since many of our mission territories benefited from *Missio* grants every year, it seemed right and just to help them.

Hans Hienkens fitted the bill. He had personal experience in the Philippines. He possessed excellent judgment. He spoke both German and English fluently. He was more than capable of handling the task: heading the Asian administration at *Missio*, interviewing mission bishops and other missionary personnel visiting Aachen, maintaining a steady flow of correspondence and formulating priorities for *Missio's* grants.

When I spoke to Hans about this, he was of two minds about the appointment. On the one hand, he welcomed the challenge. He acknowledged he was under-employed in Los Angeles. On the other hand, he had created a circle of personal friends in Los Angeles and had enjoyed their luxurious style of living when staying in their homes. But his main concern, he told me, was his diabetes.

"I suffer from a pernicious kind of diabetes," he said. "My American doctors have worked out a mix of medicines that keeps me alive. They have me under observation."

"Well," I replied, "you are right to be concerned. But surely, those medicines are also available in Germany. And among German doctors there will be specialists, too."

He hesitated, but finally agreed.

Hans started his new job just after Christmas in 1980. Then, hardly two weeks later, on January 15, 1981, the shock: He suffered a massive diabetic attack – and died.

It happened in the evening in his Aachen apartment. Apparently, he collapsed just after speaking on the phone to friends in Los Angeles. He was still using the medication he had brought from the USA. Nobody knows why at that moment he could not give himself the injection that would have saved his life.

His death hit me hard.

Was I to blame?

Would he still be alive if I had not moved him from Los Angeles?

On reflection, I decided to just accept the fact. I had done my best when making the appointment. I had been convinced that the arrangement would both do justice to Hans and serve the best interests of the Society and its missionary work.

Chapter 16

The future of Missionary Societies

*A*s Vicar General I played a role in an important international discussion concerning the future of missionary societies such as Mill Hill.

Missionary societies had sprung up during the nineteenth century in response to the discovery and opening up of new countries in Asia and Africa. Religious orders, such as the Franciscans, Dominicans and Jesuits, had been sending out missionaries for centuries. But there was a need for simpler, totally mission-oriented organizations to step in, and these had been the missionary societies. However, there were clouds on the horizon.

Because mission societies had come in with the wave of Western colonialism, many people in the Third World saw them as relics of an unwelcome colonial past.

In 1967, Fr. Ivan Illich, a renowned theologian and long-time vice-rector of Catholic University of Puerto Rico, called for a moratorium on North American and European missionaries invading Latin America. In 1971, Rev. John Gatu from Kenya, chairman of the general committee of the All-Africa Conference of Churches, stated that all foreign missionaries should be withdrawn from Africa for some years to allow local churches to develop on their own. In 1973, Cardinal Mulala of Kinshasa, Zaire, proclaimed that mission in Africa should be done by Africans, not by foreign missionaries. These and other "Go home, missionary" calls made many members of our Society uneasy.

There were undeniable arguments in favour of a "Western withdrawal." In the late 1970s, the Malaysian government expelled 40 Mill Hill missionaries from its country, affecting three of our dioceses there. Interior mission stations suffered for years – but local vocations increased phenomenally and soon the parishes were thriving again. The Catholic community seemed much healthier without Western input.

With its heavy emphasis on building structures – schools, hospitals and cathedrals – the Western approach carried the aura of business efficiency rather than spiritual enlightenment.

On the other hand, it was ridiculous to claim that the mission had been accomplished. While the Church had made an impact on South America, only a tiny percentage of the Asian population had accepted, or even heard, the Good

News. And the young indigenous Christian communities in Africa could not possibly cope with the demands of meaningful expansion.

All of this pointed to a real crisis. What were the real mission priorities in our complex post-colonial world? Did missionary societies such as Mill Hill still offer the best answer? Should we adopt new targets and new strategies?

Or, even more fundamentally, should Mill Hill hand off the torch and die?

This question was not academic. In fact, Cardinal Vaughan, the founder of Mill Hill Society, had foreseen this development. He wrote in 1866, when the society still existed mainly as a college:

"It must ever be borne in mind that a foreign missionary college is, by its very nature, only provisional and introductory. The end must be kept in view: ... to provide everywhere good native clergy.... It may be said, therefore, that the duty of a foreign missionary college is to work towards its own extinction, by rendering its own existence superfluous through the formation of a sufficient native clergy."

I felt that the situation demanded action.

The SEDOS Seminar

In June 1978 I attended a research workshop organized by *Pro Mundi Vita* in Louvain, Belgium. *Pro Mundi Vita* was an international study centre that did research on the Catholic Church to aid church reforms initiated by Vatican II. The topic of the workshop was the future of mission.

On my return to London, I suggested to our General Council that we should take the initiative in organizing an international seminar on the question. Noel Hanrahan, our Superior General, armed with *Pro Mundi Vita* material, spoke about this to the annual meeting of Superior Generals of Missionary Societies. He found allies in the Superior General of the Maryknoll Missionaries and the Superior General of the Bethlehem Fathers.

They adopted the proposal and submitted it to SEDOS (Service of Documentation and Study), the Roman secretariat established by religious orders specifically to study developments related to religious life and the apostolate. They also promised to fund an international research seminar on the future of mission.

To make a long story short, at the start of 1979 I was invited to Rome to attend the planning meeting. There I met Willie Jenkinson, a Holy Ghost father and executive secretary of SEDOS; Bernard Lang (Maryknoll); and Mary Motte (Franciscan Missionaries of Mary). I shared with them my experience in India of organizing such research seminars. After all, I had participated in major all-India seminars, such as the ones on Non-Christian Scriptures and the Bible, on Muslim Apostolate, and on Priestly Formation. I had also been an organizer of the All-India Seminar on Vatican Renewal in which nearly 400 delegates

General Assembly of the SEDOS seminar convened in Rome in 1981.
In the photo below, that's me in the middle taking part in a discussion.

represented India's 100-plus dioceses and 300-plus religious congregations.

The most productive formula we had found in India included these six steps:

• To invite key persons to write research papers

• To share copies of all these papers with all participants at the central seminar event

• To allow the participants to personally evaluate the contents of these papers and, based on this judgment, spontaneously form discussion groups on the key findings

• To allow the groups to report to general assembly sessions followed by general discussion (This would bring out the main findings of collective reflection.)

• To collect the findings on main trends and conclusions in a final report to the general assembly which would again be discussed and then adopted – with amendments, if needed

• To publish a book with all the original research papers, the conclusions of specific groups, and the final seminar statement

This process, though cumbersome, allowed maximum creative input from all participants. The planning group accepted my suggestion. Experts from all over the world were invited to send in research documents, and 42 eventually did so. Their contributions were wide-ranging and rich.

The planning group then felt overwhelmed by the amount of material. They panicked, I think.

Without involving me any further, they devised another procedure. In July-August of 1980, the documents were sent to 18 persons residing in Rome, no doubt members of headquarters of various religious congregations. Two persons looked at each paper and decided what was important and what was not. Their opinions were collected and used to devise the structure of the seminar.

The seminar, the actual event, took place in Rome on March 8-19, 1981. Roughly half of the participants were the experts. The other half was made up of "professional mission organisers": heads of religious congregations, administrators of mission centers, staff of funding agencies, and promotion offices. Indeed, a very worthwhile group of 110 men and women.

But I was aghast when I found out the methodology.

A big disappointment

We participants did not see any of the actual research papers. The contents of the seminar had been chopped up into eight topics. The topics were discussed on consecutive days. After a short introduction in the general assembly on each day, we were divided into ten pre-arranged discussion groups of about ten participants each; we had no freedom to choose the groups to which we might want to belong. The discussion paper on the topic of the day consisted of a catalogue of short, disjointed excerpts lifted from some of the original papers – which were thus presented out of context. There was a one and a half hour discussion on each topic. Then we had time for "personal reflection." Afterwards, in the afternoon, there was another short discussion and reporting to the general assembly.

I protested strongly to the organisers, recalling my mother's injunction: "You have a Dutch mouth!" - by which she meant "Dare to speak your mind!" True creativity had been cut out. The process led to superficial, disjointed, often trivial conclusions. No major new trends were discovered, no major new insights gained. Many of the crucial questions were - really - ignored and remained unanswered. My protests were in vain.

The seminar did bring out some overall issues that corresponded to what the organisers had gleaned from the original papers. These included the need of distinguishing four elements of mission: proclamation, dialogue, inculturation, and liberation. It also highlighted the central role of the local churches.

But the fragmented nature of the whole event is reflected in its final conclusion: the Agenda for Future Planning. It presents more than 100 observations/proposals/questions spread over nine subsections.

In spite of being tied down in the pre-planned, often incoherent and rambling workshops, some of us managed to meet on what we considered principal areas of mission.

I took part in such a crucial workshop on mission to, and dialogue with, Islam. Direct contact with Islam was and is truly one of the greatest tasks facing mission. Yet in Pakistan, for instance, no priests, religious or lay catechists had any depth of knowledge of Muslim belief and practice. Only a handful of priests and religious had real empathy with Islam, could talk directly to Muslims about their religion, were actually "in dialogue." The same applied to Indonesia, India and Bangladesh, each with vast Muslim populations.

Our Muslim group concluded that it was time to allocate far more resources in finance and personnel in outreach to Islam. Today, more than three decades later, with Islamic communities in turmoil in many countries, we can see how prophetic our concerns were.

We submitted the findings of our workshop to the Steering Committee and the General Council. But — as was the case with the work of other such spontaneous groups — our report and its conclusions were omitted from the published documentation of the seminar. Apparently, they did not fit into the pre-determined concerns of the organisers.

Another issue emerged. The traditional "Christian countries," such as found in Europe, were rapidly turning into "mission territories" themselves. A new secular culture had begun to dominate education, the press, TV and political institutions. The Christian message proved incompatible with and irrelevant to modern secular ideals. And, predictably, the Church had not woken up to this fact. While it allowed "inculturation" in foreign lands, it did not attempt to adapt either its preaching or practices to this whole new God-shy world.

With hindsight, I am wondering - admittedly without any hard proof - whether conservative Cardinal Angelo Rossi, prefect of the Congregation for the Evangelization of Peoples, did not steer the direction of the seminar from behind a screen. He may have planted some of his own men among the Roman experts who decided which topics needed discussion - to prudently avoid issues and proposals considered too radical. Who knows?

Chapter 17

Bishops appointed by Rome
to block Church renewal

*I*n this chapter, I will sketch the experience of Church renewal and the strangling of renewal as I witnessed it in the Netherlands. Bishops played a key role in each process.

But let me start by describing typical Dutch strengths and weaknesses.

Now, I realise that we Dutchmen have one grave defect. We take everything far too seriously. I remember how, in 1960, on the eve of the Second Vatican Council, Rome produced a document that prescribed that all teaching in major seminaries should be done in Latin. Ridiculous, of course, and overruled by the Council almost immediately. But a friend of mine, compatriot and professor of theology, heroically began to lecture in Latin on the day after the decree had been issued. The performance was a disaster. But the effort to put the decree into action in this radical way was typically "Dutch."

When decisions are made, the Dutch expect them to be put into practice. I do not know why. Could it be centuries of competition as fishermen, merchants and world traders? When a dyke burst, the whole village had to turn out and shore it up. When herring were spotted out in the North Sea, the whole fishing fleet would sail out on an hour's notice.

Life in Holland was not maintained by speech but by action. A favourite slogan even today is: "Words don't count. Only deeds!" The typical Dutch reaction to any problem is: What can we *do* about it? What can we do *today*? The Church in Holland is riddled with action groups supporting any cause in any part of the world.

The reforms initiated by the Second Vatican Council were eagerly welcomed in the Netherlands. They resonated with typical features of the Dutch middle class: awareness of one's responsibility for the common good, respect for freedom, acceptance of critical views, willingness to initiate change. An ebullient and confident middle class formed the spearhead of the faithful in the Catholic Church in Holland. They produced the prodigious vocations that enabled the

Dutch to shoulder 10 percent of the post-war missionary effort of the Church. They had been trained in leadership through their flourishing Catholic organisations. They ran their own educational and scientific institutions and controlled the publicity.

No country in the world participated in Vatican II as Holland did. Every single document was analysed and discussed by four discussion groups in each parish!

The process was keenly supported by the open-minded bishops of the six Dutch dioceses of the time. Cardinal Alfrink, who presided at various public sessions of the Council, once clashed publicly with powerful champion of conservatism Cardinal Ottaviani. He had Ottaviani's microphone turned off when the latter exceeded his time limit. Bishop Bekkers of 's-Hertogenbosch broadcast a weekly update on Council proceedings on Dutch Catholic radio. He never minced his words. His vivid accounts of the battles going on in Rome between progressives and traditionalists galvanised the nation.

The Catholic community in the Netherlands were thrilled by the prospect of a Church lining up with the values they had come to cherish in modern society. I call it the "Open to the World" model of the Church. In my own talks and lectures, I used to expand on the merits of such a fresh approach to being Church.

However, the euphoria soon subsided. Popes Paul VI and John Paul II managed to stem the growth of this new shoot. But why and how did they do this?

Bishops appointed to subvert progress

In line with Vatican II guidelines, the Dutch bishops established a "National Pastoral Council" of priests and laity to advise them on church matters. The Pastoral Council met regularly in Noordwijkerhout from 1966 until 1970. Their proposals were revolutionary. Fr. Joannes Gijsen, a church historian, was one of the opponents to the direction the Council was taking. Apparently, he regularly sent letters to Rome, denouncing the "heretical" vision favoured by the Council.

In response, when the Bishop of Roermond died in 1972, Pope Paul VI, bypassing the candidates recommended by the diocesan senate, appointed Fr. Gijsen as the new bishop. The reaction to his appointment was one of outrage.

The Dutch Catholic community knew him only too well as a negative and destructive personality. Cardinal Alfrink, Archbishop of Utrecht, even went to Rome to contest the appointment, but without success. This increased the outrage the laity was feeling over Gijsen's appointment, as the whole move was recognised as a way to impose a traditional agenda.

And, sure enough, after his consecration, Gijsen initiated a regime of terror in the diocese.

All recent reforms were abolished. Progressive parish priests were dismissed. Pastoral councils disbanded. A new old-style major seminary was established in

Roermond city. Its staff were archconservative.

When I visited the college some years later I met Adriaan Boekraad, MHM. He had taught me philosophy in the 1950s. He had now become bitter.

"The Church in the Netherlands has been ruined," he confided to me.

Haye van der Meer, the professor of theology, had written his dissertation under the famous Karl Rahner. In it he had shown that women can and should be ordained. But when I congratulated him on that publication, he told me:

"I disown the book. It is a sin of my youth."

The same treatment was meted out to the Diocese of Rotterdam. In 1970, Pope Paul VI appointed the conservative Adriaan Simonis as the new bishop. Again, dismay among the faithful.

As it happened, I knew Simonis personally. We both studied at the Biblical Institute at roughly the same time. I met him a couple of times in the Roman boarding house for Dutch diocesan priests. Sometimes we had a glass of beer together, after lectures, in a pub not far from the Institute. He was actually a kind person by disposition and could be very unassuming. When I saw him later at Bishop's House in Rotterdam, he had just come back on his bicycle from visiting a local parish.

I have never fully understood Simonis. His traditionalist stand came partly from his rural family background, partly from his deferential dread of superiors. His personnel manager at Bishop's House, whom I had gotten to know in other contexts, once confided to me:

"Simonis is a hare, living in constant fear. He trembles at the least rattling of swords in Rome."

But the bishop's greatest theological blunder, in my view, was a statement he made on Dutch radio when interviewed about Rome's rejection of women in Holy Orders.

"Men are active, are leaders by nature. Women are passive," he said.

"How do you know?" the interviewer prodded him.

"Well," he said. "Look at what happens right at conception. The female ovum is lying passively in the womb, the male sperm fights its way in and captures the ovum with a sting!"

In 1983, Pope John Paul II appointed conservative Simonis to be Archbishop of Utrecht. Two years later, Simonis invited the Pope to visit the Netherlands, and a real storm broke out.

It should not be forgotten that the Dutch are democratic to the core. Democracy flourished in the Dutch "states" and "townships" from the early Middle Ages. It was laid down in its constitution when it gained independence from Spain in 1648. Maintaining democracy required great skill of heads of state in the Dutch Republic. Leaders were respected for competence, not because of their status. John Churchill, a military leader and the first Duke of Marlbor-

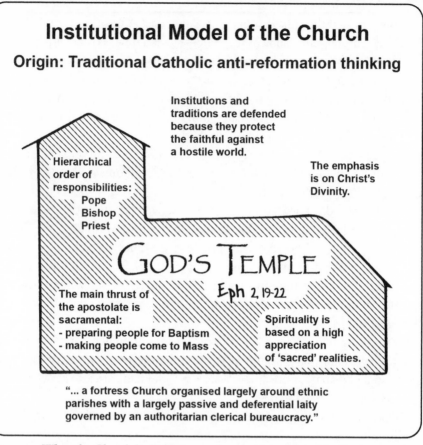

Institutional Model of the Church
Origin: Traditional Catholic anti-reformation thinking

Institutions and
traditions are defended
because they protect
the faithful against
a hostile world.

Hierarchical
order of
responsibilities:
Pope
Bishop
Priest

The emphasis
is on Christ's
Divinity.

GOD'S TEMPLE

Eph 2, 19-22

The main thrust of
the apostolate is
sacramental:
- preparing people for Baptism
- making people come to Mass

Spirituality is
based on a high
appreciation
of 'sacred' realities.

"... a fortress Church organised largely around ethnic
parishes with a largely passive and deferential laity
governed by an authoritarian clerical bureaucracy."

What the Church looks like now: the structure imposed by Rome.

ough, observed in the early 1700s that the Dutch were good soldiers, but were difficult to lead; the reason for every single move needed to be explained to them.

In Holland, episcopal candidates had always been nominated by the diocesan chapter from among the diocesan clergy. Since there were about 500 priests in each diocese, there obviously were more than sufficient candidates. After Vatican II, the process was refined by allowing wider consultation, in which even the laity were involved. Rome's disregard of this process deeply wounded Catholic democratic sensitivities.

Consequently, Rome's indifference to the Dutch way of doing things, coupled with the Pope's appointment of Simonis as Archbishop, led to a spontaneous and sizable protest. Thousands of angry Catholics gathered in the Maliebaan in front of Archbishop's House in Utrecht on May 8, 1985. It led to the foundation of the progressive "*Acht Mei Beweging*," the "Eighth of May Movement," which would instill hope in the Catholic community for decades to come.

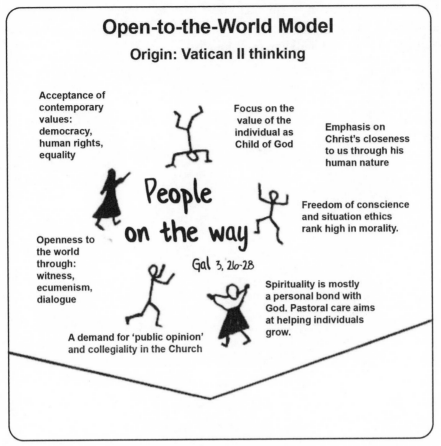

Open-to-the-World Model
Origin: Vatican II thinking

Acceptance of contemporary values: democracy, human rights, equality

Focus on the value of the individual as Child of God

Emphasis on Christ's closeness to us through his human nature

People on the way

Gal 3, 26-28

Openness to the world through: witness, ecumenism, dialogue

Freedom of conscience and situation ethics rank high in morality.

Spirituality is mostly a personal bond with God. Pastoral care aims at helping individuals grow.

A demand for 'public opinion' and collegiality in the Church

What the Church should be like...

Rome, however, continued its deliberate process of appointing reactionary bishops: in Haarlem, Breda, 's-Hertogenbosch, Groningen. This practice has had disastrous effects on the Catholic communities. Many stopped going to church. The vast majority of churchgoers openly disagree with their imposed hierarchy and the doctrine they proclaim.

Polls in 2008 showed overwhelmingly liberal views even among weekly church attendants: "Artificial means of contraception are perfectly alright" (84%); "Couples may live together even if they are not married" (86%); "Gays and lesbians are free to live as they choose" (91%).

When the Bishops' Conference began to sack progressive scholars from Catholic institutions, Catholic University of Nijmegen – until then the pride of the Catholic community – declared in 2004 that it would no longer be a Catholic university. The board felt this change was necessary to protect the academic freedom of its staff.

Similar stories, I know, can be told about what has happened in other countries. Rome's campaign to smother efforts toward Church reform led me to adopt as my fourth commandment for Church renewal: **Appoint open-minded, pastoral bishops, not hard-line traditionalists.**

Part III

Fighting the `Anti-Sex Bug´ in the Church

Chapter 18

The octopus
of sexual repression

*D*uring my time at St. John's College in Hyderabad, I held many jobs: professor of sacred scripture, chief librarian, head of the English academy, editor of the college magazine, director of summer training projects, and spiritual guide to numerous students.

One of the students, whom I will call Samuel, was a youth from Kerala.

I still see Samuel sprawling awkwardly in an armchair facing me. Tall, light-tanned complexion, 18 years old, nervously wiping his shining black hair aside as he throws anxious glances at me.

"Tell me," I said.

"I'm getting white stuff from ... well, my front," he said, pointing at a spot between his thighs. He waited, still looking at me. "From my penis."

"So?"

"It's like curdled milk... "

He waited again, then blurted out:

"I told my neighbour (the student living in the room next to him). He says I've committed a serious sin. Against chastity."

For a moment I was stunned. Where should I start?

Samuel wasn't the only one to reveal abysmal ignorance about sex and utter confusion about sexual morality. Other students harboured similar problems and, strangely enough, all those students hailed from the Indian State of Kerala. Our local Telugu-speaking students from Andhra Pradesh were much better informed in matters of sex.

Why was that, I wondered?

When I visited villages, Telugu mothers would proudly cradle their babies in their arms. If I showed an interest in her child, a mother might smilingly say "*Magadhu!*" – "It's a boy!" – while lifting his nappy to show the baby's sexual equipment.

Where did that disarming Telugu openness about sex come from?

One reason I discovered is that the Telugus live in close-knit village communities or town neighbourhoods. Tiny mud-wall or brick houses are stacked one against the other. Homes are often one-room establishments in which parents, teenagers and children sleep huddled together, some stretching on low *manzams* (beds made of ropes strung between a wooden frame), others simply lying on the floor, wrapped in a blanket and resting on a reed mat. Small children are often naked when ambling around the house. As they grow up, they see the adults undress before taking a bath. They notice them make love in the morning, or at night. The monthly periods of girls and grown up women are keenly followed by the whole family.

Moreover, our Catholic communities in Andhra Pradesh are firmly embedded within an overwhelmingly Hindu culture. And the main idol worshipped in Hindu shrines and temples throughout Andhra Pradesh is a short or tall shining, black-granite pillar of stone, the *lingam*. It represents the erect male member of the god, Shiva. An elongated saucer-type ring made of stone at its base stands for the *yoni*, the female sexual organ. The *yoni* will have a spout on one side so that libations that are poured out over the *lingam* collect in the *yoni* and can easily be drained off.

People in Andhra Pradesh refer to sex with few inhibitions. The Telugus freely speak of a man's *lingam* and a woman's *yoni*. Family names include the word "penis," such as *Mahalingam*, "large penis." There are even villages called *Lingampalli, Rasalingam, Lingamguntla*, and so on.

Things are quite different in Kerala, as I was soon to find out. Meanwhile, I bought a 208-page complete guide on sex called *Marriage Technique* by two Indian doctors and loaned it to Samuel as well as to other students from Kerala who needed it. The booklet provided detailed information on all aspects of human sexuality, with sketches and diagrams. The dedication on the front page read: "A perfect pilot for your frail little bark to save it from being shipwrecked in the whirlwinds and whirlpools of unenlightened sexuality." Prophetic words indeed!

Spotlight on a Catholic paradise

The State of Kerala adorns the southwest coast of India with a green carpet of fertile lowlands and flourishing hills and mountains. It boasts the highest literacy rate in India. Christians form 20% of the population, whereas the overall Christian percentage of the whole of India is only 2.3 %. And most Christians in Kerala are Catholic, of one kind or another.

Fishermen along the coast and coconut workers belong to the Latin rite. They were converted by the Portuguese. The *Syro-Malankara* rite is a branch of Jacobites who in 1930 were reconciled to the Catholic Church. The *Syro-Malabar* Catholic Church, on the other hand, derives from early converts when Christian missionaries evangelized India during the first three centuries after Christ. All these Catholic communities have precious old traditions while also taking part in making our world church come of age during the 20th century.

I began to understand Kerala much better when I explored it thoroughly some time later. You must know that I utilised the six-weeks breaks at college during the hot season to methodically visit the homes of my students. I did this on alternative years for Andhra Pradesh and for Kerala. With the help of the students, I would draw up a complex travel plan. I would journey to a particular village on one day, then stay with the student's family for a full day, spending two nights in the village. Then I would spend another day traveling by bus or bullock cart to the next town or village. There, too, I would stay for a full day. In each place I would get to know the particular student's home: his parents and siblings, the local church, the school, the family source of income. It was tiring, but also revealing. My students and their families seemed to be always happy to welcome me.

In this way I exhaustively visited hundreds of villages in remote places tourists will never see. I prayed with people, ate with them, slept in their homes, joined in feasts and funerals, walked with them under the scorching tropical sun and, occasionally, swam with them in a cool refreshing river. I shared their hopes and fears, and began to understand the Indian way of looking at things, the local perspective, the point of view from which they would judge persons and situations. And, I can honestly say that I came to love them— the people of Andhra Pradesh no less than the people in Kerala.

Allow me, for the purpose of this chapter, to focus on the fascinating *Syro-Malabar* Catholics living on the slopes of hills and mountains. And I will pick up the story again about Samuel, my student who was ignorant about sex. I will sketch his family whom I visited at the time, adapting circumstances and using fictitious names as I will do throughout this chapter.

Thomas Kurukkalil, Samuel's father, owns a tea estate. He is a tall, soft-spoken man with kind eyes. He does not say much but commands the total respect of his family. Samuel's mother is named Abrianna, a college graduate like her husband, of light complexion and long black hair which she ties up in a knot on top of her head. She is very happy to meet me. Samuel's 16-year-old brother, Roshan, and 14-year-old sister, Sona, are also intrigued. Both of them study in a local high school and will attend college later. All have a reasonable command of English except for the live-in maid, Prafulla, who speaks only Malayalam.

The Kurukkalil homestead lies not far from picturesque Munnar, in the mountain range known as the Western Ghats. Sitting on the veranda, chatting with the family, I look out on a bush-covered valley stretching away. I can see other houses in the distance, the nearest one a 15-minutes walk down the road. Homes are isolated in this area.

The Kurukkalil home has a spacious lounge, a kitchen, a bathroom and a large bedroom for the parents and smaller ones for the children or guests. Before the evening meal, the family says their daily prayers. A candle is lit before a statue of Our Lady. We are all on our knees. The full rosary is recited in Malayalam, with Thomas intoning the Our Fathers before each decade. It is followed by the litany of Our Lady and a long list of special intentions to be prayed for.

At the crack of dawn the next morning, the family rises. While Thomas goes off to work on his tea plantation, Abrianna, her teenagers and I walk to church. It takes half an hour along winding paths that cut through fields and orchards. Other families join us on the way. When we arrive in the parish church, lauds is just beginning. At this time, in the 1960s, the recital is still done in the liturgical language, Syriac. After 20 minutes, Mass begins. It is sung, again in Syriac. In spite of it being an early weekday morning, the church is packed.

Samuel belongs to an exemplary Catholic family. So why his ignorance about sex? The isolation of the home may play a part but the main culprit is the intense, devotional Catholic ethos which blocks an open recognition of sex. The parents are afraid of the topic. It is being repressed. Samuel is paradoxically the victim of his "devout" Catholic upbringing.

And repression breeds revolt and excess. It lies at the root of many cases I come across.

Religious Sisters from Kerala

Sister Lily is novice mistress in a formation house. She hails from a Catholic family like Samuel's. She confides to me, during a train journey to Trivandrum, that she has returned from a Catholic charismatic conference in Cochin. What's more, she tells me "a holy priest has exorcised me."

"Why?" I ask.

"When I was 12 years old," she says, "my younger brother had a friend staying with us for some months. That boy, who was just one year older than me, used to enter my room at night and creep into bed with me. We were both naked. We used to fondle each other and, at times, make love. I didn't really know what was going on. Later I understood that it had been very bad. When I confessed it to a priest, he told me I had sunk deep into mortal sin. It's one reason why I became a religious sister. To make up for it."

"Why the exorcism?" I ask again.

"At times I wake up at night. I see a black demon hopping about and sitting on my chest. When I switch on the light, he has gone. But I know I'm not fully healed. The devil still has a hold on me. I feel his claws because I have meddled in sex. I was hoping that the holy priest – she mentioned his name – would drive him out for good."

"Did it work?"

"I hope so," she replies with a sigh.

Another religious, Sister Aranga, shares her own story when I question her about sex education in Catholic Kerala.

"People mean well, but it's bad," she says. "Last year I took part in a renewal seminar for religious in higher education. Both men and women attended. I met a young priest lecturing in Aleppey and we had some very interesting conversations. He told me that, though he was 35 years old, he had never properly seen the body of a woman."

"So," I said, "how did you respond?"

"Well," she smiled at me. "This may shock you, but I, too, had never seen the body of a man. In sculptures, yes, but not alive. So we arranged to meet in his room when nobody was about – during one of the conference sessions. Both of us undressed. We took time to examine each other's bodies. We did not touch each other, of course. Just looked."

"Wonderful!" I said.

"I'm glad you think so. We both felt we needed to do this. To grow up and be mature."

I witnessed a more depressing outcome of keeping sex in the dark by what Theyya told me a few days before she was getting married. Her mother had died early. Her father had been a strict man, but he often left his children at home.

"My brother Kurian and I often felt lonely," she said. "Our aunt was there, but she would always go to bed early. Kurian and I comforted each other by sleeping together night after night. We made love not really knowing what we were doing. It's a wonder I never got pregnant."

"Anyway, you are getting married...," I said.

"That's the problem. My father has arranged it. I don't love the man he has found for me. I will always love my brother, Kurian. I will have to go ahead with the wedding, but it won't work. Kurian will remain my real husband. "

An older woman, Akka, told me with a chuckle:

"In those Christian homes, parents don't realize what happens to their young daughters."

"Like what?"

"Well, when I was six years old, my uncle who was just a young man at the time, would pick me up and fondle me. He would then put me on his lap. Since I wore nothing under my skirt, he would push it aside and rub my naked bottom over his genitals. Nobody else noticed."

Such examples, all true, will be enough to make the point. And I assure you that I did not seek out such information. I just came across it. And I connected it to the alarming ignorance about sex displayed by some students from Kerala.

The Catholic obsession

Anyone who knows the Catholic Church will have recognised that what I have been narrating regarding the Catholic community in Kerala applies equally to traditional Catholic communities anywhere in the world. Fear of sex and the attempt to repress it are, regretfully, international Catholic phenomena. Catholics in Kerala are not more beset by the sexual muddle than Catholics elsewhere. The problem does not lie in a country or its culture, but in traditional Catholicism.

I knew it only too well from my own country, Holland. In the twentieth century the Dutch Catholic Church was reasserting itself after centuries of Protestant persecution. The Dutch Catholicism I grew up in was fiercely loyal and totally committed to their faith. At the time 14,000 Catholic missionaries from the Netherlands evangelized Asia, Africa and Latin America – the largest national group of Catholic missionaries in the world, matched only, at one point, by the Irish. Dutch Catholics were thorough. They meant business. Unfortunately, this also applied to sexual morality.

* * * * *

In my own family, as I have narrated in an earlier chapter, my mother was one of nine children. None of these children received any sex education. They were warned, again and again, that indulging in sex was sinful – a mortal sin! – but sex itself was not explained. Sex was haunted by fear and hidden in darkness. My mother once told me that as the oldest child in the family she accompanied *her* mother, my grandmother, to a conference in the parish church. The preacher was the renowned Father Henry de Greeve.

"He preached for an hour," my mother said. "Thumping his fist on the pulpit, he roared, 'The world wants sex, dirty sex. But I warn you: Sex will drag you to hell! Everlasting hell!'"

"Then he shouted, 'I tell you parents, to save your children from hell, keep them green! Yes, keep them *green*!'"

But keeping children ignorant is a recipe for disaster.

One of my aunts, Caroline, two years younger than my mother, only found out during her wedding night what intercourse means.

"It was a drama," my mother said. "Caroline was shocked. Sickened. Disgusted. She cried the whole night. The marriage was scarred for the rest of her life."

Two other sisters of my mother were incapable of starting and maintaining a normal relationship with potential partners. They were doomed to remain spinsters for life. Three of my uncles fled into religious life, joining a congregation of teaching brothers – with varying degrees of success.

"I was lucky," my mother said. "When I got engaged to your father, he dis-

*My mother (back row, second from left) poses with her parents
and her eight brothers and sisters.*

covered my anxiety and ignorance about sex. He gave me booklets to read that
explained everything. I had to read them in secret because my father would have
taken them from me."

My grandfather, in fact, in spite of fathering so much offspring himself,
firmly adhered to the traditional Catholic policy of sexual repression. One day
he cycled with some of his children along the Apeldoorn Canal. It was summer.
Some half-naked men were swimming in the water. As soon as he saw this, my
grandfather shouted down the line: "Look left! Look left!" – that is, away from
the canal. Nudity was absolutely tabu.

On Saturday evenings all the children would be given fresh underwear.
Of course, with such a large family, girls crammed into one bedroom, boys in
another, changing your vest could reveal breasts and changing nickers even more
unspeakable body parts. So granpa arranged a strip-and-cover ritual. He would
wait till all of them were standing near their pile of fresh clothes. Then he would
blow a whistle and turn off the main light switch in the house. In total darkness,
vests and nickers were taken off, fresh ones put on. Sin averted! Imagine the
spiritual damage that could have been done if anyone saw his or her own body,
or that of a sibling!

Fear of the naked body also reigned supreme in convents. One nun confided
to me that sisters were ordered to wear a designated *chemise*, a kind of night shirt,
when taking a bath. They were allowed to wash their nipples and genital area
under the *chemise*, but on no account were they allowed to look at such things.

Once, when I stayed in a hospital for eye treatment, another nun who was also a nurse narrated how she had been visited by her superior.

"Sister," the superior said. "I pity nurses like you."

"Why?" she asked.

"Well, nurses like you have to wash other people's bodies. You are seeing so much sin every day..." She meant seeing the genitals of women and men!

Murderer with many arms

Such things were still in my mind when I was invited to take a short trip on a fishing boat off the coast of Kerala. The sea was calm. I admired the rugged fishermen as they sought out and located their net left overnight across a tidal underwater flow one mile from the shore.

When the net was pulled up from the water it revealed a mass of glistening wriggling sea creatures: sardines, carp, lobsters, crabs and – to my delight – an octopus.

An octopus lives on the bottom of the sea. Having no bones, it can flatten itself and squeeze through narrow slits. It is a master of camouflage and disguise. It can change the colour of its skin at will, turning speckled and light yellow on light yellow sand, grey when slithering on grey rocks, green when hiding among weeds. But all the time its eight arms are ready to strike out and strangle unsuspecting victims. The octopus lies in hiding, unseen, till it kills with deadly ferocity.

This stealthy strangler, I saw, was the perfect image for the insidious Catholic obsession with sex and hostility to sex. Hiding under clever guises of pious camouflage, the octopus of sexual repression wreaked havoc with its many strangling arms. It held teenagers in a state of terror of its unseen threat. It snuffed out the joy of sex in the bedrooms of Catholic couples. It doomed timid Catholics to avoid marriage altogether and drove more adventurous Catholics, by rebound, to explore incest, pornography and other sexual excesses.

But where did this unchristian sex-demolisher come from? And how had it managed to infest the soul of traditional Catholicism? I was determined to find out.

Chapter 19

Screwed up sex guru

*I*t took me years to fully pin down the culprit. The main engineer of Catholic disgust with sex proved to be Saint Augustine, who lived in North Africa from 354 to 430 A.D.

His influence on later centuries is truly enormous. Quotes from his more than 100 writings dominate medieval theology. Augustine is the Church Father most admired, revered and studied to the present day. And there is much in his thinking that truly deserves credit.

Unfortunately, however, his warped ideas on sex have blighted Catholic doctrine ever since and have spoiled the sex lives of innumerable Catholics.

So who was Augustine?

Augustine was born a full citizen of Thagaste, a Roman settlement in what is now called Algeria. His father, the Roman colonist Patricius, married Monica, who was a Bedouin girl and a Christian. Augustine excelled in the schools of rhetoric that existed at the time. He had a gift for language and literature, he soaked up Greek philosophy, and dabbled in fringe religions. He soon became a teacher of rhetoric himself, first in Thagaste, then Carthage, Rome and Milan. During this time he joined the sect of Manicheans as a "hearer." It is here that he acquired his lasting contempt for sex.

Mani taught that the world is divided into two opposing camps: the world of light, life, goodness and beauty on the one side, and the world of darkness, death, evil and ugliness on the other. These worlds are constantly at war with each other, with gods and spiritual powers on each side leading the battle. The earth is a middle ground that has fallen under control of the powers of evil. Our mind is a spark of light caught in the ugly mess of dark, sinful matter. Chief rulers of the earth are Ahriman, the Prince of Darkness, and Âz, the Demoness of Sexual Lust. She was also the creator of human beings, according to the Mani mythology.

Listen to this excerpt of Mani's instructions:

> When Âz created the body of Adam, she placed inside him her own vices: lust for copulation, passion and bad-mouthing, hate and sin, rage and

The earliest depiction of St. Augustine: a seventh century fresco in the Lateran Palace in Rome.

pollution, hostility to religion, thieving and lying, robbing and evil-doing, obstinacy, vengefulness, sorrow and despair, pain and ache, poverty and destitution, illness, old age and stench.... And Âz filled Eve's mind, so that she would become even more thieving, monstrous, lusty and desirous than Adam, and seduce that male with desire. In this way Âz arranged that humans be born in the world from those two creatures – Adam and Eve – and be filled with sexual lust and desire and behave with rage and vengeance and without mercy ....

When Augustine became a Christian in Milan, he renounced Manichaeism but, as we will see, traces of its beliefs stuck to his mind. He returned to North Africa, was ordained a priest and became Bishop of Hippo. Hundreds of his sermons have been preserved. Through his eloquent letters and persuasive treatises he soon put his stamp on the thinking of the Church in his time. And remnants of that thinking can be seen clearly today in the Church's attitude toward sex.

In the next section I will reconstruct some of Augustine's teachings in the form of an interview. Augustine's replies will be based, almost word for word, on his writings: *Sexual Desire, City of God, Marriage, Sermon on the Mount, Against the Letters of the Pelagians,* and *The Grace of Christ.*

Interview with Augustine

Imagine we are back in Hippo, 420 A.D. Augustine has graciously allowed me to ask him some questions. I have been led into his inner lounge and offered a seat on a wooden chair studded with pillows. Augustine sits opposite me, his stately figure enhanced by his grey hair and purple-embroidered toga, his fierce eyes sizing me up.

After a brief opening chit-chat I come to the point. We have both agreed to take off our gloves and call a spade a spade.

Bishop, do you still adhere to the teachings of Mani?

"Certainly not! There is only one God and he is good. Everything he created is good. Evil comes from the devil and from human sinful actions."

What about sex in us? Is it evil?

"Sexual lust, yes. You see, sexual passion is something foreign to us. Procreation itself is alright. It comes from God. But now procreation is tainted by the shameful excitement of our sexual organs. That excitement is an evil intruder!"

An intruder? How come?

"Just think about it. You control all the members of your body but not your sexual organ. If you see a beautiful girl, you feel attracted to her and become sexually aroused. Was that your intention? When your foot, arm, finger, lip, or tongue make a movement, they do so because you tell them so. You control them by your will. Not so with your sex organs. They do what they like." (*Desire*, Book 2, Ch. 53)

Isn't this just a spontaneous reaction of the body?

"No, no, no! You got that wrong. Sex is different. And Sacred Scripture confirms it. Have you not read in Paul's letter to the Romans? 'I do not understand my own actions. For I do not do what I want, I do the very thing I hate.... It is no longer I that do it, but sin which dwells in me. For I know that nothing good dwells within me, that is in my flesh.' The evil in our flesh is the sex drive. It is the sin Paul speaks about."

But surely our sexual desires, too, are created by God...

"Not so. Before Adam and Eve sinned, in paradise, they would have been able to produce children without foul sexual passion. Their sexual organs would have been stimulated into activity by willpower alone, just as the will controls other organs. In paradise, the husband could have relaxed upon his wife's breasts with complete peace of mind and bodily tranquility, without being excited by the allurement of lust. His sex organ would not have been activated by tumultuous passion, but brought into service by the deliberate use of his will power. When the need arose he would simply erect the organ at will and dispatch semen into his wife's womb with no loss to her virginity." (*City*, Book 14, Ch. 26)

Without the wife losing her virginity?

"Indeed. Why do you look surprised? In paradise there would have been no need of lusty carnal copulation."

Augustine then goes on to say that if people had not sinned, they would have had children as a direct gift from God without intercourse (*Marriage* §2). And, he tells me, they would have been spared the sinful sexual desires they now feel (*Pelagians* 1, 31-32).

Sex in marriage

A servant comes in and tells Augustine that a middle-aged couple has entered the house and urgently asks for his guidance. They are called Albus and Fabiola.

"They are very upset," the servant declares. "Fabiola is crying."

Augustine decides to meet them immediately. He invites me to come along. We walk to the reception room in the atrium at the front of Augustine's villa. I am introduced to the couple. Albus solemnly wears a dark red toga. Slender black-haired Fabiola has wrapped an orange stola over her long white tunic.

The four of us are seated on simple stone benches, and Albus tells Augustine:

"We want to consult you on some delicate matter... concerning relationships between husband and wife."

Immediately I offer to withdraw, but both Augustine and the others urge me to stay.

"Nothing to hide!" Augustine says. "It concerns generally accepted Christian teaching. So, what's the matter, Albus?"

"Fabiola and I have had four children in previous years. Now, after her menopause, we can't have children anymore. And Fabiola refuses to have intercourse with me. 'It's wrong, it's dirty, it's a sin!' she tells me. 'Augustine, our bishop, clearly says so in his sermons.' Is that true?"

Fabiola looks pleadingly at Augustine.

"Yes, it is true. Sexual intercourse carries a curse," Augustine asserts. "Sexual intercourse passes on Adam and Eve's original sin to every child that is born." (*Grace*, Book 2, §42)

"But what's the harm if no child can be born anyway?!"

"Well, think about it. Sexual intercourse is tainted by the sinful pleasures of the flesh. It should be avoided in marriage as much as possible. Live together as brother and sister!" (*Desire*, Book 1, Ch. 27; *Marriage*, §1 & §6)

"Didn't I tell you?!" Fabiola says to Albus.

"Shut up!" Albus growls at her. "You're only a woman, inferior in mind and morals, totally subject to me. I make the decisions!"

"Well, Albus," Augustine intervenes. "You have a point. Women are inferior by nature. And wives are subject to their husbands by human and divine law." (*Heptateuch*, Book I, § 153; *Concupiscence*, Book I, Ch. 10)

But then he continues:

"However, in this case Fabiola is right. All sex is tainted with sin. A good husband loves what's spiritual in his wife, her gifts as a human person. But he hates in her what makes her a *woman*, her mortal sexual flesh." (*Mount*, Book 1, § 41 & 42)

A Roman couple, Lucius and his wife, Publicia, are depicted in this 2nd century tombstone.

As I take my leave, I remember that Augustine himself enjoyed turbulent sexual relationships. As a young man he kept a mistress whom he took with him to Carthage, Rome and Milan. In 385 A.D. his mother, Monica, persuaded him to get engaged to a 13-year-old girl, which he did. Augustine then dismissed his mistress. But although she had given him a son called Adeodatus, and he had taken her to bed night after night for 18 years, he never bothered to mention her name in his books. During the time he had to wait for his future bride to grow up, Augustine took another mistress to satisfy his sexual desires.

Escaping from misguided teachings

Augustine's teachings left their mark on the 16 centuries of Christianity that followed his time on Earth. He was declared to be a "Doctor of the Church" by Pope Boniface VIII in 1298. His insights about God have been beneficial to some extent. His misgivings about sex have played a different role. They have caused, and are still causing, unspeakable damage.

When, through evolution, God created us to be male and female, he made us sexual beings. There is nothing shameful or disgusting about this. Of course, we need to use our sexual powers responsibly, like any other gift we possess. But sex is good. Sex, too, is a gift, not evil.

Augustine is wrong when he states that original sin is passed on by sexual passion in the parents. He misleads Christian parents by telling them that the physical expression of a loving relationship in marriage can be justified only by the need of producing children.

Through his flawed ideas, Augustine has contributed greatly to the stranglehold of the octopus on so many Catholic lives: shame about sex, disgust with sex, repression of sex.

So my fifth commandment for Church reform is: **Abandon the misguided repression of sex advocated by St. Augustine.**

Chapter 20

Lightning strikes from Rome

*I*n July of 1968 our professor of moral theology, Fr. Eddie Bennett, was away to give a course in northern India. He had asked me to open his mail and forward to him any post that might be significant.

One day a heavy envelope came in. It had been sent by the papal nunciature in New Delhi. Intrigued, I slit it open at the edge and found a document. It was a copy of detailed instructions from the Roman Congregation for the Doctrine of the Faith to all moral theologians in India. It announced the imminent release of the encyclical *Humanae Vitae* ("On Human Life") by Pope Paul VI. This proclaimed that all artificial forms of family planning were in conflict with Natural Law and should therefore be avoided in all circumstances.

We were all aware that a papal commission of experts had, for a number of years, been studying the question of artificial birth control. The signs had been positive. The commission recommended (with a majority of 68 to 4!) that Catholic couples should be allowed to, responsibly, use artificial methods in planning their families. It looked as if Rome would soften its stand against contraceptives. But the opposite happened.

In spite of the advice of his experts, the Pope condemned all artificial means:

> Any action which either before, at the moment of, or after sexual intercourse, is specifically intended to prevent procreation – whether as an end or as a means... is wrong. It is never lawful, even for the gravest reasons, to intend directly something which of its very nature contradicts the moral order, and which must therefore be judged unworthy of man, even though the intention is to protect or promote the welfare of an individual, of a family or of society in general. Consequently, it is a serious error to think that a whole married life of otherwise normal relations can justify sexual intercourse which is deliberately contraceptive and so intrinsically wrong.

I was stunned. I could immediately see the devastating impact it would have on poor families all over India.

St. Augustine's footprint ran all over the text. Had he not taught that the only legitimate purpose for intercourse lay in procreation? Sex desires did not come from God, he claimed. They come from evil, from original sin, from the devil. Medieval scholars had linked this notion to their perception of "Natural Law," a law which the Creator was alleged to have enshrined in nature.

A devastating blow for the poor

If Indian church authorities were to adopt the Roman prohibition of any form of artificial birth control, it would worsen the plight of millions of people. Since the Church ran many hospitals and clinics it might affect all their patients, Catholic and non-Catholic alike.

Moreover, I had personally gotten to know the over-sized Catholic families in our neighbourhood. In the slums of nearby Ramanthapur, a family of seven lived crammed in a reed-covered mud shack. The father, a casual worker, was a drunkard. The mother lay always sick in a corner of the hut. The children's only hope of survival was the fact that parishioners, including myself, paid for them to have food and go to school.

Then there was an Anglo-Indian family with nine children: one son and eight daughters. They lived in a two-room houselet on the man's meagre salary as a member of a small brass band.

I had also gotten to know recent converts Mary and Joseph. Joseph was a carpenter. He was a Hindu of low-caste origin who applied for Baptism because he wanted to marry Mary, who was a Catholic. I was involved to some extent in the preliminary instruction, and later in his Baptism itself. They were gentle, unassuming people, genuinely lost in a harsh world. I could not help seeing in them an Indian incarnation of the Holy Family. They would have jumped at a stable if it were offered for accommodation!

I visited them in their tiny reed-matted, lean-to hut in Ramnagar. They lived in the shadow of a Parsi Tower of Silence. This burial tower was a two-story hollow building covered with a lattice of iron bars instead of a roof. As you may know, Parsis believe that human bodies should neither be interred nor cremated. They deposit the naked corpses of their dead on the roof trellis so that birds of prey can pick off the flesh, and the bones fall down into the pit below. The whole area around the Ramnagar Tower of Silence stank of corpses. Mary and Joseph lived in a place normal people would shun as hygienically and religiously unclean.

As I entered the hut, I found Mary with her latest child. She was a girl. A two-year-old boy was sitting on the dust floor looking at me with large inquiring eyes. I was offered a mug of tea. Joseph told me he had a temporary job on a building plot. Mary narrated that she had paid a visit to her parents' home in a country village.

"I wasn't welcome," she said with tears in her eyes. "I wasn't welcome in the home I grew up in. When I came near the door, I overheard my mother say to

A grandmother with her daughter and two grandchildren, belonging to the Lambadi tribe in the Indian state of Andhra Pradesh, sit in front of their communal hut wearing all their wealth in homemade jewelry.

the others: 'I hope that's not Mary who is coming. For God's sake! What can I give her to eat?!'"

"My mother has had seven children," she added by way of explanation. "My father died."

I did not know what to say.

"Look where we live. Joseph is not getting a proper wage. They take advantage of him. How can we survive?" she said.

And with a weary look on her face, she added:

"Father, in my whole life I have never known comfort."

I will never forget what she said. These words still ring in my ears after so many years. I hear them as a reproach when I enjoy comfort myself. I wish I could have done more for them.

I was called out to Osmania General Hospital in Hyderabad some time later. Mary and Joseph's third child was dying. I found them in the emergency clinic for children, standing helplessly near a cot where the baby lay linked to a life-support machine. Its emaciated body was still breathing. Dysentery, I was told. I prayed over the baby. It died soon afterwards.

This illustrates the major problem compounding abject misery in India, namely the number of children born to poor parents. Undernourished mothers did not have time to recover from the hardships of childbirth. Over-population and poverty added to the burden of feeding, clothing and educating children. Family planning was essential to help the poor rise above starvation level, as the government of India recognized.

But what support did the Church offer? Nothing. People like Joseph and Mary were forbidden to avail themselves of a condom or an IUD (intra-uterine device) provided by the government. So were the other one-third of the population, 200 million at the time, who lived under the poverty line!

St. Augustine had won. He had the Pope on his side!

Many priests refused to continue hearing confessions, saying they could not follow the Pope's guidance. The fog cleared somewhat when at least ten national bishops' conferences declared that, in spite of the Pope's words, couples could follow their own consciences and that confessors should respect such decisions. The bishops who stood up against the Pope were in Austria, Belgium, Canada, East Germany, France, Indonesia, the Netherlands, Scandinavia, Switzerland and West Germany. Their position was supported by prominent theologians such as Karl Rahner and Bernard Häring. Unfortunately, the Indian bishops were undecided.

I entered the fray by publishing articles in the Catholic weekly *The New Leader* and *The Malabar Herald*. I explained that "Natural Law" for human beings is our power of reason. We regulate our bodies by such artificial means as a kidney transplant, a pacemaker for the heart, a wooden leg.

The hut that Joseph and Mary lived in was similar to this one, only smaller.

I also reminded Catholics that papal encyclicals are not infallible. I was promptly attacked by traditionalists. According to Father Anthony Gomes of Goa, Pope Pius XII stated that though some persons assume popes do not teach infallibly in encyclicals, they claim full assent of mind and will. In other words, they are infallible in practice.

I am quoting this to show how a question of life or death for ordinary people like Joseph and Mary was now deteriorating into squabbles about the authority of encyclicals.

The next time I visited Joseph and Mary they had moved to the Victoria Leprosy Hospital in Dichpalli, hundreds of miles north of Hyderabad. Joseph had been found to be infected with leprosy. He was treated in Dichpalli as an outdoor patient. With Mary and children, he had been given a hut to live in on the hospital grounds – grand accommodation compared to their previous hut in

Ramnagar. The hospital employed him as a carpenter in their workshop, where he fashioned crutches for other patients.

Mary and Joseph were reasonably happy in spite of the prospect of having to leave the premises once he had fully recovered. If ever there were underdogs, this "holy family" was one of them! Victims of fate - and also of St. Augustine.

Why had Paul VI stuck to an absolute ban on contraceptives?

He did not dare to change direction, it emerged, because "the teaching *traditional since Augustine* and restated by Popes Pius XI and XII was 'the plain teaching of Christ,' who warns against false leaders and 'calls for sacrifice and self-denial.'"

Years later I visited Cardinal Simon Lourdusamy in Rome. I had known him when he was Archbishop of Bangalore. Now he functioned as the Prefect of the Congregation for the Evangelization of Peoples. He told me, in confidence, that my name was found on the list of "troublesome" theologians compiled by the Vatican Congregation for the Doctrine of the Faith. I am sure that I was granted that "honour" from the time I spoke out about family planning in India.

My sixth commandment for Church reform is:

Grant parents total freedom to plan their families responsibly.

Chapter 21

The ordination of women

As we have seen in the previous chapter, poor families were the victims of the Church's adherence to the Augustinian anti-sex legacy. It slowly dawned on me over the years that, in fact, all women were victims of this Augustinian prejudice that portrayed them as somehow tainted by sex.

Like Eve, every woman, just by her possessing a sexually attractive body, was capable of seducing men to sinful carnal lust, according to Augustine's logic. Moreover, women ranked lower as human beings.

"It is the natural order among people," Augustine taught, "that women serve their husbands, because the justice of this lies in the principle that the lesser serves the greater.... This is the natural justice that the weaker brain serve the stronger."

Such a judgment was all the more detrimental in a country like India. For women were repressed, socially as well as culturally. Proverbs will illustrate the point.

A proverb has been called "the wit of one person, but the wisdom of many." Proverbs are brief, rhythmic or melodious expressions of generally accepted values. The Telugu people of India honored proverbs as containing principles and deep-seated convictions of their "inner language." An appropriate proverb would prove a point and even settle an argument.

Among a well-known collection of 8,500 Telugu proverbs I found more than 100 expressing judgments about women that are contrary to modern values and Catholic teaching. More disconcerting was the fact that 29 of them could be identified as commonly used even in our Christian communities. Some samples will speak for themselves:

- A boy born is like gold; a girl, dust on the road.
- Even if she is the maharaja's daughter, a woman is subject to her husband.
- A woman is spoiled by going outside the house; a man if he stays at home.
- Within her threshold she remains a woman; outside she is a donkey.
- It is better to be born a shrub in the desert than to be born a woman.

The popularity of such proverbs clearly demonstrated a failure to accept the full human and Christian dignity of women.

The root of the problem lay in generally accepted Hindu religious beliefs. I discovered that the *Manusmriti*, the Hindu classic laying down every person's duties, teaches that a woman should always be subject to a man: first to her father, then to her husband, finally to her son. Women cannot pray or sacrifice independently. Their redemption consists solely in faithful servitude to their husbands. Women are by nature fickle, greedy, unreliable and unfaithful. They should be kept at home and under control. Here are some quotes from the book:

• "The faithful wife must constantly worship her husband as a god, even if he be destitute of character, or seeking pleasure elsewhere, or is devoid of good qualities."

• "Women have no sacrifices or fasts ordained for them. Neither are they called upon to perform the *sraddhas* (rituals)."

• "[Women's] only duty is to serve and worship their husbands with respect and obedience. By the fulfillment of that duty alone they attain heaven."

• "Woman was created for seducing man and hence there is nothing more detestable than a woman."

This was still the generally accepted persuasion of Hindus all over India, in spite of the efforts of the government and enlightened circles to bring about a change. The same degrading of women persisted in many Catholic circles, too. The husband dominated.

Why can't women be priests?

While I became aware of this general paternalistic climate, I also made another discovery. The Church in India was preparing a research seminar titled "New Ministries in India." I was asked to study the possibility of more imaginative lay ministries for women.

When I delved deeper into the question, I found out the abysmal reasons for which women had been excluded from Holy Orders.

• "Women are inferior to men by nature."

• "Women are not created in the image of God, as men are."

• "Women are not perfect human beings and thus cannot represent Christ."

• "Women have always been forbidden to touch sacred objects or wear sacred vestments."

• "Women will soil the sanctuary during their monthly periods."

• "Women are not perfect members of the Church."

Reading this shocked me to no end. On reflection, I realized the damage done – through the centuries. Jesus had established a radical equality between men and women. Men and women receive the same Baptism. To all disciples he said at the Last Supper: "Do this in memory of me!" But the Church had

perverted Jesus' intention because of the prevailing social discrimination against women of the time.

While working in India, I met a religious sister who was principal of a large college for girls in a small town. I will call her "Rosita" in this account.

The college had a chapel, and each morning at 6.30 six sisters from the convent, ten Catholic teachers and more than 150 students from an adjoining hostel for village girls would come to attend Mass. A priest from the local parish would come to conduct the service.

"The parish priest is angry with me," Rosita told me. "I contradicted him in public. He was wrong. But now, to punish us, he has stopped sending a priest for the past week. What is more, he has taken the key from the tabernacle so that I cannot even distribute Holy Communion – as I am allowed to do when a priest does not turn up to say Mass. Us women, we are at the total mercy of men!"

It was the kind of story I had heard before. I also realized that Rosita belonged to the Reddy caste, while the parish priest was a *Khamma*. Conflicts between the two castes were common. But more was at stake.

I knew the priest. Rosita was in many ways intellectually superior. She had graduated from university with distinction in science and math. He was not that well-educated. I reflected also that Rosita was a compassionate person, always at people's service. So she possessed all the qualities needed to make a good priest. She would have done very well presiding at the Eucharist. But here she was, at the mercy of a man just because the Church withheld ordination from women for ridiculously outdated reasons.

Later I heard from her that the priest had resumed saying Mass in the college chapel, but for some weeks he would give Rosita only "half a host" at Holy Communion – to show his continuing displeasure with her. It was a ludicrous gesture, of course. Jesus is as much eucharistically present in half a consecrated host as in a complete host – which Rosita realized.

This incident graphically demonstrated – on a local scale – the petty disdain held by the official Church towards women.

My campaign

I will not repeat here all the ramifications of my original discovery. I have extensively narrated them in my publications *Did Christ Rule Out Women Priests?* (1977), *The Ordination of Women in the Catholic Church* (2001), *No Women in Holy Orders?* (2002) and *What They Don't Teach You in Catholic College: Women in the Priesthood and the Mind of Christ* (2020). These books also contain the solid academic evidence endorsing women's ordination that I collected over

◀ *Sister teaching catechumens in a small village, sitting in front of their local prayer hut.*

the decades. Moreover, I uploaded thousands of supporting documents on my website www.womenpriests.org.

For the seminar called "New Ministries in India," I prepared a paper in which I showed that women can and should be ordained. Excluding them from Holy Orders was, I argued, due to a "social myth" that held women to be physically, intellectually and morally inferior to men.

In 1975 I submitted these cautious recommendations to the Indian Bishops Conference:

> The ministry of the diaconate should be opened to women. This could be done with the understanding that lady deacons be entrusted especially with the nurturative aspects of the apostolate: consoling the dying, Baptism, distribution of Holy Communion, apostolate of teaching the youth, and of reconciliation.
>
> In some special cases, women could be ordained priests with apostolic tasks that could only be fulfilled by them. I am thinking here especially of work among the Muslim women, pastoral work in female wards and in other spheres of life not so easily accessible to men. Women working in such spheres should have the power to hear confessions, give the sacramental absolution, celebrate Mass, and administer the anointing of the sick.

My seventh commandment for Church renewal is this: **Give women full access to Holy Orders.**

Chapter 22

Creating a training institute
for religious sisters

*W*omen traditionally have been undervalued in the Church both because they were deemed intellectually inferior and because they were rated to be sex-ridden creatures. Third-century Church Father Tertullian declared every woman to be a second Eve, but not in a complimentary way: "You are the devil's gateway, you are the first deserter of the divine law, you are she who persuaded him (Adam)..., you destroyed so easily God's image, man."

Remember Augustine saying that men should hate the sexual nature of their wives? Medieval scholars described women as "animals that menstruate" and "dirty creatures." And this is why Church law forbade women to touch sacred vessels or sacred vestments, preach in church, or distribute Holy Communion. Incredibly, most of these prohibitions weren't lifted until 1983.

Fortunately, I was in a position to do something about this while stationed in India.

Congregations of religious sisters all over India were running many vital institutions such as schools, clinics, hospitals and homes for the disabled. In Andhra Pradesh alone, at that time, 1,800 religious sisters looked after 40 hospitals, 550 schools and colleges, 55 boarding schools for boys and girls, and 10 homes for the elderly.

The beneficiaries of hospitals and schools were as much as 90 percent non-Christian. And to pre-empt any misunderstanding: no attempt was made to "convert" such persons. The aim was simply to help those in need and serve the welfare of people.

But, whereas some religious sisters attended universities and colleges to obtain teaching degrees and medical qualifications, their personal education in faith and spirituality was often woefully inadequate.

In one novitiate of a so-called "indigenous" congregation, I found that novices received only two short pep talks a week by the local parish priest. They did not receive any grounding in scripture, theology, spirituality or liturgy. The local staff, their superior and novice mistress were ignorant themselves. The situation was not much better in other congregations.

When I was asked to become moderator of the CRI – the Conference of Religious in India – for Andhra Pradesh, I saw it as an opportunity. Fortunately, our local CRI was headed by three intelligent and farsighted superiors: Sr. Josepha Rachamalli, JMJ; Sr. Felix Albuquerque, SCCG; and Sr. Amandine Marneni, FMM.

With their help I began a programme of systematically urging congregations, especially indigenous congregations and the bishops who supervised them, to send talented young sisters for higher studies in theology, scripture, church law, religious life and other disciplines. It worked. Gradually the Indian novitiates and juniorates began to be staffed by qualified teachers.

While that would help in the long term, more needed to be done in the here and now. We had to provide a more thorough formation to the hundreds of young religious who each year emerged from their novitiates.

The answer was a training institute which we called *Jeevan Jyothi* (life and light).

Finding premises

Like *Amruthavani* before it, *Jeevan Jyothi* began its life in St. Patrick's School in Secunderabad. We offered a three-months course to a group of 30 young sisters from ten different congregations. They attended talks in a classroom temporarily provided by the school. The lectures were given by qualified priests and religious who at that time worked in the Hyderabad/Secunderabad area, mostly in St. John's Seminary and in various religious institutions.

For years I myself and the CRI committee looked for a better and more permanent place to house our new institute. Eventually, we located a promising house in Begumpet. The house was spacious, and it was surrounded by a large garden that offered the possibility of future expansion. The property was for sale for a number of reasons, partly because it lay close to swamps that created the enduring nuisance of mosquitoes.

But to make a long story short, we acquired the property. The CRI committee members were pleased with the new location and, over time, new buildings were added to provide accommodation to many generations of young sisters.

On August 16, 1975, *Jeevan Jyothi* was formally registered as a charitable society in Andhra Pradesh. Next, we had to build its teaching staff.

Recruiting resident lecturers

Jeevan Jyothi began to offer annual formation to groups of 50 sisters. "Annual" meant that the course lasted for ten months. This was brilliant, but due to lack of resident teaching staff the temptation was to resort to a system of "block courses," that is, courses by specialized teachers who often came from other parts of India to present short, intensive lectures on one topic or another.

Right: *That's me teaching a class of sisters, and a few men as well.*

Below: *Sisters talk in the garden during a break between classes.*

For example, two weeks Scripture (the letters of St. Paul), one week theology (Christology), one week liturgy (the Eucharist), two weeks church history (the Reformation), etc.

Though such block courses could have advantages if used judiciously – for instance, to introduce the students to exceptional experts – they could not form the substance of a thorough teaching programme. For these block courses acted like short, intensive bursts of information that could not be properly digested by the students. New insights are easily forgotten, lost in a succession of ever-new topics. Real growth in understanding requires a gradual, long-term exposure to systematic teaching.

Moreover, the block courses tended by their very nature to be brief, compressed and generalised. For some of the students, they were repetitions of what they had already heard. I felt that good theological/scriptural teaching at *Jeevan Jyothi*'s level should focus on select topics which were thoroughly explored, rather than superficial, general introductions.

Teachers of block courses invariably found that the time given to them for their lectures was too short to do justice to their material. They would therefore either cram heavily compressed teaching into hour after hour of lecturing, or resign themselves to a half-hearted, simplified presentation.

As for the students, four lectures on the same topic each day for six days on end would prove far too heavy and congested. The "block system" in fact deprived students of the time for private study and weakened their motivation to pursue any topic in depth. It derailed real learning. New knowledge acquired during lectures should be assimilated by the students through personal reading, library research, preparing essays, and expressing their views in carefully tailored personal assessments (exams).

You see from what I am writing that I felt strongly about this. I knew from my own teaching in St. John's College that students need time, often many months, before grasping complex issues, such as the function of "literary forms" in a correct understanding of scriptural texts. In the block course system, the needs of the students or the requirements of this level of studies were not sufficiently taken into account.

However, the problem *Jeevan Jyothi* was facing lay in the lack of trained staff. At the time there was hardly a single religious sister in the whole of India qualified in ecclesiastical studies, such as theology, sacred scripture, church history or whatever. So I made up my mind to recruit such staff from abroad.

In the summer of 1974, during a short break in the Netherlands, I appealed to the national conference of religious there. I also visited the headquarters of individual Dutch congregations. In the end, I managed to obtain the services of two very capable sisters, both doctors in theology: Dr. Sr. Angela Nijssen of the Sisters of Charity of Tilburg and Dr. Sr. Gabriel van den Heuvel of the Sisters of Charity of Schijndel.

Sr. Gabriel became the dean of studies; Sr. Angela was principal professor of theology. With the help of some lecturers from St. John's College, they could offer full one-year academic courses to the students.

At the official inauguration of the new *Jeevan Jyothi* building, I publicly announced among its main purposes: to enable more religious sisters to enjoy good theological courses; to stimulate the appointment of more religious to full academic theological qualifications; and, last but not least, to promote the ordination of women to diaconate, priesthood and episcopacy.

Chapter 23

Finding God in a loving partner?

While I was working in India, I came across another major issue: priestly celibacy. Some of the students I had helped train in the seminary left the priestly ministry a few years after their ordination and got married.

I am thinking, for instance, of Father Bandi Shoury, who hailed from the *Mâla* caste. He was sent for higher studies to Catholic University of Louvain. After qualifying with an MA in Scripture, he lectured for some years as my successor in St. John's Seminary in Hyderabad. However, then he fell in love. He married and had two beautiful and intelligent daughters, both of whom studied medicine.

I am confident Shoury would not mind me mentioning him by name. He died in 2016, but throughout his life, though he was barred from performing priestly duties, he provided excellent service to his community. He taught religious classes in local schools and ran a number of charities, such as a local orphanage for poor children. He resented very much that the Church did not allow him to preside at the Eucharist because of his marriage. The inscription on his tombstone reads: "Here lies an eternal priest, a loving husband, an adorable father and a faithful friend."

Later, as Vicar General of the Mill Hill Missionaries, I came across many other cases. One concerned one of our English fathers who, while attending a renewal course, had fallen in love with a woman from Canada. I went to visit him in Toronto, where he had obtained a temporary job while preparing for marriage. The problem was, the woman's family would consent to her marriage only if he obtained proper dispensation from Rome. He had already applied through the local diocese - 10 years earlier! - but had never received a reply.

I arranged a meeting with the chancellor of the diocese through which the application had been submitted. He turned out to be a young man, qualified as a doctor in church law. I urged him to put pressure on the case because of the serious pastoral needs involved.

"No use," he told me, shrugging his shoulders. "Pope John Paul II is deliberately withholding all dispensations to stop the avalanche of requests the Vatican has received."

When he said "avalanche" he wasn't exaggerating. Indeed, 3,000 to 4,000

Bandi Shoury, one of many who left the priesthood to get married, talks with children in an orphanage he ran after he was laicised.

such applications flooded in from all over the world when John Paul II was Pope.

Priestly celibacy?

During the final years leading up to my priestly ordination I had been made to promise celibacy for the rest of my life. Because it was a promise to God, it was called a "vow." I had willingly accepted this obligation because it was a requirement if you wanted to become a priest. Church Law prescribed it. Later I began to realize that my promise might have been invalid.

My ignorance about women, sex and marriage invalidated my commitment.

Classic moral theology teaches that a promise, even if made under oath, ceases to be valid by ignorance or erroneous knowledge. This applies to errors affecting the content of the promise or the purpose of the promise. A marriage vow by a woman who does not know anything about intercourse, for instance, is invalid. A promise to donate money to a leprosy hospital is null and void if the hospital does not actually materialise. Thomas Aquinas says that such promises or vows collapse; they fold up "from within." They have no substance. They are hollow, empty, non-existent and non-binding.

It gradually dawned on me that that was the situation I, too, was in.

* * * * *

In February of 1975, I was in an extremely busy period. Workloads oppressed me from every side. They almost killed me.

I had a full-time lecturing job in St. John's College at Ramanthapur. I carried all the responsibilities of being Planning Director of *Amruthavani* Communication

Centre in Secunderabad, with 60-plus staff members dependent on me. I was a member of the National Council of the All-India Bishops' Conference. I gave regular part-time courses at the National Biblical Catechetical and Liturgical Centre in Bangalore. And I was completing some new theological publications.

When I say it almost killed me, I am not exaggerating.

I realised this one day when travelling on my Jawa 250 motorbike from St. John's College to *Amruthavani*. Indian roads were narrow and chaotic at the time. I had to maneuver my way through buses, lorries, water buffaloes, and children running across the road without warning while trying to avoid deep holes in the tarmac left by the previous rainy season. Fatal road accidents occurred frequently. Well, on that day, just before a major road junction, I experienced a moment of mental oblivion. My mind went blank. I did not know where I was. My vision was blurred. I felt utterly confused.

I stopped the motorbike and pushed it to the side of the road. I staggered to a tea stall that happened to be close by and sat down on a stool. Holding a mug of tea, I felt my mind clearing.

I realised the significance of what had happened. It was a warning sign. It would be suicide to ignore it. Survival mattered more than pushing on, regardless. I knew I needed a good break.

So when I had recovered a little, I turned the motorbike round and returned to St. John's College. I went to see Father Fred Moss, the acting rector at the time, and told him what had happened.

"Enough is enough," he said. "You're overdoing things. Cancel all your lectures and other commitments. Take two weeks off."

I followed his advice. Next day I flew from Hyderabad to Chennai, which was then called Madras. In Madras I dropped into a tourist office and they advised me to book in at the Mahabalipuram beach resort, just south of town. I went there the same afternoon, finding accommodation in a small tourist lodge.

Mahabalipuram is blessed with wonderful white sandy beaches lined with palm trees stretching along the coast. There were very few tourists at the time. It was truly a paradise. I loved walking along the sea and taking an occasional dip in spite of the high coastal waves. The only people I met were the occasional Tamil fishermen hauling in a net or other guests in the lodge. I had time to rest, and sleep, and think.

After a few days I began to put my thoughts down. I made decisions about my work. But I also reflected on my sexuality. Here is one of the entries in the "self definition" I drew up at the time:

> I never want to forget that I am also "body." I accept my body in its fullness; with all its limitations, its feelings, its possibilities. I reject the inadequate spirituality of my early years in which there was no healthy place for sex. I see sex as a beautiful gift from God to me. I realise there can be no question of sin in sex unless I harm myself or others through what I do.

My motorbike was a practical and reliable means of transportation while on mission in India. That's St. John's College behind me.

Love and intimacy

There were other guests staying at the tourist lodge. I was the only single person and the only European. All the others were Indian couples. But not all was *kosher*, as I soon found out while eating a delicious Tamil *thâli*: a wide round plate with boiled rice heaped in the middle with vegetables, curries and chutneys arrayed around it.

"Many of them are businessmen bringing their mistresses from Madras," a friendly waiter whispered to me.

I could easily see who they were: middle-aged men in smart suits with young girls in colourful saris. But there was a happy, married couple, too. They had two small children. Husband and wife obviously were in love with each other. They looked at each other's faces, chatted and laughed.

I felt a pang of envy. Their closeness was something I missed. I was paying the price of being celibate. What was the cost?

Was I doomed to a life of loneliness? Would I be forever deprived of intimacy? I had been privileged in the past because I had enjoyed close emotional intimacies. One had been with my mother when I was rather young and sharing with her and my brothers constant hunger, dysentery and humiliation during four long years in the Japanese POW camps. The other had been with my older brother, Carel. With him I had been able to share all my secrets: my fears, hopes, daily adventures, plans for the future, my latest dream. And you'll recall he died while in college.

The dread of loneliness fell all the more on me through a near-death experience.

I was walking along the sea in Mahabalipuram early in the morning, admiring the waves splashing in at regular intervals. The sun stood not yet too high. Seagulls skillfully sailed through the steady breeze. Nobody else was on the beach except for a single Tamil fisherman and some nervous crabs digging themselves into the sand.

I reached a small bay, and the water looked tempting. It was soothingly warm. Being a keen swimmer, I walked in and was about to swim out into the deep when the fisherman dropped his line and came running up to me. His gestures were unmistakable. He frantically waved to make me come back. I went back onshore, unsure of what was wrong.

The fisherman did not understand my Telugu, but he explained his reason by what he did next. He cut a piece of wood from a dead palm tree branch and threw it into the water. The wood circled on the water for just a few seconds, then was sucked under and swept out 40 yards into the sea. I had been on the point of swimming straight into a dangerous undersea current!

I thanked the fisherman. Later in the lodge I heard that a Scotsman had drowned in more or less the same location a year earlier. I had been lucky to escape the same fate. Out in those coastal waters there is no one who can pull you out.

I had almost died, but there was no one with whom I could share my feelings of delayed shock and intense relief.

This gave me much food for thought. Here I was, far away in a foreign country, with many responsibilities on my shoulders. I worked from early morning to late at night. I had dreams of building up some important new structures for the Church in Andhra Pradesh. I endured pressures from colleagues, students, staff at *Amruthavani*, distrustful bishops and angry critics. I was creatively involved in developing new correspondence courses for Hindu inquirers, new Christian films, radio programs and spiritual books.

But in all this I was deprived of the possibility of sharing my hopes and fears on a deep personal level.

Is God a rival?

Traditional teaching on celibacy stressed that a priest should choose between God and a human partner. They would quote St. Paul's words:

> I would like to see you free from all worry. An unmarried man can devote himself to the Lord's affairs, all he needs worry about is pleasing the Lord. But the married man has to devote himself to the world's affairs and devote himself to pleasing his wife: he is torn in two ways. (1 Corinthians 7,32-33)

Now, I realize there is truth in that. Not being married gave me more freedom and flexibility in some of my missionary apostolate. I could see this in the restraints put on Anglican missionaries I knew. Their wives might develop special health problems. They had to find suitable schools and colleges for their children – which might be challenging if they were stationed in rural parishes. But the reverse was also true.

I got acquainted with a Methodist couple in Secunderabad who were top-class missionaries, each in their own right. And whenever I visited them I was struck by the support they could give each other. They would discuss plans together. If anything went wrong, they went through a shared process of honest analysis, searching prayer, healing and emotional repair. And it did not in the least stand in the way of their relationship with God. In fact, I recognized that God was in both of them, in their sustaining, comforting and loving each other.

One of my priest colleagues at St. John's College, whom I shall call Phil, a warm-blooded enthusiast from Manchester, fell in love with an American woman. Phil was teaching Catholic theology. She worked in a Pentecostal parish in Bombay. When they got married, I went out of my way to call on them at their home in a neighbourhood of slums. Looking after the down-and-outs was their mission. They were both intensely happy. Again I found a deep level of sharing: shouldering joint responsibilities for people and carrying each other in their commitment to God's love.

Married couples do not always enjoy the fruitful and life-giving intimacy that should be theirs. But where it was present, I reflected, it surely was a gift from God: God revealing himself as love in and through the loving partner.

In a truly Christian marriage, God was not a rival for each partner. God became more intensely present and real in the profound affirmation of self-worth imparted by genuine deep sharing and intimacy. Thus, Augustine's brash principle – "Celibacy is a more perfect state of life than marriage" – was as much a fallacy as his other teachings on sex.

As I stated before, I had come to realise that the promise of celibacy I had made before ordination did not really bind me. It had, somehow, been forced upon me. On the other hand, I did not want to upset the crucial priestly tasks I was engaged in. I felt that my commitment to priestly and missionary service should take priority. So while acknowledging my right to marry, I decided I should abstain from marriage or physical relationships with women because of the actual situation I was in.

At the same time, I also affirmed my personal appreciation of marriage

Time spent at Mahabalipuram Beach provided me with a much-needed opportunity to relax and think deeply about my life and my future.

and my right to be married if I were to come across the right person and if circumstances would change.

This is one of the notes I made while in Mahabalipuram:

> God has made me a man. He gave me the physical and psychological make-up that enables me to give and receive life-long and intimate love. Whether I actually marry or not, depends on circumstances and my free choice. But at all times I want to be the kind of person who can or could sustain such a generous and mutually liberating partnership. Meanwhile, my basic vocation to love will make me give all women the respect and affection they deserve.

And my eighth commandment for Church renewal is this:

Allow priests to benefit from the support of a loving spouse.

Part IV

Helping Catholics Become Adult Believers

Chapter 24

Teaching on three fronts

When my term of office as Vicar General of the Mill Hill Missionaries ended in 1982, I found myself in a precarious situation. As a Dutch citizen, it had been difficult to obtain a residential permit to live in India even two decades before.

But in 1982 the government of India was putting even more obstacles in the way of Christian missionaries wanting to work in their country. Hindu nationalists had turned more militant. Just a few months earlier a prominent SVD Father, Fr. Engelbert Zeitler, was almost expelled from India, and efforts to regain him his residential permit resulted in much unwanted publicity for the Catholic Church.

I went to India for six weeks as a tourist. After considering all the implications in discussion with those who knew the situation well, I came to the conclusion that it would be inadvisable for me to start a process of wrangling about a residential permit. That would be awkward for the local church. At the same time, it was clear that I still could make an important contribution to the apostolate in India. So some compromise solution needed to be found.

The solution proved quite simple: The Indian government allowed non-residents to come into the country on a three-months tourist visa "for any legitimate business" (which included teaching and training purposes). The tourist visa could then be extended by another three months. After this, the same person could apply for a new tourist visa only after a lapse of six months.

Back in London, I put a proposal before the Mill Hill General Council. I suggested that I divide the year into two periods. From January to June I would operate from Hyderabad in India, and from July to December from London. During the Indian period, I would be involved in giving courses as a guest lecturer. During the London phase, I would concentrate on teaching in the Missionary Institute, promoting the communication apostolate in our Mill Hill missions all over the world, and focusing on writing books on Biblical spirituality.

In mid-November I received the official letter from our Superior General confirming that my proposals had been fully accepted.

Turning my plan into reality proved to be an arduous and at times adventurous and convoluted task.

Housetop Centre in London

To begin with, I set up a communication centre in the middle of London from which I could operate. Through the good services of a friend, I secured a small but well-located house near Paddington Station. I also was lucky enough to attract Sr. Jackie Clackson, FMM, whom I had gotten to know in India, as a team member. Jackie was professionally qualified as an art teacher. She had also studied communication in the French city of Lyon, Irish Dublin and at Dominican University College in Ottawa. She could run the Centre even during my six months absence in India every year.

We decided to call the Centre "Housetop," referring to Jesus' injunction that we should proclaim the good news "from the housetops." Over the course of time, our team would be expanded by the addition of volunteer workers who gave their energy and time.

Our communication centre was involved in a range of apostolic ministries. With the help of my team, I provided counselling to people who were caught in the new religious sects. I developed educational videos that could be used in countries all over the world. I wrote books and articles on Biblical spirituality and church reform.

My Indian safaris

I spent the first half of each year (1984 -1990) in India on a tourist visa. It meant having an extremely varied programme. A typical commitment would be giving a ten-day theological updating course to priests of a particular diocese. I gave such courses in Cuddapah, Nagpur, Kumbakonam, and other dioceses whose names I have forgotten.

At other times the requirement would be seven-day retreats for religious or for diocesan clergy. Since India had 90,000 religious sisters at the time, and 100 dioceses, these retreats took me all over the country. Among other things, this travel gave me precious insights into the Catholic Church in India.

Also every year I would have regular slots for extended courses at the major renewal centers in India, such as the National Biblical Catechetical Centre and *Sudeep* in Bangalore, *Jeevan Jyoti* in Secunderabad, and *Mater Dei* in Goa.

My journeys through India offered a number of unexpected adventures. Once travelling from New Delhi, our small Fokker aircraft lost a wheel in flight. After circling for a long time over Kanpur airport, it managed to land safely on one wheel. However, it took some days before another wheel was brought in from elsewhere and we could continue our journey on the plane.

Another time, taking off from Pune to fly to Mumbai, I was again in a small Air India Fokker plane. It was the monsoon period, and our little 30-passenger aircraft was being tossed right and left in fierce winds. As I looked outside through a small side window, I observed mist and rain. The plane seemed to

The original home of Housetop Centre, Homer Street 10, in London: Our offices occupied all three stories and the basement of the building at right, between 1983 and 2000.

climb with difficulty. Then I suddenly saw walls of sheer rock rising up in front of us – part of the Western Ghats.

My heart stopped beating. But the plane managed to surge up and emerge over the top. However, two days later, I read in the paper that another plane flying the same route from Pune had crashed into the mountain during a monsoon storm. Everyone on board died.

During a series of conferences in Calcutta I was supposed to stay at St. Xavier's Jesuit College, as I had done before. I had sent a telegram about my time of arrival, but the plane was much delayed. It arrived at the airport around 2 a.m., and it took another hour for a taxi to take me to the College. I found the College in total darkness and hermetically closed. All gates in the high perimeter wall were locked. Through gaps I could see ferocious guard dogs patroling the inner area. It took a long, long time before, via a microphone near the front gate, I established contact with the Jesuit minister. He recognised me and let me in.

I travelled in a small bus on a 13-hour night journey in Eastern Tamilnadu. I sat on a hard narrow bench, pressed on all sides by a mass of local men. Most were trying to sleep. It was very uncomfortable.

But then I suddenly felt a hand slide under my belt, stroking my skin right down to my buttock and up along my back under my shirt. I froze. What to do? I could not even see who was doing this. I did not want to cause a disturbance and perhaps lose my seat. Why was the chap doing this? Was he gay and trying

Me (under the arrow) taking part in a conference of Catholic experts on dialogue with Muslims. The meeting took place in Patna, India.

to make contact? In the end, I firmly gripped his hand, squeezed it and turned it away. Peace returned.

A bishop in the northeastern Indian city of Kohima invited me to give a course to his priests. I accepted. He told me that, because of some local tribes fighting a guerilla war against the Indian garrisons, outsiders needed special clearance from central government in Delhi to be permitted entrance. He told me that he would obtain such clearance for me. But when, in Delhi, I boarded the plane to Kohima, security police warned me I needed the clearance. I told them it had been arranged. However, on arrival in Kohima I found out that the clearance had not come in time.

I was promptly arrested. By interceding with the local governor, the Bishop then managed to change it to "supervised house arrest" in the Bishop's own mansion. All turned out well.

On one occasion, three of us, all Scripture experts, gave a one-week course to nine Indian bishops. The course was conducted in secret; no one should know that even bishops needed instruction! We updated the bishops on the correct principles of interpreting the Bible. While my companions were more diplomatic, I went out of my way to debunk popular myths. It resulted in much frank talk and heated exchanges. But in the end, even the traditional Archbishop of Agra confided to me that he had "learnt a lot" and that he preferred my straightforward style to the soft-peddling used by the other lecturers.

I'm animating a discussion during a course at a renewal centre in India.

The Missionary Institute

The Missionary Institute of London had been founded in 1968 as a collaboration among missionary societies, such as Mill Hill, the Missionaries of Africa, the Divine Word Fathers, the Comboni Fathers, the Milan Fathers and others. The Institute was physically located in Holcombe House in Mill Hill. It brought students together, not only from European countries, but also from many African and Asian nations. The Institute was affiliated with both Middlesex University and the famous Catholic University of Louvain in Belgium.

During the first semester of each year, that is from September to December, I taught at the Institute as a professor of Sacred Scripture. My subject was mainly the letters of St. Paul. I presented these in three main sections: General Introduction, Paul on Justification, and St. Paul's Sources. I designed the last section to disprove German theologian Rudolf Bultmann's contention that Paul, not Jesus, was the founder of Christianity.

I tried to ensure maximum participation by the students through inserting debates within my lectures and by giving them essays to do which were both instructive and relevant to contemporary issues.

Chapter 25

Bringing priests 'down to earth'

*P*riests were often my audience in renewal seminars. Both as Vicar General of the Mill Hill Missionaries and as the travelling lecturer of later years, I often found myself facing priests who were outdated in their thinking.

To understand the problem, come with me and meet Fr. Norbert Pryor who, at the time, lived in our Mill Hill retirement home in Freshfield. I had looked forward to my encounter with him. He had ministered in India for most of his life, and some Telugu priests I knew in Andhra Pradesh had been singing his praises. In their eyes he was an example of the perfect priest. Not so.

The Norbert Pryor I met was confused and disgruntled. He fiercely rejected all Vatican II reforms.

"Priests have been relegated to the status of boys polishing people's shoes!" he complained.

He refused to ever concelebrate at the altar with other priests:

"Concelebration has been invented for the comfort of sacristans," he groaned.

Fr. Anton Zuure, retired in Vrijland, had been a caring parish priest on an island in Lake Victoria. The area belonged to Jinja Diocese in Uganda.

"Anton loves devotions," the local Bishop once told me. "When I offered to send him an assistant priest to help in his parish, he replied, 'No! Rather send me a statue of St. Joseph.'"

On return to the Netherlands, Anton could not cope with the renewed Church he encountered. Being the militant person he was, he joined Dutch reactionary groups that fought against every kind of reform.

During visits to our houses of formation I had made it a practice to visit the small communities of nuns who looked after the cooking, washing and upkeep of the house – to thank them for their help. When I visited the community of nuns in Hoorn, one of them confronted me regarding the new post-Vatican-Council custom of giving communion in the hand.

"It's a disgrace!" she said. "Communion should be given on the tongue!"

"Why?" I asked. "In the early Church, people received communion in the hand. The Vatican Council has simply re-instated the ancient practice."

"No! No!" she cried out. "Only a sacred priest is allowed to touch a consecrated host. Even Jesus, when Jesus himself distributed communion, he gave it on the tongue!"

"How do you know?" I challenged.

She went to her bedroom and returned with a leaflet in German produced by an archconservative Catholic group. The leaflet attacked the practice of communion in the hand. As its centerpiece it showed a picture of the Last Supper. This portrayed apostles kneeling devoutly in front of Jesus who takes white round hosts (!) from a paten (!) and puts them on the apostles' tongues. The article claimed that the drawing faithfully represented the vision of two stigmata-carrying visionaries: Anna Katherina Emmerick and Theresa Neumann. I translate an excerpt into English:

"When in 1927 the Swiss priest Alphons Büchel asked Theresa Neumann how (in her vision) the apostles went to communion, she replied, 'Jesus himself broke the host into smaller pieces and then placed a piece into the mouth of each apostle.'"

The 'sacred' person 'anointed by God'

Apart from some obviously primitive ideas about Jesus, Neumann's vision exemplified the traditional image of the "sacred priest" shaped especially since the Middle Ages. The "man of God" will always wear his Roman collar. He carries the unerasable stamp of the priesthood that makes him a living ambassador of God. He remembers this whenever he mixes with people. He will avoid making lay persons his close friends, especially women. He will not go to the cinema or read frivolous novels. Every day he faithfully recites Lauds, Matins, Vespers and other hours of the Holy Office.

In my lectures and conferences I would explain this priestly model in a diagram.

I would then describe the different model discovered by priests in our own time. In fact, I would point out, this new model was far closer to the ideal of the religious leader Jesus had in mind. The New Testament presents the Eucharist as embedded in the world. This shocking fact may never be forgotten. Jesus Christ did not come from a priestly family, nor did he receive the priestly ordination prescribed in Leviticus 8:1-36. He offered his sacrifice not in the hallowed Temple precincts, but on Golgotha, a contaminated mount of execution. He wore no priestly garments. His altar was a beam of ordinary wood. The author of the letter to the Hebrews explains at length that Christ thus abolished and replaced the cultic worship of the Temple. The curtain that shielded the Holy of Holies was torn in two. The theological and spiritual significance of Christ's action cannot be overestimated, I would say. For in one stroke he made the whole world sacred and liberated the whole human race from distinctions based on a sacred status.

The early Christians were deeply conscious of the unusual situation in which they found themselves. They celebrated the Lord's Supper in ordinary homes, breaking the bread and sharing the wine in vessels used in their households. Those who presided were dressed like everyone else. They grasped that Christ's words, "Do this in commemoration of me," implied also a commemoration of God becoming incarnate in ordinary everyday life, transforming the "profane" world by turning it upside down, ignoring temples – because the people themselves had become God's Temple.

As polls in Europe showed, many priests were adopting the more "down-to-earth" model. While treasuring their priestly task, they did not see themselves as different from everyone else. They did not feel comfortable wearing a cassock or black suit and clerical collar. They wanted to mingle with people rather than stand out from them.

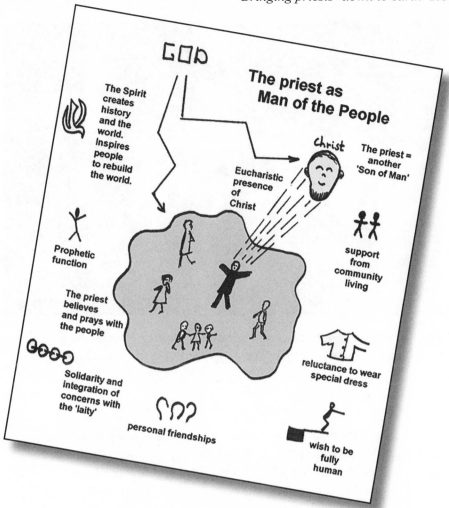

Yes, they realized they were spiritual leaders. They had to bring about change in society. They had to help people discover God and live in harmony with the spiritual "Kingdom" Jesus preached.

But how could they do this if they did not know people intimately? If they did not experience their challenges and dreams? Were lay people not their allies, equally called to priestly, prophetic and royal roles in their own stations in life?

The clash between the various images led to confusion and struggle. In the talks I gave I tried to help priests understand what was going on. Although my personal sympathy lay squarely on the side of the "man of the people," I always stressed that neither of the two concepts was correct in its extreme form.

"We, priests of our time," I used to say, "have to find the balance between the two. We should be both 'men of God' and 'men of the people.' And we should learn to deal with the mix-up the two models cause in the minds of colleagues, friends and recruits. We should learn to allay the trauma and heal wounds."

I was honored to preside at a church ceremony in which my brother, Aloys, and his wife, Nelleke, renewed their marriage vows, at Arnhem, the Netherlands, in 1986.

Disagreement in the Vatican

It did not help that the new ideal of the priest was frowned upon in Rome. Pope John Paul II rightly often extolled the utter dedication required in a priest. But in his many talks and letters he also kept stressing the "sacrality" of the priest.

"[Priests are persons] for whom the Holy Mass, Communion, and Eucharistic adoration are the center and summit of their whole life," he said.

"The world looks up to the priest, because it looks up to Jesus! No one can see Christ; but everyone sees the priest, and through him they wish to catch a glimpse of the Lord! Immense is the grandeur of the Lord! Immense is the grandeur and dignity of the priest!"

That is why Pope John Paul II ordered all priests in Rome to wear clerical dress at all times. He defended the priesthood as "a sacred and perpetual vocational state, not just a profession – which is the reason for the state of celibacy required of priests."

Finally, to cap it all, in August of 2000 the Vatican Congregation for Divine Worship issued new instructions that stressed that "sacredness" surrounds the Eucharist. The sanctuary should be treated as a *sacred* area within the church. The altar is a *sacred* table and should be treated as such. The ambo, from which the Scripture is read, is a *sacred* lectern. The chalice and the paten that hold the consecrated bread and wine are called *sacred* vessels. The priest wears *sacred* vestments and is himself a *consecrated* person. Even the chair on which he sits in the sanctuary shares in his *sacredness*. It has to be "visibly distinguished from chairs used by others who are not clergy."

I wonder what the son-of-man Jesus would have thought about that? Or the apostles re-enacting the Last Supper in people's homes, wearing everyday clothes and consecrating standard bread and wine in household vessels?

Chapter 26

Treating the faithful as adults

*M*y purpose as a teacher throughout the years was primarily to promote adult faith formation among the laity. Now, I know that many may not grasp what this means or why it was, and still is, of such importance to the Catholic community, so I offer the following explanation.

After World War II, enormous changes affected the Western world. Previously, Mass attendance had been good in Catholic communities. But it slumped to less than 30% in most countries. Teenagers and young Catholic couples drifted away from the Church.

The causes of church decline were numerous: in people's eyes, science was winning the battle over religion; society had become mixed, pluriform and fragmented; people were asserting their own autonomy over traditional morality; they were becoming "fulfillment-seekers" rather than obedient followers. Meanwhile, the official Church refused to update its views on family planning, women's equality, lay participation in church governance. At the root of it all was the fact that educated Catholics were discovering their own responsibility as adults while the ecclesiastical institution still treated them as children. This eroded faith.

Most Catholics were instructed in doctrine through a catechism that was imposed on them in primary and secondary schools. Texts had to be learned by heart, rather than key beliefs discussed and explored. At Sunday Mass, the priest preached homilies that consisted of often repeated and predictable assertions. There was no room for questioning, for debate, for coming to accept a point of faith after mature reflection. But we know faith can become one's own conviction only after much thought and a personal "adult" decision.

In other words, most teenagers and Catholic adults were supported in faith only by an immature indoctrination.

Reform would not happen unless religious leaders could be made to change their mindsets. My aim was to persuade priests, teachers and other religious educators that they should help teenagers and adults rediscover their faith and make it a "personal conquest."

"Don't stand there shivering! It's not cold unless I tell you it is!" (A cartoon I commissioned to make a point about treating the faithful as adults)

My principles for deepening people's faith were as follows:
- Don't preach. Provide information.
- Respect people's doubts, people's need to search, each person's individual pace of learning.
- Realise the importance of people's own experiences.
- Encourage people to think for themselves, to make their own decisions when they are ready for them.

What I learned in India

The courses I gave in India were often addressed to priests. They were either the clergy of a particular diocese, or priests attending a renewal course in a pastoral centre. I used to teach them that an important part of the liberation Jesus brought consisted in helping people discover their own self-worth.

Persons belonging to lower castes or outcasts suffered not only from all the injustices heaped on them by society. They also were hampered by their lack of self-esteem. They could not imagine themselves being successful, wealthy, respected. This was proved by some interesting experiments.

After partition in 1947, many Sikhs moved to the Punjab, taking over land from Hindus. Farm production increased rapidly. The Sikh farmers took major new initiatives in irrigation and local organisation. In the 1960s there was an enormous upsurge in agricultural output: wheat production tripled between 1966 and 1970. The rice crop increased during that same period, from 280,000 tons to two million tons. Researchers attribute this success to the inner attitude of the Sikhs: "They knew they could do it."

The local government of Maharashtra State apportioned new land to poor families. Men could choose the size of the plot they wanted. Caste people asked for plots of many acres in size. Low-caste persons generally asked for a few "cents" of land, equivalent to about 100 square yards. The upper caste families flourished. Lower caste families struggled to even keep their mini-plots going. This was due to both the lack of education and, mainly, the lack of belief in themselves.

Research in Andhra Pradesh showed that low-caste Christians developed an unhealthy mindset of "dependence." They would often complain:

"We cannot improve our situation. We need help, but nobody comes to give it to us. Whatever we do is useless. See how miserable and poor we are. Why do more people not come forward to give help?"

The temptation for priests and other spiritual leaders was to give in to that dependence, rather than help people better their own situations.

I used to point out that Jesus was fond of the image of "seed." The kingdom of heaven is like a mustard seed which is the smallest of all seeds. It can hardly be seen. It is just a speck on the hand of the sower. And yet it grows out into a great tree, Jesus said. Good seed that falls on fertile soil produces a wonderful increase: some 30-fold, some 60-fold and some a hundredfold. It is as if Jesus is saying: "Don't worry about the future harvest. Concentrate on the seed."

We should prod every individual to jump out of his or her bag of self-pity and prove their worth.

And it can be done. I had an interesting experience myself. One day, when I was celebrating an Indian-style Eucharist sitting on the floor with a group of students, I decided to do a foot-washing, as Jesus had done at the Last Supper. I wound a towel round my waist, took a bowl with water, and knelt before each one of them. Then I washed their feet.

Now, you should know that people's feet are considered very dirty in India. No one will ever touch another's sandals. Sandals are left outside a house. People will wash their feet before entering the house. So foot-washing is an incredibly powerful symbol. When I washed the feet of one of the students, Johannes Gorantla, he cried and cried. After Mass he told me that he never thought anyone would consider him worthy of such an honour.

Johannes belonged to the *Golla* caste, the shepherds. They are one of the lower castes. They had the reputation of being stupid, essentially useless, unworthy of respect. Telugu proverbs make the point:

• "There's not anyone in the world who has not beaten up a shepherd."
• "However good a person a shepherd may be, he will always remain a fool."

I am sure Johannes would not mind me mentioning him by name. He died in 2007. He certainly jumped out of the bag of self-deprecation. He became a priest. He was sent to Rome for higher studies. Later he served as Bishop of Kurnool Diocese for nearly 20 years.

The right leadership strategy

"It's easy for you to talk, but many people need paternalistic guidance," priests would tell me. "They are confused, they are poor, they are helpless. Unless they are led by the hand and told what to do, they will not manage."

Unfortunately, this style of leadership was, and still is to a great extent, favoured in Catholic hierarchical tradition. It breeds leaders who are mainly concerned with maintaining order.

This leads to what is called "management by control." It starts from certain basic assumptions:

"Most people are weak and inclined to make mistakes. Therefore, in order to help people to stay on the right path, some use of force will be necessary. They need to be controlled, directed, even threatened with punishment to make sure they reach their goal. Moreover, the average human being prefers to be directed, wishes to avoid responsibility, has relatively little ambition and wants security above all. It is the task of the leader, therefore, to shield these people from as much harm as possible and to guide them step by step with regard to their duties and responsibilities. At all costs the established order should be maintained, and this can only be achieved by effective control from above."

I had an experience in India that illustrated this approach dramatically. It happened when Fr. Joop Jansen, MHM, was a parish priest in Anantapur District. He was respected as a saintly and committed priest by his parishioners. But he was an extreme "paternalist."

One day he was scheduled to bless three marriages in the chapel of an outstation. After the sermon, Fr. Jansen summoned the three couples to step forward to the altar. He placed them next to each other in a row, then went from couple to couple and directed them to exchange marriage vows. Then, according to Indian custom, he instructed each groom to hang a necklace round the neck of the bride. For Telugus this seals the marriage. As he was doing this, some prominent parishioners came forward and tried to alert him to something. But he shouted at them and sent them back to their places.

When the Eucharist had been completed, and the married couples processed out of the chapel, there was pandemonium. It seems that Fr. Jansen had married the grooms to the wrong brides! Panic and confusion.

You should know that in India marriages are carefully planned by the families. Sensitive negotiations are involved with the dowry the bride should bring in, on the wedding ceremony, and so on. It is not just two individuals who get married, but two families. By matching the wrong grooms to the wrong brides, Fr. Jansen had ruined all such arrangements. Moreover, the question arose: Were these marriages valid?

Now, Fr. Jansen showed who was in charge. He made the congregation sit down again and he declared:

"What I've done, I've done. I acted in the name of God. These marriages are valid. OK, I may have been confused, but God is not. It is God who sealed these marriages through a sacred sacrament. The new couples should now live together as loving husbands and wives. No further discussion. The matter is closed! Their families should support them."

Fr. Jansen was wrong, of course. It is the free exchange of consent that brings about the marriage, not the blessing by the priest. The couples had been constrained to act as they did. The marvel is that people accepted Fr. Jansen's verdict. And somehow – I was told – the unexpectedly bonded couples made successes of their wedded lives.

As we can conclude from this debacle, Fr. Jansen's behavior is hardly an example to be followed. Spiritual leaders should see their function more in the line of encouragement and stimulation. The right model is "management towards dynamic growth." Proponents of this model have assumptions upon which they base their judgement:

"It is natural for people to be creative and do well if only they get a chance. External control and the threat of punishment should be avoided. People will naturally exercise self-direction and self-control in the pursuit of objectives to which they are personally committed. And why will people be committed to such objectives? Mainly because of the rewards associated with their achievement. The average human being will be much happier if he or she can truly grow and is given proper responsibilities. Many more people than we might think at first are capable of carrying such responsibilities in a creative and productive fashion. In fact, most people realise their potential only partially. The proper way of guiding people is therefore to help them work out things for themselves."

People's moral autonomy

In March of 1998 the Council of the European Bishops Conferences convoked a consultation in Vienna regarding "Sects and Fringe Religious Groups in Europe." Because of my involvement in counselling members of "sects and cults," I was delegated to represent England.

I presented a paper in which I sketched the social and cultural world of Europe which had radically changed the way in which even Catholics would normally think and act. This was the background against which many youngsters were "taking refuge" in fringe religions, I explained. Features of this new reality included: God seemingly disappearing from everyday life; living in a mixed, pluriform, fragmented society; people changing from being "security-seekers" to "fulfillment-seekers;" and, last but not least, people's own autonomy taking over from prescribed traditional morality.

I suggested that the Church should acknowledge this new reality and build on it. It needed a new kind of evangelization to plant the Gospel in this new fertile soil.

I was fiercely opposed by some participants in the consultation. In particular,

Johannes Gorantla was a member of one of the lower castes (the shepherd caste) in India. He was a seminary student of mine, and when I washed his feet in a ceremony he cried and expressed feelings of unworthiness. Some years later, he was ordained a priest, then rose to the position of Bishop of Kurnool.

a young Polish bishop, using an interpreter, stated that he was appalled at my giving in to secular degeneration. Instead, we should instill into people's minds the age-old trusted Catholic beliefs and practices. We should not give in to Satan! It shook the assembly. Later, the Italian professor commissioned to edit our papers for publication in a book approached me, asking whether I wanted to withdraw my paper, or amend it substantially in view of the Bishop's criticism. I said, "Certainly not! I believe that what I said is correct."

Many processes in our time boost the central role of the individual in society: better education, a growing awareness of one's democratic rights, enlightened discussion in the media, a rising standard of living. All these things conspire to make the individual the focus of society.

One element of this individualisation process is a slow de-coupling between morality and religion. It does not mean the end of morality, but a change in its underpinnings. Many theologians now agree that morality is basically autonomous. Concrete moral rules of conduct, they say, cannot be derived directly from religion. God made us autonomous, by creating us in his image. Religion only plays an indirect role, namely through its providing a set of norms that inspire, guide, criticise and coordinate.

The Catholic Church is perceived to take an ambivalent attitude towards individual moral autonomy.

On the one hand, the Church applauds the growing discovery and vindication of people's personal rights and endorses the dignity of conscience, freedom of choice, and the liberty of the children of God. It also approves the rightful autonomy of every creature, obviously under responsibility to the Creator and the Gospel. On the other hand, the official Church lays down detailed norms of sexual morality that are felt by many to contradict a valid personal autonomy.

The sociologist Andrew Greeley maintains that since the Encyclical *Humanae Vitae* (1968), the Vatican has lost its credibility as a teacher of sexual ethics. Many have left the Church. Many don't take it seriously on sexual matters anymore, not even its own members, not even devout ones.

Greeley cites data from the USA showing that ever more Catholics practice artificial birth control, live together outside marriage, and condone pre-marital sex. In 1963, 88% of Catholics believed pre-martital sex was always wrong; in 1988 that number had fallen to 18%. A similar situation exists in the urbanised world. Urbanised people are comfortable about the Church speaking out on questions of human rights, but are much less comfortable about public pronouncements on ethical issues which affect their intimate personal lives or encroach on their moral autonomy.

I pleaded in Vienna that the Church should fully recognise the value of human and Christian autonomy. It should reformulate moral guidance to do justice both to the demands of Gospel morality and the genuine adult responsibility of each individual. The official Church bodies, I stated, will need to change their image of being patriarchal, male-dominated, and autocratic.

Later that day our session was concluded with a Eucharist. We trooped to the chapel. As it happened, I had been selected to be one of the two priests flanking the main celebrant at the altar. When I entered the sacristy, I found out that the main celebrant for the day was the Polish bishop who had so fiercely lambasted me. While we put on our vestments, he glared at me, but did not say anything.

During Mass he gave me the hug of peace, but whether he meant it I will never know. He is probably still praying for my conversion!

But one thing I'm quite sure of is that maturing Christian people must not be treated like children; their autonomy and dignity must be respected by the hierarchy of the Church. So, my ninth commandment for Church reform is this: **Respect and promote the adult dignity of every member of the community.**

Chapter 27

Wielding my pen

*I*n the course of my life I have reached tens of thousands of people through my writings, all of which were based on research.

I passed through Rome in early 1978. I had been a member of the Catholic Biblical Federation from its foundation, originally as the delegate for India. So I paid a visit to my old friend, Fr. Jos van de Valk, the secretary of the Federation, in his Roman offices. He told me that he was facing a catastrophe. The International Assembly of the Federation was scheduled to take place in Malta just two months later, but a key speaker had dropped out.

"Please," he pleaded with me. "Can you fill the gap?"

"Yes," I said.

I decided I would talk about "Biblical spirituality." What is it that makes *Biblical* spirituality different from, let us say, Franciscan spirituality or Ignatian spirituality? In record time I produced a quite appealing interpretation, even captivating – if I say so myself. After showing that all Christian spirituality has to be "Biblical" to a great extent, I highlighted its four main elements: experience of God; searching the Scriptures; witness of the Spirit; and transformation of life.

As luck would have it, the other key speaker at the Assembly was the dull Prof. Prosper Grech, an Italian expert on the Letters of St. Paul. In his broken English, he tried to explain that the Greek word *pistis* (faith) has six slightly varying meanings in Paul's Letter to the Romans. His speech was broken up into numerous points and paragraphs. For instance, under the third meaning of *pistis* (fidelity), he announced, "Well, here we have to note nine points. Point one is..."

It may have been scholarly, but for this international audience of parish priests, students, religious sisters and college lecturers, it was a total disaster. I looked at their faces. Some were asleep. Some yawned. Some looked on in disbelief. When, after one and half hours, the professor came to an end, everyone sighed with obvious relief.

So my lively and down-to-earth presentation after the break was a roaring success. For I had peppered my text with vivid examples from exciting persons:

Basil the Great, Charles de Foucauld, Thérèse de Lisieux, Queen Bridget of Sweden, Francis of Assisi and others.

When I finished, the response was overwhelming. My talk was published in at least nine international publications, with translations into Dutch, Chinese and other languages.

Charismatics

Another major opportunity to promote familiarity with Sacred Scripture among Catholics arose in 1984. At that time charismatic renewal groups had sprung up all over the world.

My first encounter with charismatics in India some 15 years earlier had left me sceptical. I was not convinced by the charismatics' uncontrolled "speaking in tongues" or their glib assertion of miracles. But gradually I changed my mind. I realised that a direct, almost tangible, experience of God's Spirit is healthy in a Christian's life. Moreover, I had come across cases where a "baptism by the Spirit" had in fact liberated some persons from deep psychological traumas.

As it happened, I knew some of the charismatic movement's top brass, such as Mr. Piet Derksen in the Netherlands. Then, previously, I had gotten to know Fr. Fio Mascarenhas, SJ, and Fr. Gino Henriques, CSSR, national leaders of the Charismatic Renewal in India. In England I was in touch with the local chairman, Chris Whitehead.

I do not remember the exact channel, but somehow I was invited to speak about Scripture studies at the International Charismatic Convention that took place in Rome from April 30 to May 5, 1984. It was a huge event: hundreds of participants from all over the world, mainly leaders of prayer groups. My task was to explain to them how to make the reading of Scripture trustworthy and fruitful.

This would require introducing an element of instruction. I presented the outline of a comprehensive plan to do so. But I was given only one hour for my talk and discussion. I realised that I would not be able to do justice to the subject during the convention itself, so I had prepared four diagrams and 30 pages of text, which were distributed to all the participants.

My presentation was later published as "Scripture in our Life" in the charismatic manual, and in international magazines such as *Word & Worship*, *Koinonia*, *Scripture Bulletin* and *Priests & People*.

Helping preachers use Scripture

Listening to sermons over the years, it struck me that most preachers did not really know how to make the biblical message relevant to their audiences. I myself had learned much from the imaginative biblical conferences of an American retreat preacher in Rome, and the spellbinding sermons of a parish priest in

Nijmegen, the Netherlands. So I developed a course, both for the seminarians I was teaching at St. John's College in Hyderabad and groups of priests being updated at the National Centre in Bangalore. The course was quite creative and took most of my students by surprise.

The first part of the course dealt with the whole purpose of Scripture to enlighten people's lives, its power coming through images and stories.

Then I spelled out 12 different techniques. I explained how "simple free narration" differs from the "story-reflection-story" approach. I worked out how a biblical personality could be painted in a straightforward "portrait" or brought to life with pertinent ruminations. I presented how scriptural "motifs" and themes could be used in sermons. Other categories included imaginative elaboration, meditating on a law, unravelling a proverb, giving witness or speaking a prophecy. Whenever I taught this course, I had my students play out the various techniques.

When I turned the course into book form under the title *Communicating the Word of God*, its English edition was published both in the UK and in India. This was followed by publications in French (Paris, 1982), Chinese (Hong Kong, 1985), and Spanish (Estella, 1988).

Another practical course I developed aimed at making readers in church present the Scripture readings as effectively as possible. In particular, I showed how it is often necessary to de-code difficult words, customs or the context. For instance, Matthew 9,18 reads: "While he was speaking to them, behold a ruler came in and knelt before him...." Who is speaking to whom? The context shows us. So a more intelligible, de-coded text reads: "While *Jesus* was speaking to *the disciples of John the Baptist*, a *government official* came in...." The course contains many other useful hints and suggestions.

As a book, the course came out under the title *Yes, Read the Word to Others, but Make Them Understand*. Apart from the Indian and UK editions, a Dutch version was published in the Netherlands.

Rescuing the Old Testament

In my renewal courses for older priests, I frequently found that the books of the Old Testament were considered an abomination by them. I remember talking to a parish priest with 20 years of experience in the ministry. Rome had just announced that the offensive and barbaric bits in the Psalms had been eliminated from the Office.

"Tell me," the parish priest asked me, "why has the Church not long ago got rid of the whole Old Testament?"

"It is part of the inspired Scriptures," I answered.

"I don't know what's inspired about them," he retorted. "The narrative sections are riddled with violent, cruel, racist passages that are in conflict with the values of the God of Love we know through the New Testament. The books of Wisdom are out of date, the prophets unreadable."

I realised he was not alone in thinking like that. In fact, most of the priests I got to know hardly ever referred to Old Testament passages in their sermons or instructions. Using these passages required pruning and clarification. I tried to explain this through my courses - which grew into a book, *God's Word to Israel*.

In the first half of the book I showed how the Old Testament narratives grew from oral traditions, with all their often raw and coarse content, into ever larger written texts. In the second half I presented ten rules of interpretation. These contained principles to distinguish the "primitive shell" from "inspired teaching." But I knew I had to go further, and this led to another publication.

Christian preachers should make creative use of Old Testament narratives and reflections in their sermons and conferences. After all, 85% of Sacred Scripture is found in the Old Testament books. What we should do, I argued, is take the ancient texts and examine them through the lens of our New Testament understanding. This approach often reveals deep insights and new dimensions of meaning.

Take, for instance, the horrible belief going back to St. Anselm that God could not forgive Adam's sin without a bloody sacrifice. And a human sacrifice would not do. So the Father sent his own divine Son to become human and expiate for our sins by bleeding to death on a cross. It is an atrocious heresy, of course. As Scripture repeatedly asserts, God's forgiveness comes as a free gift. Jesus explains his own death not as caused by a bloodthirsty Father, but by his being faithful to his mission. He was the Good Shepherd who does not run away from the wolf, but who is prepared to die for his sheep. When the priests and scribes plotted Jesus' death, Jesus did not run away. In that sense he did his Father's will.

To bolster the presentation, I pointed out how God consistently condemned human sacrifice in the Old Testament. Children were buried under the walls of towns as foundation sacrifices - a practice that persisted for at least four centuries. Children were killed as offerings presented to idols. I depicted in detail the appalling shrine, close to Jerusalem in the valley of Hinnom, where children were sacrificed on a regular basis.

In the book and in my presentations, I showed how stories and images from the Old Testament could vividly underpin the New Testament message. To help people discover this approach, I published 20 examples in *Inheriting the Master's Cloak*. Other editions followed in India, the Philippines and Taiwan. The book won a Catholic Press Association Award in the USA for "best adult spiritual reading."

Chapter 28

Counselling victims of sects and cults

*I*n 1985 Bishop Gerald Mahon, the area bishop for Central London, asked me and Jackie Clackson on behalf of Cardinal Hume whether we could provide pastoral care for families involved in the so-called "sects and cults." The official name for them was "new religious movements."

The reasons we were asked to deal with this is both because of my theological qualification and because Jackie and I had many years of experience with Eastern religions. We said "yes" to his request. In the decade that followed we helped literally hundreds upon hundreds of families from all over Britain.

It is difficult to fully fathom why, at the time, so many youngsters left their traditional church communities to join sects that often were bizarre and extreme. A number of factors can be identified. The West was beginning to enjoy a boom of material wealth, which left many feeling spiritually empty. Traditional Christian communities which often ran on external practice rather than interior depth could not meet the spiritual need. Ancient religions from the East seemed to offer greater potential. At the same time, the emerging secular and individualist society left sensitive persons feeling vulnerable and lost.

Without wanting to over-generalise, the typical cult featured **a dominant leader**. He or she was usually the founder of the group who totally controlled all that went on. For example, Maharshi Mahesh Yogi, who founded Transcendental Meditation; Ronald Hubbard, who crafted Scientology; and Sun Myung Moon, who established the Moonies.

Sects were often imbued with **Eastern spirituality**. Many sprang from Hinduism: *Hare Krishna*; *Ananda Marg*; *Sahaja Yoga*; and the *Brahma Kumaris*. Others originated from Islam, such as *Subud*.

Stress was often put on the value of belonging to **a new community**. Contact with one's natural family was forbidden or discouraged. In some sects, sexual discipline was strictly imposed. In others, the rules were relaxed. Notorious among the latter were the Disciples of *Rajneesh*; the worshippers of the Welsh goddess Rhianne; and the Children of God, invented by Mo Berg.

Indoctrination was practiced by most sects and cults. This usually relied on a master handbook written by the cult leader. Local communities would have their trained teacher who would pass on instructions from that handbook. At times key passages from the handbook had to be learned by heart. Some cults imposed "sleep deprivation" on their candidate members, allowing them only a few hours of rest at night. This ensured that their capacity of critical thinking would be reduced.

Another common feature was that cult members would be given **a new identity**. They were told to dismiss their past existence. They received a new name and were given the distinctive dress. Other cult members became their brothers and sisters, as opposed to their siblings by birth.

I will not distract you by hundreds of detailed accounts, recorded in our diaries, of our contacts with actual cult members, nor with their families, parish priests and friends. Rather, in this chapter I will focus on the "Catholic" sects we came across at the time. In the following account I will use fictitious names for the individuals involved, to preserve their privacy.

The *Sede Vacante* splinter group

In July of 1986, Marcia came to see us. She had gotten entangled in a small group centered round Britons Catholic Library in Bloomsbury Square in London. Its leader was Australian-born Martin Gwynne (his real name).

The beliefs of the group were inspired by extreme traditionalist *Sedevacantist* thinking. This amounts in short to these tenets: According to Canon 188 § 4 of the 1917 Code of Church Law, clerics lose their positions in the Church by public apostasy. The Pope and all the Bishops in the world apostatised publicly by signing some of the documents of the Second Vatican Council. Therefore, since Pius XII's death in 1958, the See of Rome is vacant. All Catholic bishops have lost their rank, and no Catholic Bishop anywhere in the world can validly ordain priests.

Martin Gwynne added his own doctrines, as explained in his book, *Complete Catholic Handbook for the Latter Days*. It contends that no one can be saved unless he or she is part of his small community of followers. Members were subjected to penance, fasting and prayer services day and night.

Apart from Marcia, who came out of the sect eventually, we got to know Steve, who lived with his wife, Donna, in a retirement home. Gwynne persuaded Steve "for the good of his own soul" to leave Donna and join his community. We do not know what happened next. Later that same year, the Anglican Bishop of London rang us about a woman who had joined the group under suspicious circumstances. I advised him to take a tough stance. He did. Three days later he went to the police, who raided the community residence and found that the woman was being kept against her will. She came out.

Peter III is Pope of the Palmarian Catholic Church (since 2016). The Palmarians are a Catholic sect founded in 1978 by a Spaniard who claimed to be ordained as Pope by Christ himself.

The Order of Divine Innocence

In September of 1995, Pete Farrow phoned us from his home in Durham. He and his wife had joined a branch of the Family of Divine Innocence. Because of its strange practices, he had come out, but his wife was still a member. He was worried about her and his two teenage daughters.

Pete was right to be worried. The Order of Divine Innocence had been founded by Patricia de Menezes in Blackpool, England. This woman had become a Catholic in later life and then began to suffer from religious illusions. She imagined that Mary frequently appeared to her with the Infant Jesus in her arms. Patricia held childlike conversations with them. After making an appearance to Patricia, Mary supposedly told her on one occasion:

"I am the Immaculate Mother of God, Mother of the Hidden and Mystical Wounds, Mother of England and Mother of the world. I come to gather in all my children everywhere. It is only in a mother's arms that a child is safe. My arms are open to receive you so tenderly. No one who comes to me will be lost!"

The overall message was "The first rule is Love, the last rule is Love, and all the rules in between are Love." But the community she formed was expected to follow a rather strict routine of observances and prayers. Deviation was not tolerated. Patricia claimed Jesus had fully endorsed her brand of religion:

"This spirituality is the Perfect Original Spirituality of the Church Herself. This Order, the perfect Order of My Divine Innocence, is the First and last Order! The Alpha and the Omega, I AM. This Order is *my order*! This Order is Perfection! The Order of *my* Divine Innocence precedes all orders, and supersedes all orders. It is the original perfect Christian Universal Order of

God!"

As luck would have it, I met Pete's bishop, the Rt. Rev. Ambrose Griffiths, the bishop of Hexham and Newcastle, on some other business. I talked to him about Pete's ordeal, and the bishop said he would be happy to meet Pete in person. That meeting helped Pete and may have saved some other families as well.

The Palmarian Catholic Church

In September of 1993, a representative of a mental health centre in Cumbria approached us. A woman in the centre's care seemed to be suffering from a mental breakdown. She claimed to be a member of the Palmarian Catholic Church. They wanted some background information.

The Palmarians are a breakaway Catholic sect. They took their origin from the Spanish accountant Ferdinand Clemente Dominguez y Gomez, who claimed to have been ordained as the Last Pope by Jesus Christ himself. This ordination took place on the night when Pope Paul VI died, August 6, 1978. He took the name Gregory XVII. He resided not in apostate Rome, but in the sacred place of *el Palmar de Troya* in Spain.

Palmarians rejected the reforms initiated by the Second Vatican Council. They claim that Catholic doctrine was enriched with many dogmas proclaimed by Pope Gregory XVII and enshrined in the Palmarian Creed. Members must wear a brown scapular of Our Lady at all times. Dress should be decent. At prayer, women must have their heads covered, skirts must be four inches below the knee, sleeves must be long, and they may never wear trousers. The penitential Palmarian rosary consists of 50 Our Fathers, 50 Hail Marys, 50 Glory Bes and 50 of Hail Mary, Most Pure.

We do not know if the counsellors were able to relieve the woman in the mental health centre from her anxieties.

Opus Dei

In April of 1988 a certain Mrs. Black rang us. She said she was worried about her son, whom she found out by chance had joined *Opus Dei*. Now, I had a good friend who had become a member of *Opus Dei* and was aware of their good intentions. Should *Opus Dei* be treated as a "sect"?

A highly strung Spanish priest, José Maria Escriva de Balaguer y Albas, founded the organization. He adhered to a rather world-hostile spirituality and practised a somewhat violent mortification. His vision was establishing a "new way of sanctification for the faithful in the midst of the world." Thousands of well-meaning youngsters joined the group. They were attracted to the high ideals held out and the complete commitment demanded in one's efforts to attain those ideals.

But, whatever the good intentions of its leaders and recruits, *Opus Dei* at the time exhibited some features of a cult. This manifested itself in its recruitment techniques. Future members were carefully targeted. Friends who were members already would hide this fact so that, at a cleverly orchestrated retreat, the earmarked individual could be more easily coached into commitment to the movement. Once inside, group pressure and instilling a sense of guilt could be used to ensure the person stayed in.

A case in point was Charlotte, who approached us in September of 1989. She had been tempted to join *Opus Dei* but pulled back from it. Friends kept putting pressure on her: "You are resisting God's grace."

"Can I refuse to enter with a clear conscience?" she kept asking me.

I said she could. I gave the same advice to two other ex-members who were troubled by a sense of guilt.

In June of 1994, Mrs. Wilby told us that her niece in Belgium was in trouble. The niece's husband was being drawn into *Opus Dei*. It began to claim most of his time and money. It was disastrous for the family, she said, especially for the children. What could we do to help? After consulting experts we came to the conclusion that *Opus Dei* was not likely to consciously want to pull married couples apart. A more likely cause was a problem in the relationship. We put Mrs. Wilby in touch with people who might be able to help.

In February of 1995, Mrs. Marshall asked our help to get her 31-year-old daughter out of *Opus Dei*. She said she was looking for an "exit counsellor" who could do so. Exit counselling was a rather forceful technique sometimes paid for by parents to "liberate" their children from a sect. We told her that exit counselling was not the right thing to do. It turned out that the daughter had already been a member for 11 years, and that she rarely came to see her mother. We told Mrs. Marshall that she should talk frankly with her daughter to find out if everything was all right, but that, in the end, she should respect her daughter's free will.

Opus Dei has grown out to be a powerful organization in the Church. Archconservative Popes John Paul II and Benedict XVI rightly judged it to be an ally. In 1982 Pope John Paul II established it as the first and only personal prelature in the Church, with jurisdiction over people rather than a geographic area. With separate branches for men and women, the organization has been headed since 1982 by a prelate elected by its members. The prelate can establish seminaries and promote students to Holy Orders.

My own hope is that the membership – recruited as it undoubtedly is from intelligent and sincere people – will gradually come to recognise its duty to promote genuine reform on all levels of the Church's life.

Other Catholic sects we dealt with were *Regina Laudis*, the New Apostolic Church, the Society of Saint Pius X, and the Catholic Counter-Reformation.

Chapter 29

'Walking on Water'

*O*ne of the stated purposes of our Housetop Centre was to produce tools for religious education that could be used both in our European home countries and our Third World mission territories.

I wondered at the time, in the 1980s, what would be the perfect tool for adult faith formation. Jackie Clackson, my team member in Housetop, and I studied various available options. We realised we would need to combine new information with an element of "parable" to stimulate participants' imagination, followed by a process of discussion and reflection.

Jackie was an artist with a BA degree in Art & Design. In the months leading up to our opening of Housetop, she had studied the use of creative media for catechetics in Lyons, France, and Toronto, Canada. Slides were the favoured medium at the time, and Jackie was a skilled photographer. So we started looking at the potential of slides for the parable element. In fact, for one or two years we used to organise "prayer sessions" in our basement chapel. These sessions consisted of an opening prayer, a display of a series of slides prepared by Jackie, reflection in silence, discussion, and closing prayer.

Jackie's slide presentations were beautiful. They ranged from showing the sun rising over the horizon and throwing ripples of light across the sea, to delicate close-ups of flowers, insects and mushrooms in a spring forest, to faces of agitated men and women in crowded streets. While Jackie projected her slides, she would play matching music in the background.

The prayer sessions were a success. They attracted a wide range of keen participants. But the element of focusing on parts of Christian doctrine was missing. Also, for maximum effect, the slides often needed an inspiring introduction.

Moreover, change was in the air. Video was rapidly replacing slides. Because of its presenting *moving* images, video was far better suited to telling a story. And video was gaining in popularity everywhere.

In 1989, experts at an international meeting in Rio de Janeiro described video as "a wildfire, expanding uncontrollably in all directions, defying economic assumptions and crossing all cultural barriers." Reporting on the video revolution all over the world, *Time* Magazine stated in September of '89:

"From the highest peaks to the deepest jungles, the eyes of the world are glued to the wondrous and irrepressible offerings of the VCR (video cassette recorder)."

There was hardly a place on earth where video was not making inroads, *Time* reported. In some countries, video was people's answer to heavily censured state television. In other countries, video could bring programmes to areas not covered by TV networks. Often video became the poor man's cinema, presented in video parlours that spread to slums and villages.

A good number of priests at the time thought that the use of video in the pastoral ministry was no more than a gimmick, a giving in to the latest fad. But we came to a different conclusion. Video proved, in fact, an entirely new medium ideally suited to support pastoral programmes. Video could help pastors and religious educators communicate more effectively in an audio-visual culture.

So we produced videos like *The Seven Circles of Prayer, Prayer in Your Home* and *Loaves of Thanksgiving*. They were a great success in the UK, but because the stories were presented in an English setting, they could not be used in Asian or African contexts. The production of these early courses proved very useful as a training exercise for me. I learned how to combine video and course book. This taught me how to write film scripts, and it familiarised me with the various stages of a professional production.

But it fell short of our main objective: to support adult faith formation in Third World countries.

International co-production

We faced what seemed like insurmountable challenges. If even in England we had to struggle to find the financial resources needed for making videos, how could missionary dioceses find funding for such a purpose?

Moreover, did the emerging Christian communities in Asia, Africa and Latin America have the local talent needed to create content and story? And if we thought of cooperation between various mission countries, how could we use the same basic material while yet doing justice to the immensely varying local cultures? It was a daunting task.

So I started a long process of worldwide consultation. We needed to find the right principles that an international production would have to adopt. Eventually it led to an eight-day seminar organised for us by the catechetical commission of the Indonesian Bishops' Conference in January of 1988. The seminar took place in a retreat centre on the slopes of the active volcano Merapi on the island of Java. It brought together persons with media expertise, theologians, Scripture scholars and religious educators from all the Indonesian islands, and from some other countries as well.

At the start of the conference I explained my plans and my queries to the assembled experts. I outlined a project of international co-production which I provisionally called "Sitting at Jesus' Feet." Heated discussions in the general sessions and small groups followed over the next few days. As the days progressed, I began to see how we could successfully develop the project.

• One catechist pointed out that in any culture stories from other countries or even continents could be used as long as they were *human interest stories.* People can understand other people wherever they live in the world.

• A Jesuit priest who worked as a TV producer in Germany made me see that, even if a story is the main element of a video presentation, short *slots of instruction* could be inserted at the right intervals, just as advertising slots are routinely inserted in televised narration. These educational slots could link to more complete information in the course book.

• Last but not least, an Indonesian film producer showed me how a locally filmed story could be used in another region as long as the script used *voice-over narration.* This means that, for instance, in a scene depicting a row between a husband and wife, we do not hear the actual words spoken by the two, but a summary by the voice-over narrator who may say: "Her husband Mario is furious because she bought a new fridge without his consent, but she replies that looking after the kitchen is her responsibility, and he should support her rather than always criticise." Discovering this technique was a breakthrough.

Several sponsors helped us to obtain the financial resources necessary to fund our educational programs. Left to right: a representative of AMA (the Netherlands); Heinz Hödl of DKA (Austria); me; Barbara Pauli of Missio München (Germany); Ferdinand Luthiger of Swiss Lenten Fund; a representative of Missio Aachen; and Walter Ulmi of Swiss Lenten Fund.

• We also learned that the original film could have more than one soundtrack: one for background noises, such as the hissing of a boiling kettle of water, and another one for the voice-over narration. To adapt the film to another country, all one needed to do was to translate the voice-over narrator track into that country's language and overwrite that new language track over the original language track.

I realised a truly international set of catechetical video courses could be produced as long as we adopted these principles. Bingo!

With my team, I drew up an audacious project for the production of what we now called the "Walking on Water" series. I managed to get financial backing for the program from a consortium of agencies that included AMA in the Netherlands, *MISSIO* in Germany and *Katholische Jungschar* in Austria. As a member of the Catholic international media organizations UNDA and OCIC, I could give wide publicity to the project and so attract partners from several continents. (UNDA was the International Catholic Association for Radio and Television, while OCIC was the International Catholic Organization of the Cinema and Audio-visual.)

Creating this new network took many letters, journeys, consultations – too long to enumerate. But in due course our project assumed truly international proportions. Cooperating in the project were co-producing centres in Taipei, Taiwan; Nagoya, Japan; Waegwan, South Korea; Helsinki, Finland; Warsaw, Poland; Varanasi, India; Yogyakarta, Indonesia and Montréal, Canada.

The General Assembly of the 1990 International OCIC Congress in Bangkok adopted this resolution:

> The General Assembly of OCIC welcomes the initiative of the "Walking on Water" programme in which more than 25 countries in all continents will co-produce a series of videos on Scripture and Christian life. The General Assembly considers this a pilot project that could clarify principles of future cross-cultural production and distribution. It requests the General Secretariat of OCIC to explore with Housetop ways and means of evaluating the programme in depth before the next General Assembly.

When the 1994 OCIC-UNDA Congress took place in Prague, we advertised the series to its 500 participants from 136 countries. During the Congress I distributed a summary of principles that should guide cross-cultural co-production: "Getting Video Co-Production Right: A Challenge to Christians." We also ran three workshops on "Walking on Water," recruiting 160 feedback advisers from many countries worldwide.

Censorship from Rome

One of the nine "Walking on Water" courses dealt with discrimination against women. It was called "Respecting God's image." The background story

Discussing the Arab version of one of the films in our "Walking on Water" series during a meeting in Beirut, Lebanon, are (left to right) Fr. Jusuf Halit; me; and Jusuf el-Khalidi, the producer.

on the video presents the leadership role of a courageous Indonesian farmer's wife who broke with centuries-old tradition to lead her village out of prejudice and poverty. I will call her "Ratna." The story is based on a true event. I wrote the script for the filming of this story after having visited Indonesia on a fact-finding trip.

The village in question lies in a valley surrounded by mountains and hills. In this account, it did not have a good supply of water for its fields. On one occasion Ratna boldly entered the all-male council of village elders and demanded that they ask the government for an irrigation canal that would need to be dug. Reluctantly, the head of the village gave in. A request was made. The government replied saying it granted permission to dig the canal, but it could not supply bulldozers or other modern equipment. The elders decided to reject the project, but again Ratna stepped in. She stated that the canal could be dug with standard tools.

When the council refused to accept her proposal, Ratna began digging the canal on her own – with a simple spade and a reed basket to remove rubble. For two months nobody came to help her. Then gradually, one by one, other villagers joined in. Finally, after nearly a year of back-breaking work, the canal was completed. The villagers now had irrigation for their fields.

Then I started writing the accompanying course book. I aimed to refute traditional Christian biases against women. In particular, I showed how, contrary

*A scene depicting women at work from our video
titled "Respecting God's Image," filmed in Indonesia*

to medieval convictions, Scripture does not teach that women are subject to men. Rather, the origin of the cultural subjugation of women lay in Greco-Roman thinking. Women were considered inferior to men by nature, just as some human races were considered fit for slavery by nature.

The New Testament message of true equality was revolutionary and daring. The early Christian community had the right vision: of a society where men and women could be truly equal. Unfortunately, as the centuries went by, Christians slid back to pagan ideas. Slavery was tolerated. Other nations were colonized. The Jews were persecuted. Women were denied their rightful place.

The course reflects on the reasons for this sad history. We consider how key biblical texts, such as the story of creation and passages in Paul, were used to justify social prejudices. These mistaken interpretations of Scripture are corrected in "Walking on Water." The way to a new Christian commitment in embracing genuine human equality must begin from a recognition of past errors.

After completing designing the course book in September of 1992, I submitted the draft, as usual, to the Archbishop's House in Westminster to obtain the *imprimatur*.

I was in for a shock. I was told the book could not be given church approval for publication because of strict guidelines received from the Vatican.

The reason, I found out, was a short section in which I outlined that the traditional reasons for excluding women from Holy Orders were not based on valid theological grounds. I predicted that the Church would one day change her mind and start ordaining women. Msgr. George Stack, the Vicar General of Westminster, informed me that in order to receive the *imprimatur* that section had to be removed from the book.

I found myself in a quandary. What to do? Removing that section went against my deep scholarly convictions. It offended my freedom as a Catholic theologian. It did an injustice to the people who would follow the course, people we were supposed to treat as adults.

On the other hand, if I did not receive the official Church *imprimatur*, the text might run into trouble in the many co-producing countries. The section on women's ordination was not indispensable. The course would fight discrimination against women also without that section.

So reluctantly, gnashing my teeth, I had to give in. I omitted that section and received both the *nihil obstat* ("There is no objection against the book") and the official *imprimatur* ("Let it be printed").

Chapter 30

How to make sense of God

Religion seems to fall apart in our secular world. And uncertainty about God lies at the heart of it. The gravity of the crisis was brought home to me by the frank confession of a theologian-turned-atheist.

In the early 1960s I had gotten to know "Fred," as I will call him, in Rome. I met him by chance in a students' tearoom. Well-tanned, cascading black hair, sparkling eyes. Like me, he had been ordained a Catholic priest and obtained a doctorate in theology, but from a different university than the one at which I studied. We had many interesting discussions. Then our ways parted though we kept in touch through correspondence. For decades he served his diocese in a number of demanding ministries. He explained his mental turmoil in a long letter:

> Something terrible happened on my 60th birthday when I went to church. The gospel that day was on blind Bartimaeus and his prayer, 'Lord that I may see.' I suddenly discovered I was more blind than Bartimaeus, ignorant and idiotic, people laughing at me and thinking me crazy for following my naïve belief that God exists. I decided it would be better to be an honest atheist than a hypocritical Christian....
>
> My mind today revolts against seeing Jesus as son of God. Reason is my only light, and rationally I can see him only as a fatherless human being.... God, supposedly in heaven, is a useless father utterly blind to the miserable plight of millions of children he has begotten. How can we call him 'Father'? A tree is known by its fruits. I am proving myself to be an agnostic, if not an atheist. And I consider the biggest curse in this world the proliferation of *Godmen*, organized religions, especially the Churches, the blind leading blind credulous people.

The lengthy letters I sent him did not make him change his mind. I pointed out various reasons to believe in God, working them out at length. For instance:

• Scientists accept "truth" as a norm which they have to obey. The atheist Bertrand Russell treated truth as his god. But he and others never could explain what makes truth so fundamental. From which source does truth derive its immutable nature? It requires a deeper dimension.

• Our life on earth is shrouded in mystery. We are faced with profound questions: Why do we exist? What do we live for? Science cannot provide the answers to such ultimate questions.

• Look around you. See the complex structure and elaborate organization of the universe. Puzzle over the mathematical formulations of the laws of physics. Stand perplexed before the arrangement of matter, from the whirling galaxies to the beehive activity of the atom. Ask why these things are the way they are. Why this universe, this set of laws, this arrangement of matter and energy? Indeed, why anything at all?

Everything and every event in the physical universe must depend for its explanation on something *outside itself* – something non-physical and supernatural. Now, you might object that evolution explains everything. But the point is, it doesn't. Evolution explains *connections within the universe*, not the universe itself.

As I said, my arguments did not make Fred reconsider. Moreover, I discovered that other factors were also at work, such as unfair treatment by church authorities.

Anyway, his witness and others like his that I came across vividly demonstrated the religious crisis we are facing.

Birth of a new course

The practice of religion and belief in God are shrinking in our world. It is undeniable. Catholics worldwide needed to tackle this challenge as a top priority.

So I designed a course that helps people re-discover God in our modern world. It presents Christian faith to the kind of people we have become today: secular and scientifically minded. The majority of people in the West still believe in God, but the image is confused and frequently contradicts implicit or explicit tenets of people's secular convictions. Research showed the need for a new presentation which would provide compelling reasons why belief in God makes sense even in a secular age.

This course, we knew, had to offer a reasoned witness. Its main purpose was to help people *think* about the issues involved. The arguments of atheists and agnostics would be presented alongside modern Christian reasoning. The presentation had to be kept within short chapters, and in semi-academic form, to accommodate people's reduced attention span.

To do justice to this aim, I set up the course to be larger than the previous *Walking on Water* courses. Instead of having just three parts, *How to Make Sense of God*, as we titled it, has five parts, each confronting a key area of discussion:

• Mystery – Do science and religion exclude each other?
• Creation – Does evolution say it all?
• Conscience – Where does our conscience come from?
• Encounter – Is "Incarnation" just an illusion?

Sung Tsu Shou was film director of the section of our educational video that was filmed in Taiwan. The video is titled "Journey to the Centre of Love."

• Love – Are human suffering and a loving God compatible?

When I wrote the 340-page course book, I made sure it was based on a wholehearted acceptance of the positive values of our own age: the freedom and autonomy of the individual, the raising of living standards through technology, respect for human rights, and accepting the sciences as a tool in our search for truth.

But, of course, I pointed out why only by recognizing the presence of "Ultimate Mystery" as a deeper dimension could we make sense of our world. The professional cartoonist Tom Adcock contributed excellent drawings, which are both humorous and enlightening.

I am happy to report that the Catholic Press Association of the United States and Canada recognized the book during their National Convention in Philadelphia in 1996. *How to Make Sense of God* ranked third in the "Popular Presentation of the Catholic Faith" category.

The story re-told in video

I realized that the course needed a very strong "parable" component on video. This eventually resulted in a film called *Journey to the Centre of Love*. It, too, has five parts of 35-minutes duration, corresponding to the five parts in the book.

After researching various possibilities, I opted to make the film around a story that would take place partly in England and partly in Taiwan. Before writing the script for the film, I did extensive research in England. I also travelled to

Taiwan with my colleague Hubert de By. Our partners at Kuangchi Media Centre in Taipei allowed some of their staff to be our local guides. One was a lovely young Chinese woman called Zhang Min. I can still see her before me in my mind's eye: her silvery pink face, long black hair, brown eyes, a smile on her lips.

For the story I had in my mind I needed a community of fishermen on the coast. Zhang Min took us in her jeep to various villages. None of them would do: The houses looked dirty, rubbish was floating in the harbors, beaches were littered with abandoned cardboard boxes and tins. In the end, we located a small fishing port that could be used at least for part of the story. But I was still disappointed.

While we were at lunch slurping up our noodle soup in a small roadside restaurant, I said to Zhang Min, "Let's go back to Taipei."

"OK, sir," she replied. "But we are not far from a tourist attraction: Sun Moon Lake. Why not go there? You'll like it."

"Fine by me," I said.

When we got to the inland Sun Moon Lake, I realized I had discovered a source of wonderful new locations that could be used in our film. Along its banks lie Wen Wu Temple, ports for fishing barges and tourist ferries, and a guest house with superb views of a mountain range across the water. I made copious notes. We agreed to stay there overnight before returning to Taipei.

When I wrote the giant script for the 2 hours and 45-minute film, I spread the Chinese story over three main areas: the city of Taipei, the coastal harbor village, and Sun Moon Lake.

With funding received from sponsors we were able to enlist top professionals for the production. Our two film directors were Sung Tsu Shou in Taiwan, who had directed 26 Chinese feature films, three of which received nominations and awards; and Laurens Postma in England, who had directed acclaimed dramas and documentaries for the BBC. Our two leading artists were acclaimed actors: Wu Mai Ling acted in a popular Taiwanese serial, and Marcus Atkinson in modern theatre.

The video won three awards:

• The Tenth International Catholic Film Festival, held in Warsaw (May 18-23, 1995), awarded its Grand Prix to Housetop's TV film *Journey to the Centre of Love*.

• At the 1996 International Film Fest in Columbus, Ohio, USA, the film received the Columbus Award, which is internationally recognized as a hallmark of superior quality.

• At the 30th Houston International Film Festival of 1997, the film won the Bronze Award. The significance of this award is clear when one knows that the film ranked third among 4,150 category entries that were competing from 31 countries.

But not everyone was pleased with our production. A theologian from the U.S. sent me an angry letter.

"Pope John Paul II will be pleased with your effort to prove that God exists," he wrote. "But in your section on 'Conscience,' you give priority to a person's own power of reason. You laud the 'freedom and autonomy God gives us to make our own decisions.' You scorn the authority of natural law God laid down in creation, and of the lawgivers he appointed to guide the faithful."

This letter would prove to be an ominous foreshadowing of the inevitable clash that would darken my world.

Part V

The Clash – and Renewed Resolve

Chapter 31

Inner turmoil leading to action

*A*s I approach this phase in my story I must confess my inability to do justice to everything that took place in the months and years surrounding my decision to resign from the priestly ministry.

How will I be able to describe the complex processes going on in my mind and my heart?

How can I relate the never-ending discussions with friends, family, colleagues and authorities? How can I summarise the hundreds upon hundreds of letters I wrote and received, many of which still fill voluminous files on my shelves?

Regardless, one of the things that is certain is this: An extensive and intricate network of relationships was shaken to its core.

In previous chapters of my life story, I have recorded my growing unease with the way Roman authorities were ruling the Church. Time and again they had shown a lack of pastoral empathy with ordinary people's lives. They had consistently rejected calls from bishops, priests and the laity to reconsider outdated rules and regulations. They were determined, it seemed to me, to quell the legitimate voices of loyal and competent theologians who disagreed with them. Under Pope Paul VI and especially Pope John Paul II the Vatican had turned into a conservative dictatorship that was determined to suppress any attempt to reform.

Things came to a head on May 22, 1994, with the publication of Pope John Paul II's *Ordinatio Sacerdotalis*. In that encyclical the Pope stated:

> Although the teaching that priestly ordination is to be reserved to men alone has been preserved by the constant and universal Tradition of the Church and firmly taught by the Magisterium in its more recent documents, at the present time in some places it is nonetheless considered still open to debate, or the Church's judgment that women are not to be admitted to ordination is considered to have a merely disciplinary force. Wherefore, in order that all doubt may be removed regarding a matter of great importance, a matter which pertains to the Church's divine constitution itself, in virtue of my ministry of confirming the brethren (cf. Lk 22:32) I declare that the Church has no authority whatsoever to confer priestly ordination on women and that this judgment is to be definitively held by all the Church's faithful.

Pope John Paul II, therefore, more or less declared that the exclusion of women from Holy Orders was part of revealed doctrine. He stated that he, as head of the Church, "*definitively*" (Did he imply "infallibly"?) proclaimed the issue resolved. No further discussion should be tolerated, he stated.

Rome's utter rejection of women's ordination shocked me. In one fell swoop, millions of faithful Catholics, mainly women, who fervently hoped the Church would change its stance on the issue, were pushed aside. They were virtually pushed out of the Church because the companion document, *Responsum ad Dubium*, stated that rejection of the Pope's declaration amounted to placing oneself outside the communion of the Church.

Moreover, the Pope was so obviously mistaken. Though no one has a strict right to ordination since it is a call and gift from God, excluding a whole class of human beings from ordination is a clear form of discrimination. The Church cannot, for instance, accept the exclusion of all Africans or Australian Aboriginals from the priesthood. The exclusion of women, which has no valid basis in either Scripture or Tradition, amounts to an intolerable act of discrimination.

My mother's anger surged up in me. She had never had the opportunity to study theology, something she would have loved to do. But from her young years, she felt in her a profound dissatisfaction with the way women were treated in the Church. She refused to be "churched" (a revolt unheard-of in those days). She would protest at all statements from the pulpit that seemed to put women down, insisting that the priest come to our home for further discussion.

On one occasion she argued strongly with Professor Lucas Brinkhoff, OFM, who was a member of the International Liturgical Commission after Vatican II, telling him that the new vernacular translation, "Pray, brethren," excluded all women in the congregation. Brinkhoff disagreed, but when my mother went to Mass the next morning (at which Brinkhoff happened to be the celebrant), his face turned red when he saw her sitting in the first pew. He could not bring himself to say "Pray, brethren." Interestingly enough, a directive from Rome followed after a few months, urging pastors to use inclusive expressions, such as "brothers and sisters."

I have always seen in my mother the perfect example of the *sensus fidelium*, the spontaneous knowledge of what is right or wrong in the consciousness of the faithful. Although I had come to my conclusions about the ordination of women independently of what my mother thought, I knew that I carried in me traces of her deep exasperation!

And this was not the only issue that enraged me.

Married priests

In the matter of obligatory celibacy for priests, I found Rome's harshness distinctly un-Christian.

The core of our Christian belief is that God is love. It is through love that we experience God (1 John 4, 7-8). Tenderness, mercy and love – the way Jesus himself loved – is our greatest commandment and should be the distinguishing feature of the Christian community.

But the authorities in Rome had created a climate of legal discipline and fear in the Church.

For that reason I could not agree with the way Rome treated married couples by imposing obligations which few couples could observe without carrying an intolerable burden. Homosexuals, who are, after all, born that way, were not allowed to be true to the way they were *created by God*, to use theological parlance. People were made to feel guilty, confused about themselves and lacking in self-respect. They were deprived of the joy of inner Christian freedom.

The area in which I felt this most was with regard to Rome's treatment of priests. A great part of my ministry had been devoted to teaching and forming seminarians. Throughout my 39 years of service I had observed how the insistence on mandatory celibacy ravaged the Church's priesthood. The official motivation for imposing celibacy is that married life is not compatible with the priestly ministry. Priests had begun to realize that this is wrong but Rome simply refused to acknowledge the error. Many committed priests I had known abandoned the priesthood in order

Me in 1996-97 wondering what to do... I was in the process of deciding whether to resign my priestly ministry in protest of the Church's appalling policies against women in the priesthood.

to marry and so were lost to the ministry.

Rome was also totally insensitive to the inner agony of so many good priests and the women with whom they had fallen in love. I had witnessed this in many cases from close by.

And I felt all this on a personal level. I knew that in my own case, too, I had been unjustly ensnared into compulsory celibacy by the Church. We were told celibacy was an implicit vow made to God when we accepted the sub-diaconate.

Remember, I was only eleven years old when I entered the minor seminary. Then, in subsequent years, I had been deprived of the opportunity to get to know girls or young women. Meanwhile, I was confronted constantly with the stark choice of giving up my priestly vocation if I did not give up marriage. I was caught in a trap.

Since I have always been serious about my vocation, I had no other option than yielding to the Church's pressure. Moreover, as I said earlier, I could not realistically judge the benefits of the other option, of being married, because I had been deprived of getting to know women on a personal level. Moral theology teaches that one is not bound to keep a promise if one has been deceived about the full implications of the promise. Already, while working in India, I worked out with my spiritual director that the "implicit vow" had been totally invalid in my case.

So I fully empathised with the agony of priests dedicated to their mission who fell in love and who knew, in their minds and their hearts, that the requirement of celibacy had been imposed by the Church, so to say, under false pretences.

All this was forcefully brought home to me by a very sad case which demonstrated Rome's intransigence. One desperate priest, Father Sean Seddon, hounded by Church authorities finally committed suicide by throwing himself in front of a train in November of 1993. Jan Currie, the woman he loved, has provided a full background account. Christian understanding on the part of the Church could have saved his life and their togetherness in love.

Dictatorial Vatican *ukase*

In 1998, another bombshell was dropped: the publication of Pope John Paul II's *Ad Tuendam Fidem*.

This "*motu proprio*," this edict, added demands of total submission to statements made by a Pope or his loyalists. Canon 750 § 2 was rephrased to read:

> Everything set forth definitively by the Magisterium of the Church regarding teaching on faith and morals must be firmly accepted and held; namely, those things required for the holy keeping and faithful exposition of the deposit of faith; therefore, anyone who rejects propositions which are to be held definitively sets himself against the teaching of the Catholic Church.

And Canon 1371 imposed a penalty on anyone who disagreed.

The official *Commentary to Ad Tuendam Fidem* (June 29, 1998) by Cardinal

Joseph Ratzinger, who later became Pope Benedict XVI, linked this explicitly to the "doctrine" that priestly ordination is to be reserved to men. He wrote:

> The Supreme Pontiff, while not wishing to proceed to a dogmatic definition, intended to reaffirm that this doctrine is to be held definitively, since, founded on the written Word of God, constantly preserved and applied in the Tradition of the Church, it *has been set forth infallibly* by the ordinary and universal magisterium....
>
> Whoever denies such truths is in a position of rejecting a truth of Catholic doctrine and is therefore no longer in full communion with the Catholic Church.

How should I respond?

Remembering the millions of faithful Catholics who firmly believed women should be ordained, I felt the time for action had come.

But what could I do?

Two months of prayer, deliberation, consultation and reflection followed.

I had before my eyes the example of a family man who quit his government job when the department for which he worked adopted a policy that went totally against his conscience. I came to the conclusion that I should do the same. In protest against the official Church's rejection of women priests, I should resign from exercising my priestly ministry.

Note the wording: *resigning from exercising the ministry*, not resigning from the priesthood. "Once a priest, always a priest." I knew my priestly vocation was valid. I did not want to abandon my mission as a priest. And, as Vatican II had clarified, the priestly mission goes deeper than fulfilling sacramental functions in church. Every priest is a prophet, called upon to proclaim the Kingdom of God. I could continue being a priest even while resigning from ministering within the ranks of Vatican-approved clerics.

At the same time, I was conscious of the negative effects my resignation might have on vulnerable groups of people. I thought of the priests, religious and lay people I had taught in India. I thought of my colleagues in Mill Hill Society. I thought of the persons I had touched through my writings, the video courses, the workshops and seminars organised by Housetop. I realised it was crucial that I explain my action clearly to each of these groups.

I had meetings with the Society leaders in Mill Hill. I visited family members and sponsors in the UK and the Netherlands. I wrote explanatory letters to key persons such as bishops and pastoral leaders in England with whom I had dealings. I sent a personal message and an information pack to all the bishops in Andhra Pradesh, asking them to pass on the information to their priests.

* * * * *

When I consulted key persons about my decision, I encountered a wide range of responses. Some urged me to reconsider. Among those was Cardinal

Hume, Archbishop of Westminster, a pastoral leader whom I highly respected. I had written him a long, five-page letter setting out in detail the reasons why I was contemplating withdrawing from exercising my priestly ministry.

I am publishing his reply because it is representative of the advice I received from Church leaders. It also provides me with another opportunity to clarify why I was taking the step I felt I had to take. Cardinal Hume wrote:

"I ask you to reconsider your decision.... When we as priests walk away from the institutional Church, we are being, to some extent, self-indulgent. Who am I to think I can do better? Who am I to sit in judgement on others? Do be careful of thinking that you are wiser than the rest of us in the institutional Church. It is always important, I find, to say to oneself, 'But I may be wrong.'"

The Cardinal was obviously well-intentioned. He was voicing the objections I had heard from many others, too. However, the three reasons he gave me for reconsidering my decision were wholly inadequate.

Stay loyal to the authorities?

Cardinal Hume's letter went further:

"It is not easy to exercise authority in an institution where sacred and holy things have been entrusted into such frail hands as ours. I do think there is much in the Church which many of us find difficult, but then I think of our Lord's words: *Do you also wish to go away?*"

It is clear that the Cardinal implied that Christ is on the side of the authorities who – poor things! – are doing a difficult job. By "going away" from them, he meant we are abandoning Christ. But is that so?

I felt strongly that this was a misjudgment. Christ was much more on the side of the underdogs. To mention just a few:

• Christ was on the side of the tens of millions of Catholics who were suffering because of the Church's total rejection of artificial contraceptives in family planning: poor parents producing more children than they could afford to look after; wives infected with AIDS because they could not protect themselves against husbands carrying the disease; educated Catholics who followed their own consciences while using contraception but who were yet burdened with a simmering sense of guilt.

• Christ was on the side of the millions of women who rightly felt reduced to being second-class citizens in the Church because the priestly dignity they had received in Baptism was denied to them in sacramental ministries.

• Christ was on the side of the tens of thousands of married priests and their wives who were treated as pariahs. As the Austrian bishop Reinhold Stecher wrote in May of 1998:

> The most disturbing example, for me, of neglecting divine commands is
> our treatment of priests who have married. In my own experience, requests for

laicisation forwarded with the bishop's urgent endorsement, for pastoral and human reasons, lie in Rome unread for ten years and even more. Consider that what is being requested is simply reconciliation with God and the Church, the possibility of having a Christian marriage and, in some cases, being admitted to non-priestly ministries. Here too all we hear is a merciless 'No' from the Vatican. What did Jesus say? Did he not make the duty of forgiveness and reconciliation the highest duty in all his words, parables, and deeds right up to his final prayers on the cross?

It was a harshness I myself had encountered in many examples when I was Vicar General of Mill Hill.

And as to quoting the Gospel, why not think of Christ lambasting religious leaders who are "blind guides, that tie up intolerable burdens and lay them on people's shoulders?"

Resisting 'self-indulgence'?

"*When we as priests walk away from the institutional Church we are being, to some extent, self-indulgent,*" Cardinal Hume wrote.

But, wait. Self-indulgence is defined as the lack of self-restraint or as the pursuit of one's own comfort and pleasure. Now, it is true that loosening oneself from the control of religious authorities does bring relief from some stifling rules and regulations. On the other hand, giving up the official support of the institution inflicts other losses, such as status, a cozy job and a steady income, to mention but a few. In fact, I was wondering whether those within the institutional Church who toe the line were not more self-indulgent than I was?

What about the self-indulgence of all those leaders who knew that some of Rome's views were clearly wrong and yet gave in to its claims so as to preserve their privileges? For example:

• The bishops in their palaces and parish priests in their rectories who played along with Rome because they did not want to "rock the boat"...

• The theologians teaching in seminaries and colleges who would lose their jobs if they said publicly what they knew to be true...

Many of those, I am sure, would not call it self-indulgence, but self-preservation in a Church bent on suppressing all dissent.

'Modesty'?

"*Who am I to think I can do better? Who am I to sit in judgement on others? Do be careful of thinking that you are wiser than the rest of us in the institutional Church. It is always important, I find, to say to oneself, 'but I may be wrong,'*" the Cardinal went on.

This part of his letter really upset me. Of course, modesty makes sense. Yes, we can make mistakes in our assessments. On the other hand, this appeal to modesty amounted, in fact, to my giving up my own power of reason. If I surrendered to this kind of thinking, I would always be forced to yield to the official point of view.

I have already recounted how, during my college studies, I had come to a recognition of my own responsibility as a thinking person. I had decided then never to accept any "party" doctrine without having tested it with my own intelligence. After all, like any other human being, I had been created in God's image. God gave me an intellect. God expected me to base my judgements, after careful scrutiny and respecting the guidance of experts, on my own intellectual assessment.

Modesty, yes, but not at the expense of rejecting my own critical evaluation of things.

Moreover, I had been professionally trained in the study of Sacred Scripture and theology. I had, so to say, become an expert myself. As the Second Vatican Council had laid down, it was not only my right but also my duty to express my findings even if they contradicted what was officially presented as "doctrine." I knew then – as I still know today – that the claims made by the Congregation for the Doctrine of the Faith and by the Pope regarding mandatory celibacy and in so many other matters were simply wrong. They go counter to Sacred Scripture, the true understanding of Tradition, and the principles of sound Catholic theology. Telling me to "shut up" because I might be wrong – without even discussing my documented reasons or my conflict of conscience - struck me as odd, indeed.

And what saddened me in all this was the realization that even Cardinal Hume, well intentioned though he was, did not grasp the importance of *listening* to what individual Catholics, even experts like myself, were saying. Our view was discounted from the beginning as "just a private view, which may be wrong." People at the top of the hierarchy were convinced that they possessed the full truth. There was no need to pay attention to the growing mismatch between the "Catholic sense" of ordinary faithful and the officially imposed belief. There was complete unwillingness to hear what competent pastors and theologians were saying.

In fact, a regime of repression had been put in place. Dissenting voices were silenced. Papal commissions were filled with "yes-men" willing to prove the party right. Bishops were chosen only from among men prepared to pledge unwavering support to a pre-determined order.

In short, advice such as given by Cardinal Hume was not the answer.

I had to act. I had to take responsibility. I had to openly express my disagreement with Rome's erroneous views.

My voice would be heard only if I publicly withdrew from taking part in the priestly ministry. And that is what I decided to do after writing a polite, short reply to Cardinal Hume and others like him.

Chapter 32

Stepping down from my official position

On September 7, 1998, I expressed my decision in a letter to the Pope. Ten days later I made my resignation publicly known through a press statement:

"I have resigned from the priestly ministry on account of a conflict of conscience with the supreme authority of the Catholic Church in Rome."

I explained that my reasons were mainly the exclusion of women from the priesthood, but also the total ban on artificial contraception, the imposition of obligatory celibacy on clergy of the Latin Rite, and the condemnation of homosexual relationships. I also stated clearly that I withdrew from the public *ministry* as a priest, not from *being* a priest.

News of my resignation and the reasons for it were widely publicised. It appeared in *The Tablet*, *The London Times*, *The Daily Telegraph*, *The Guardian*, *The Universe*, *Catholic Herald*, *The Herder Korrespondenz* (Germany), *Trouw* (the Netherlands) and *Time* Magazine (USA), to mention just a few.

Once the news was out, I received an avalanche of responses. The vast majority were positive. They revealed widespread disquiet in the Catholic community about the dictatorial methods employed by our Vatican leaders. A Catholic couple sent me this letter:

> My husband and I would like you to know how much we applaud your resignation. We appreciate the courage and the agonising that it must have taken, and we wish that more priests would stand up and be counted. We always enjoyed your contributions to *Mission Today* and *The Tablet*. As Catholics, we feel very isolated now with all this repression of freedom of thought. We can only "hang on in," making our voices heard even if we are often viewed as heretical. I'm sure the truth will prevail in the end – how long, oh Lord? How long?

And here is the cry from an anguished layman:

> You are so right that the priests "on the ground" are more in-touch with Christ's compassion than the abstract hierarchy. Thirty years ago, my wife continued to dutifully attend Mass, but could not receive Communion. Why? Because she was in a state of constant "sin" over contraception after having our three children. (We could not afford a bigger house.) Finally, a priest allowed her to go to Communion.
> My wife's youngest brother is a homosexual who believes in only one

lifelong "friend," as far as I know. He is an immensely good-hearted and generous man – and a regular churchgoer, so obviously he also has found a sympathetic priest who understands that God creates Diversity.

I joined an oriental cult because I was seeking the Holy Spirit – God – some Spiritual Reality & Love which I did not find in our local priests. [A problem] in the Vatican is to do with POWER – a power which Christ never exercised – *the control of minds.* Jesus never exercised power-through-fear, as the Church has constantly done. [Some of thier] rules are absurd and have nothing to do with Christ....

Reactions in India

As I have stated before, when I decided to publicly resign from the ministry, I had also made up my mind to minimise any pastoral damage it might do to people to whom I had ministered. And among those, India featured prominently. For 14 years I had taught in St. John's Regional Seminary in Hyderabad, and at the National Biblical Catechetical Liturgical Centre in Bangalore. Then, after 1984, I had spent six months every year for many years giving courses and retreats all over India. What impact would my resignation have on all the priests and religious I had taught, and on the thousands of lay persons who had read my books?

I realised that giving good information would be crucial. So I compiled a special dossier which I entitled "Personal Report." It contained my press statement as well as background documentation on the precise issues I was protesting about.

From two weeks before I released my press statement, I began sending out copies of this dossier with personal letters. They were addressed to each of the eight bishops of Andhra Pradesh, and to the heads of the various institutions I had been dealing with: St. John's Seminary, the Conference of Religious of Andhra Pradesh, *Jeevan Jyoti, Amruthavani, Jyotirmai,* the NBCLC in Bangalore, and so on.

I received a mixed response.

The Archbishop of Hyderabad, Samineni Arulappa, who had been a personal friend of mine, did not bother replying to my letter. But I heard later from others that he publicly condemned what I had done. Speaking at the plenary session of the Association of Theologically Trained Women of India, held at Stanley Girls High School in Hyderabad in 1999, he said that women in the Catholic Church should be content with having been given duties like Bible reading and offering communion, holding independent positions in religious orders, and managing institutions.

Other bishops were more forthcoming, especially those who had studied advanced courses in theology. I received letters of support from Church historian Dr. Leobard D'Souza, Archbishop of Nagpur; Dr. Gali Bali, Scripture scholar and Bishop of Guntur; Dr. Mallavarapu Prakash, theologian and Bishop of Cuddapah; and Marampudi Joji, Bishop of Khammam.

Many priests and religious sisters also wrote to me in support. Father Christopher Coelho, OFM, a dear old friend of mine and partner in many projects, wrote to me in October of 1998 to say that he considered me a prophet. Being the well-known artist he was, he also sent me a drawing to express his feelings.

All these messages from India moved me deeply. They also confirmed my assessment that most were sufficiently grounded in their own faith and understanding of the Church to not be negatively affected by my resignation.

Reactions from Mill Hill Missionaries

My resignation from the priestly ministry would, of course, affect my membership in Mill Hill Society. I had seen in other cases how religious men and women who protested against Rome had embroiled their congregations in the dispute.

Usually the Vatican had put pressure on the superiors of those congregations to restrain their members by "order of obedience." I had witnessed conservative superiors siding with the Vatican and imposing sanctions on the religious persons involved. I was determined to avoid such turmoil. So I decided that it was best for all concerned if my resignation from the priestly ministry would also terminate my membership in the Society. But there was a problem.

During my six years as Vicar General of the Mill Hill Missionaries practically all its 1,200-plus members had come to know me personally. I realized I needed to minimize any damage done by giving the members a good explanation of

A drawing which my friend Fr. Christopher Coelho, OFM, made for me to express his support for my speaking up for reform in the Catholic Church. It is based on Isaiah 62:1, "For Zion's sake, I will not keep silent."

We, Mill Hill Missionaries, gathered at our annual Assembly meeting in Huissen, on the 27th and 28th of October, would like to show our respect to you and our firm solidarity with your struggle against the institution of the Church that makes it impossible for you, in conscience, to continue in your priestly ministry. We wish you much strength!

Note of support from Dutch Mill Hill colleagues

why I was taking my step. And I needed to make clear that it did not in any way devaluate the missionary work of our Society or my respect for it.

So, well before I issued my press statement, I met Fr. Maurice McGill, the Superior General, and members of his General Council. At first, they tried to dissuade me, but when they understood my reasons they acquiesced. Also, at my request, Maurice sent a letter to all the members setting out what I intended to do well before word reached the media.

I received a lot of responses from Mill Hill members about my resignation. Many were positive; some condemned me for it; others rejected the validity of my reasons. Following are excerpts from a representative sample. I replied with a personal letter to each response I received.

From David Bingham in Serawak, Malaysia:

> So you have allowed yourself to be hijacked by the Politically Correct Establishment – a faction that in their own way can be as inflexibly dogmatic and as sure of the infallibility of their views as any Vatican Curia. Beware of the "feel good" factor – the white knight in shining armor galloping to the defence of the beleaguered legions (??) of ladies who want to become priests.

It should be remembered however, that your decision causes a good deal of distress to many of us who continue to soldier on. Moreover, you have to accept that if you think it is OK to snipe away at the papal teaching, plus accepting the role of a media personality, then you also have to be prepared to accept some flak in your direction.

Jaap Borst, a missionary in India and a one-time colleague, wrote as follows:

Regarding your leaving the priesthood, I respect your integrity. I have always admired not only your competence, but also your zeal for evangelization. Yet, I may perhaps also express my reasons for not following you in this kind of decision....

I surmise that the secular quality of modern thinking has diminished your perception of spiritual realities, reducing it too much to the psychological. I know I could never ever follow you on this point.

On the subject of feminism and women's ordination in particular, I was very open to women's ordination after Vatican II – I couldn't see any objections to its validity. As "Roman" thinking gradually crystalised against it, and this presently so forcefully, I began to ask myself: Have I missed out or overlooked something, some dimension? I ask myself: Is there some deeper meaning and design in sex, gender, gender roles, which in the current upsurge of feminism are not in focus?

But many others agreed with me. My former classmate Wim van Gastel, who was on fundraising in the USA at the time, wrote as follows:

I suppose all of us who do think a bit have problems with what has been going on in the Church for a good number of years.

I've never seen you as a rebel or revolutionary, but a visionary who has helped many people to see Christ as a friend, as the Good Shepherd; never as someone who threatens us with the Codex in his hands.

Honestly, I cannot understand the mentality of the Pope, a Ratzinger, etc. who are highly intellectual and spiritual, I imagine, and yet act like this due to some spiritual pride, power, triumphant Church ideas or whatever, but definitely not inspired by the Spirit. Having lived through a shortage of the traditional priest-figure in all the places I've worked in, and yet hearing all the time that the Eucharist should be the centre of our lives, is a living contradiction in the Church, and I believe that the Eucharist should not depend on the traditional priest-figure.

I am glad to report that I have always been able to maintain good relationships with Mill Hill Society. They have never made me feel an outcast.

Chapter 33

No sympathy from the Vatican

S o far I have written about the events surrounding my declaring in public that I was going to resign from exercising my priestly ministry. But, of course, long before that happened I had been working at sorting out my official position with Rome.

I wanted to avoid simply disappearing from the scene as some other priests had done, mainly to get married. Since I had been officially in the service of the Roman Catholic Church, I wanted my new position officially sanctioned and recognized. Only in that way could I efficiently continue my prophetic mission in the Church.

So, after consultation with Father Maurice McGill, Superior General of Mill Hill, I sent the following letter to the Vatican through the services of Father Hans Stampfer, who was our Procurator General in Rome.

His Holiness John Paul II
Vatican City,
Rome

39 Homer Street,
London W1H 1HL
UK

7 September 1998

Holy Father,

I, John Wijngaards, a member of Saint Joseph's Missionary Society of Mill Hill, request the indult of dispensation from the priestly life and ministry. I have come to this petition after serious reflection and prayer.

I submit to the paternal attention of Your Holiness the following reason. I find myself in an unresolvable conflict of conscience. I cannot, with personal integrity and in conscience, agree to the official position of the teaching authority regarding its ban on the priestly ordination of women.

I will try to minimise as much as possible any spiritual damage that might come to the faithful from my decision to give up the priestly ministry.

Confident of obtaining a kind hearing, I promise to do my best to remain a faithful member of the Church.

Craving your Apostolic Blessing, I remain,

yours devoted in Christ,

John Wijngaards

You will notice that in my letter there is no mention of celibacy. In fact, in a letter to Maurice McGill of August 18, 1998, I had explicitly excluded this as the reason for asking dismissal from the ministry. I wrote:

"After long reflection, discernment and prayer, I have come to the conclusion that I have to withdraw from the priestly ministry. Therefore, I request you to obtain laicisation for me from the Roman authorities and to grant me an indult to leave Mill Hill Society, in accordance with No. C 87 of our Constitution. *There is no need for you to apply, on my behalf, for a dispensation regarding celibacy.*"

A long application procedure followed that would last from September 1998 to April 1999. Hans Stampfer and Father Ludwig Jester, our Mill Hill expert on church law, had various meetings with Dom Piero Amento of the Congregation of the Sacraments. To cut a long story short: The Vatican did not distinguish cases of conscience like mine, they only handled one form of application, which centred around the question of celibacy. I was told I would have to follow this procedure.

I decided to follow suit. In my priestly life, I had discovered how ill-conceived was the imposition of legal celibacy on all priests of the Latin Rite. Moreover, I had come to the conclusion that acceptance of celibacy in my personal case had also rested on faulty assumptions. When we became sub-deacons, we were automatically assumed to have voluntarily embraced celibacy; it even was called glibly "an implicit vow of celibacy." With hindsight, I knew it had been invalid in my case. All this would come out in the subsequent process. I decided to play along.

The procedure of examination

As a person asking to be "laicised," I had become a "petitioner," a term used throughout the process. The key element, it turned out, in Rome's handling of cases of "laicisation" was a form of ecclesiastical grilling to establish the true situation of the petitioner and his genuine motives. So a long questionnaire with 44 questions was handed to me as petitioner. I had to fill in my responses and swear to them under oath in the presence of two ecclesiastical witnesses. The form was called "Interrogation of the Petitioner."

I must confess that, as I read the questions, I felt deep anger surging up in me. So this is how Rome treated priests struggling with a celibacy that had been laid upon them under false pretenses!

Priests who chose to leave the priestly ministry were forced as humble petitioners to fall on their knees and plead for pardon from the almighty Church institution! What is more, to get out of their predicament, they were morally compelled to reveal matters of conscience *under oath* to ecclesiastical judges outside the secrecy of confession! How could a priest in trouble protect himself against such a system? Now, Jesus had told us to be "simple as doves and cunning as serpents," but I decided this was not the time to rock the boat. It was time to play the game.

I still have a copy of the answers I provided. I will not bore you by showing my replies to all questions. They mainly concerned my history and previous ministry, already familiar to you from previous chapters in my story. But I present here a record of the paragraphs that mattered, with my responses.

§ 24. Did you during your time of priestly formation have an adequate appreciation of the reality of living a celibate life? Were there emotional difficulties of any kind? If so, how did you cope with these?

My formation towards a mature attitude to sexual life and celibacy has been highly unsatisfactory.

I did not receive sexual education from my parents. They were shy and felt embarrassed.

Questions I raised with my confessors in the minor seminary regarding chastity were not seriously answered.

Since I had no sisters and since we were explicitly told by seminary authorities to stay away from girls, I had no normal friendships with people belonging to the opposite sex.

Also during my major seminary time the topic was avoided. Of course, I knew the "facts of life" by then, but when I talked to my spiritual directors... my doubts were dismissed as temporary.

§ 32. When did you begin to feel dissatisfied about the Priesthood? What was the nature of the dissatisfaction?

I have never felt dissatisfied with the priesthood as such, but I have gone through a crisis on account of the ecclesiastical obligation of celibacy. As I have explained above, I had not been adequately prepared for celibacy during my seminary training. This caused a lot of turmoil in me during the first decades of my priestly life. I went through a personal search.

During a retreat in 1975 I came to the clear recognition, in consultation with my spiritual director, Fr. Finbar Connolly, CSSR, a Moral Theology professor in Bangalore, that a vow of celibacy in my case had been personally invalid.

The reasons were:

1. I had entered celibacy with substantial errors in my mind regarding the substance of the vow. Full and complete knowledge of the object of the vow was missing. I lacked proper sexual education. I was deprived of the experience of women. I did not understand marriage.

2. I had also been misled by the motive (causa finalis) of the vow since I had been under the mistaken impression that the priesthood and marriage could not go together.

However, I decided not to act on this realisation because of my sense of duty to the people who had been entrusted to me, since I was a priest.

Throughout my ministry I have, in relating to women, not allowed any friendship to become incompatible with my sharing in the priesthood of Christ. Regarding chastity and sexual ethics, I have, as a rule, acted in accordance with my conscience.

§ 35. When did you decide that you would no longer continue as a priest? What were the circumstances that led up to this decision? What were the reasons behind it?

• *The first doubt and initial conflict of conscience that arose in my mind was occasioned by Pope Paul VI's encyclical "Humanae Vitae," because it banned the use of contraceptives in marriage. I was in India at the time. As a theologian I strongly disagreed with the reasons given in the encyclical for the decision. I also deplored the spiritual and moral hardships thus inflicted on the faithful.*

• *I have also been distressed by the Holy Father's insistence on obligatory celibacy for priests in the Latin Rite. I have seen many valuable companions and precious students I had formed in the seminary, being lost to the ministry on account of this practice.*

• *When the Congregation for the Doctrine of Faith published its reasons for rejecting women from the priesthood in 1976, I published counter arguments in my book "Did Christ Rule Out Women Priests?" As a theologian, I continued researching this topic, becoming more and more convinced that there are no valid arguments from Scripture or Tradition that [say women cannot] legitimately and validly be ordained priests. I also became involved in the pastoral ministry of guiding women who are seeking their rightful place in the Church.*

I decided to give up the priestly ministry on account of the "Motu Proprio" of John Paul II, 'Ad Tuendam Fidem' (28 May 1998), and the accompanying letter by Cardinal Ratzinger (29 June 1998). Since these documents prescribe adhering to the belief that women cannot be ordained priests on pain of no longer being in communion with the Church, I felt in conscience obliged to offer my resignation from the priestly ministry.

After long prayer, reflection and consultation, I explained my situation to my Superior General, Fr. Maurice McGill, towards the end of August 1998, when I applied for laicisation.

§ 39. What are your motivations for requesting this dispensation?

The reasons that move me to give up the priestly life and apply for a dispensation are the following:

• *As a theologian I owe it to my own integrity and truth to hold my belief that women can be ordained priests. After long and serious study I am convinced that the ban on women's ordination is not legitimately founded on Sacred Scripture or Tradition, has not been arrived at after proper consultation in the Church, and is harmful to ecumenism and the spiritual wellbeing of the faithful.*

• *I see at the same time that the official Church, whose ultimate pastoral leadership and teaching authority I have to respect, obliges all Catholics to accept its own view.*

This has put me into an intolerable conflict of conscience. I can no longer represent the official Church while disagreeing with it on such a fundamental matter.

§ 40. In the final analysis, why do you find yourself unable to persevere in the Priesthood?

Once a priest, always a priest. I do not intend to give up the priesthood in as far as I will continue, to the best of my abilities, to preach the Good News of Jesus Christ. What I find it impossible to continue, in the present climate of the Church, is to exercise my priestly ministry.

I feel that as long as there is this conflict between the convictions I sincerely hold in my heart and mind as a Catholic and theologian on the one hand, and the official teaching authority of the Church on the other, I cannot resume my priestly work.

§ 41. Have you attempted civil marriage? If so, what is the name of this woman? Is she free to marry?

I have not attempted civil marriage.

§42. Do you have children?

I do not have children.

I submitted my replies under oath in the presence of two witnesses: Fathers Bill Tollan and Fons Eppink, both members of Mill Hill's General Council.

Response from Rome

In total it took 18 months before the Vatican finally communicated its decision. A letter dated February 23, 2000, conveyed the message that Pope John Paul II had graciously granted me dispensation from my priestly celibacy. But I would have to observe the injunctions laid down in an accompanying edict, called a "rescript" in Vatican parlance. This document was also in Latin. Its text is very revealing of the official Church's attitude to its priests. I will present it here in my own translation.

Congregation of Divine Worship and Discipline of the Sacraments, Protocol No: 2090/98/S

Father John Wijngaards, priest of St. Joseph's Missionary Society of Mill Hill, requests dispensation from priestly celibacy and all obligations connected to sacred ordination.

Our Most Holy Lord Pope John Paul II, on the 21st of February 2000, after having taken note of the case through the Congregation of Divine Worship and the Discipline of the Sacraments, has acceded to this request, subject to the following regulations:

1. The dispensation comes into force from the moment of its concession.

2. The written confirmation of this dispensation should be notified to the petitioner by the competent ecclesiastical superior and this should, inseparably, include both dispensation from clerical celibacy and the loss of the clerical

state. Never will it be allowed to the petitioner to separate these two elements, namely accepting the first and refusing the second. If the petitioner belongs to a religious order, this rescript also concedes dispensation from the vows. The same, moreover, brings with it absolution from church sanctions, to the extent this might be required.

3. A note about the concession of this dispensation should be entered into the baptismal register of the petitioner.

4. With regard to the celebration of a legal marriage, the norms should be applied which are prescribed in the book of church law. The local bishop, however, should see to it that the celebration is performed cautiously, without pomp and public display.

5. The church authority whose task it is to notify the petitioner of the rescript should urgently exhort him to take part in the life of God's People, in the manner that is congruent with his new state of life. He (the former priest) should edify people and show himself to be an honest son of the Church. At the same time he should be informed of the following regulations:

6. *The priest who received the dispensation by that fact itself loses all rights attached to the clerical state, all dignities and church offices; he is no longer bound by other obligations bound to the clerical state.*

7. *He remains excluded from exercising the sacred ministry, except in matters referred to in Canons 976, 986 § 2, and therefore he may not preach the homily in church. Moreover, he may not function as an extraordinary minister of distributing Holy Communion, neither may he exercise a leadership role in the pastoral field.*

8. *Also, he may not fulfill any task in Seminaries or similar Institutes. Neither can he carry a leadership role or teaching function in other educational institutions which are somehow under control of church authority. Especially, in such institutions he may not teach a subject that is properly theological or intimately connected to theology.*

9. *However, in lower-grade institutions he may not exercise a leadership role or a teaching function, unless the local bishop, following his prudent judgment and in the absence of scandal, discerns differently with regard to a teaching function. The same law applies to a dispensed priest with regard to religious education in institutes of the same kind not under control of the ecclesiastical authority.*

10. Normally, a priest who is dispensed from celibacy, and all the more if joined in marriage, should stay away from the places in which his previous condition is known. But the local bishop of the place where he lives may,... having taken the advice of the bishop where the priest was incardinated or of his major religious superior, dispense from this rule of the rescript, if it can be foreseen that the continuing presence of the petitioner will not cause a scandal.

11. In that case, a job of pious or charitable nature should be imposed on him.

12. Notification of the dispensation may either be given face to face, or

through a notary or ecclesiastical secretary or through "registered post." The petitioner must return one duly signed copy of the rescript to acknowledge receipt of it, as well as acceptance of the dispensation and the attached rules.

13. At a convenient moment the competent local bishop should briefly report to the Congregation on the fulfillment of the notification, and if some alarm has arisen among the faithful, provide a prudent explanation of it.

(This decree will stand) notwithstanding whatever may be contrary to it.

From the office of the Congregation, 21st of February 2000.

Signed by Cardinal George Medina Estévez, Prefect; Archbishop Francis Pius Tamburino, Secretary; and V. Ferrarer, Notary.

Assessment of the rescript

My request for release from the priestly ministry on the grounds of a conflict of conscience had been transformed into dispensation from celibacy and a reduction to the lay state. Release from celibacy was, on reflection, a bonus. Moreover, there was a tacit acknowledgment of the principle "once a priest, always a priest." For the reference to Canons 976, 986 § 2 meant that, in case of people needing the administration of an essential sacrament, I would not only have the right, but also the duty to exercise my priestly power.

But the overall tenor of the document was truly atrocious. It utterly lacked pastoral sensitivity.

Where was the recognition of all the faithful services I had rendered the Church as a priest during the 39 years since my ordination? No single word of thanks.

Where was the pastoral empathy about my conflict of conscience, of the inner turmoil that had forced me to take this unusual step?

Where was the concern about my future, about how I would be able to make a living, about my spiritual welfare?

Instead, was the whole emphasis not on protecting the institution from "scandal," from people being upset by hearing about my "misdeeds" or "failings" as a priest?

And then, inflicting insult upon injury, was it not bent on avoiding, at all costs, that a treacherous person like me should "infect" others through my holding a teaching post in a seminary or university?

I did get married in due course, as I will explain in the next chapter. It proved a true and precious blessing indeed. But the experience of going through this process exposed once more the people-insensitive, law-centered steamroller the institutional church had become.

Walking with interior freedom...

Reflecting on my situation, I decided not to take too much notice of this Vatican thunderclap. Yes, I had officially withdrawn from ministry within the Church – and some doors would remain closed. But I had not given up being a priest, as I had written in my statement. Also, in spite of Vatican prohibitions, I would continue to express my honest views as a theologian.

In other words, I decided in my conscience that Christ's judgment of my position differed fundamentally from the stark condemnation by the official Church. Christ wanted me to continue as a priest for those who sought my help and as a prophetic teacher in a Church so badly in need of reform.

That is what I have tried to do ever since.

Confirmation of the validity of this approach came years later. It happened to Fr. James Alison, a priest and theologian like myself, who had also been caught in the ecclesiastical juggernaut. James had discovered that the Church's assessment of his being gay was totally unacceptable from a theological point of view. It led to him being dispensed from membership in the Dominican Order. When he sought to be incardinated in a local diocese, he did not succeed.

In spite of him not having asked for it, he received the same document of "reduction to the lay state" as I had, with the prohibition to not "teach, preach or preside." James complained about all this in a personal letter to Pope Francis which reached the Pope because a bishop, a friend of James, gave it to the Pope during a personal audience.

And the Pope responded by speaking to James by telephone on Sunday July 2, 2017. In a long, friendly conversation, Pope Francis' message came to this:

"I want you to walk with deep interior freedom, following the Spirit of Jesus. And I give you the power of the keys. Do you understand? I give you the power of the keys."

Reflecting on the implications of the message, James noted that the Pope, the ultimate authority in the Church, clearly overruled the sentence imposed by the Vatican Congregation for the Clergy. James wrote:

"He clearly treated me as a priest, giving me universal jurisdiction to hear confessions. He was trusting me to be free to be responsibly the priest that I have spent all these years becoming. For the first time in my life in the Church, I had been treated as an adult by an adult, and – good Lord! – it takes the Pope himself to act like that." (*The Tablet*, September 28, 2019, pp. 14-16.)

Well, if this is what the Pope said to James Alison, why should it not apply to me as well?

"I want you to walk with deep interior freedom, following the Spirit of Jesus. And I give you the power of the keys...."

Chapter 34

My marriage to Jackie Clackson

Over the course of the years, Jackie and I had come to know each other extremely well. Even when we ministered in India, our paths had crossed a number of times.

Founding Housetop Centre together, living in the same house, and shouldering joint responsibility for many apostolic projects had brought us very close. We found that we shared the same vision and could produce results as a well-knit team. But we had also bonded on a personal level. We respected and appreciated one another and, yes, I will say it: We began to love each other.

I realise it is time to introduce her in more detail.

Jackie is the daughter of Norman Clackson, who was sales manager of the *Yachting Monthly*, and Tess Nichols. She was born on March 27, 1937, in Muswell Hill, London. Within the same year, the family moved to their new home, Coppins, by Woodside Green in Great Hallingbury, Essex. During World War II, her father served as a lieutenant-commander in the British Navy.

For her primary and secondary education, Jackie attended Chantry Mount Girls' High School in Bishop's Stortford. It soon became apparent that her strengths lay on the cultural and artistic side of life. She scored high marks for English literature, drawing, art, and music. She received special piano classes and also played the guitar. In this respect she took very much after her mother, Tess, who won first prizes at local flower shows for her artistic flower arrangements and who was given major parts as an actor in a local theatre club.

Jackie qualified as an artist at the London School of Art and Design, and as an art teacher at Goldsmith College. She demonstrated considerable skill in book illustration, woodcuts, oil painting, sculpture and pottery. During her time at college she also searched for and found God.

Jackie's mother was a Catholic, but she did not practise. Her father, Norman, as an avowed agnostic, insisted on Jackie's being educated in secular schools. So she had really grown up without religion.

Discovering God

From her childhood, Jackie had pursued a deep, personal, interior life. She kept copious notes of it in her diary. Although she consciously accepted the existence of God later during her time at college, she traces the origin of her faith to a much earlier time.

"As a child, sometimes I glimpsed a greater depth. Sometimes I sensed another dimension. Perhaps the background to an appreciation of the fullness found in silence – in my thinking when I walked through fields and forests. Or again when I sailed over wind-powered waves of an estuary along the lonely East Coast meadows, their flat cloud-filled horizons stretching between cornfields and trees – Constable country – and only river birds calling and sky larks, high beyond sight, saturating the drying marsh grass with cascades of silver sound."

In college, she was confronted with the direct question: "Do you believe in God, or not?" She did not know what to answer. It put her on a long path of searching. Then, as she tells us:

"Someone suggested an experiment. You decide that there is no God, and keep this decision up for a week. Then you will see at the end of the week whether you really do or don't need to believe in God. Looking back I can see that it was a pretty shallow kind of theology, to say the least! But for lack of anything better, I thought I'd have a go at that. It certainly did one thing for

Jackie as a teenager with her pony, "Puffin," in Great Hallingbury, England

Jackie in 1956 while completing her BA as an art teacher in Goldsmith College, London

me: At the end of that week I realised how empty and meaningless life would be without some kind of belief apart from material things... and I hadn't until then realised just how much I did pray. I knew that maybe I had no proof for others but that I did believe, and I could never again see my life stretching ahead for years without some religious belief."

Friendship with a Pentecostal classmate opened another question: "What about Jesus? Should I be a Christian?"

Months and months of further intensive search followed. Jackie visited communities belonging to a wide range of denominations. In the end she decided to become a Catholic. The rich symbolism displayed in Catholic churches and rituals spoke to her. Also, she liked the truly international nature of its worldwide community.

After some intense instructions by Redemptorist priests in her local parish, Jackie was admitted to the Catholic Church through a conditional baptism – because she found out that her grandmother, who was a Catholic, had secretly baptised her when she was born.

Missionary in India

Jackie's new life as a Catholic took a dramatic turn when she decided to become a missionary. Reading about the plight of so many deprived people in the Third World, she felt she could not just stand by and do nothing, So in September of 1962 she became a member of the Franciscan Missionaries of Mary. This is a religious congregation concerned with educational, social and medical welfare and development in all parts of the world.

She was appointed to India. From 1965 to 1969 she served as assistant headmistress of Rosary Convent High School in Hyderabad. It was a combined primary and secondary school with 4,500 girls from age 4 to 17. Jackie taught art, crafts, religious knowledge and moral science.

In the course of time, Jackie served as headmistress of Fatima Girls' High School in Kazipet, then as principal of Immaculata Industrial School in Hanamkonda. In subsequent years she was coordinator of training and formation programmes for Indian religious sisters in her congregation for three Indian states, as well as research associate at *Amruthavani*, the Catholic Communications Centre in Secunderabad.

On repatriation to Europe, Jackie went for higher media studies in Lyon (France), Ottawa (Canada) and Dublin (Ireland). As I have narrated in previous chapters, she was appointed by her congregation to work with me at Housetop, in London.

Because of disagreement with her provincial superior, Jackie applied for, and was granted, dispensation from her religious vows. Jackie ran Housetop during my long periods of absence abroad. She assisted me greatly in our ministry to victims of the "new religious movements." She designed wonderful illustrations for our *Walking on Water* video courses. We got to know each other very well, and fell in love.

So when, on February 21, 2000, I received from Rome the indult that released

Jackie on her scooter in Kazipet, India, in 1973 while visiting the homes of her students

*Jackie and me in June of 2000 in the Netherlands during
one of the public celebrations of our wedding*

me from the obligation of celibacy, the result was inevitable. We decided to get married. On May 27 of that year, we married in a simple Church ceremony in the Netherlands. We also sealed the marriage civilly in the English county offices in High Wycombe.

Since most of my family live in the Netherlands, we organised a huge party there for my brothers and sisters-in-law with their children and grandchildren. It involved a day out, with the whole clan, in a nature reserve near Arnhem. Soon after that we also organised a feast in England which brought all the Clacksons together in Waltham Abbey.

Chapter 35

Academic research to update the Church

*M*y resignation from my official priestly status forced me to reconsider my priorities. In consultation with my team of co-workers at Housetop Centre, I decided that, instead of aiming at adult catechesis, we should focus more directly on reform of the Catholic Church.

This led to the Centre being transformed into the Wijngaards Institute for Catholic Research. One of our main tools is coordinated international research, and another is providing detailed information on our educational websites.

The need for academic evidence

I had learned a lot at a Women's Ordination Conference held in Baltimore in 1978. I arranged to attend because I happened to be in the USA around that time. The event impressed me. It was well organised. The 2,000 participants were mainly highly educated women: lecturers, teachers, lawyers, physicians. I made new friends. But not everyone was so friendly.

I was the only man participating in one of the workshops. When I tried to make a contribution to the discussion, two women attacked me. They told me men should shut up and listen.

"Why are you here, anyway?" one of the women hissed at me. "From now on, it is up to us women. We will reform the Church!"

I met such aggressive people also later in life. Reform movements not open to men: "We women can manage on our own!"

I understand the frustration of radical feminists, their exasperation with "patriarchy" and "paternalism." But I have always believed that excluding men from campaigns for women's equality is a misguided strategy. It is doubtful that change will come about in the Church without the active support of men. Actually, the organisers of the Baltimore Conference agreed. Fr. Carroll Stuhlmueller, like me a graduate from the Biblical Institute in Rome, was one of the key speakers. And Rosemary Radford Ruether publicly appealed for priests like us to wear our clerical dress during a protest march outside the Catholic Bishops' Conference venue organised for the next day.

More important was another discovery. I found that many participants at the conference believed they could bring about reform simply by shouting out their demands. Apparently, they did not comprehend the roots of the problem. They did not grasp that the persons who were clinging to outdated patriarchal views were not crooks. Rather, they were well-intentioned men and women, committed Catholics who were convinced the exclusion of women from Holy Orders was based on solid scriptural and traditional arguments. Angry screams of frustration would only harden their resolve. Only solid contrary evidence could convince them and ultimately win them over to our way of thinking.

Since that time, when promoting the ordination of women, I have devoted all my energy to strengthening, widening and presenting academic research. The four books I wrote on the question, as well as 23 articles in major Catholic weeklies and magazines, offer *proof*, rather than lamentation.

The Internet as an ally

My resigning from the ministry in protest to John Paul II's *ukase* against women did not pass unnoticed in the Netherlands. One day Prof. René van Eyden invited me to present my views to a theological conference taking place in Utrecht in 2000.

In due course, Jackie and I travelled to Utrecht by car. We spent the night in a roadside motel not far from Utrecht. I did not know what to expect. I knew I had not forgotten my native Dutch, but for safety's sake I created, in Dutch, six diagrams that outlined the main arguments for admitting women to Holy Orders.

The conference took place in a large hall. The audience consisted of professors, lecturers, students, priests and so-called "pastoral workers," i.e, women who had been theologically trained and who fulfilled a wide range of functions in a parish. I was one of two main speakers. When my turn came, I set out my case as forcefully as I could. People in the Netherlands prefer a candid, down-the-barrel approach. The reaction was hugely positive. Two responses stood out for me.

One of the arguments I had used centred round the devotion to *Mary as a priest*, which could be traced to the earliest centuries. It proved that Mary, a woman, had been implicitly accepted as a priest in church tradition. A pastoral worker from Rotterdam Diocese reported that, while on holiday with her husband in Croatia, she had come across an intriguing sixth-century mosaic in the Basilica of Parenzo. It depicts Mary and Elisabeth during Mary's "visitation." Both are wearing the arch-episcopal *pallium* under a chasuble. Remember, Mary was believed to have baptised and confirmed John the Baptist in Elisabeth's womb on this occasion; she was therefore exercising her priestly ministry.

Another response came from Dr. Anne-Marie Korte, who approached me during the break after my talk. Though she was a Catholic and served as professor of religion and gender at Utrecht University, she confessed to me that

A mosaic from Parenzo, Croatia, created in 540 A.D. shows Mary and Elizabeth in priestly garments. Notice the episcopal palliums with crosses under their chasubles.

she had not realised how overwhelmingly the evidence favoured the ordination of women. She then made a valuable suggestion:

"Why don't you publish your findings on the Internet? Then you will reach far more people."

It actually confirmed something that had already struck me. The Irish reform movement *BASIC* (Brothers and Sisters in Christ) had asked me for permission to publish the contents of my book *Did Christ Rule out Women Priests?* on their website. I agreed. In that context, I also searched online for academic material on women's ordination. I found none.

So I opened www.womenpriests.org. In the course of the years, I and my team uploaded thousands of original documents to the website: resolutions by synods and church councils; fathers of the church; medieval theologians; stories of women called to the priesthood; ordination rites for women deacons; discussion of Scripture passages; testimonies to the ministry of the Magdalene; papal documents; classic books and articles on the question; and more. It grew out to become the world's largest academic Internet library on women's ordination, with introductory sections in 25 major languages.

Collaboration

I realised that our research would need to transcend international borders.

Our delegation met up in Rome in March 2017 to present our research report on "The Ethics of Contraception." Left to right are: Dr. Luca Badini (UK), Miriam Duignan (UK), Prof. Dr. Hille Haker (USA), Prof. Dr. Mary McAleese (Ireland), me, and Prof. Dr. Irene Pollard (Australia).

At that time, in order to further specific research projects, scholars would be invited from far and wide to come together in a central location, to take part in a seminar or symposium. There they would present the papers they had prepared, then integrate the findings through discussion in workshops. I myself had participated in such events organised on an all-India level.

The problem was that we could never afford to convene such seminars on a worldwide level. But how else could we have scholars from various continents take part in common research projects?

My younger brother, Guus, then professor of eLearning at Rotterdam University, drew my attention to a new development. Because eLearning was such a new discipline, experts from the USA and Europe created a joint "wiki" to which members could upload reports, information on new developments, assessments, and so on. It was known as New Media Consortium. I, too, joined and for some months experienced for myself how it worked.

I knew it was the answer to our problem. Since then we have developed our own approach. We regularly bring together scholars on specific research questions. They add data to the "wiki" assigned to the project, express their judgment on other data, and help edit the final report that resides on the "wiki." The report is subsequently summarised in a statement or declaration which, in turn, is submitted to worldwide scholarship for approval. It has led to significant results.

For example, our "Declaration on Authority in the Church" was signed by 216 professors and lecturers from more than 100 Catholic universities all over the globe. Our "Statement on the ethics of using contraceptives," which we launched on a United Nations platform, was similarly signed by 178 academics. And the work is still going on.

All findings and recommendations resulting from our research are passed on to the Pope and the relevant congregations in the Vatican. At the same time, we also publish the information in detail on our websites, mainly for the benefit of Catholic academics, pastoral leaders and educated faithful.

Leaders at the top must learn to listen. They have to free up church doctrines and practices from the accumulated burden of ancient and medieval errors that infect them. Which brings me to number ten in my commandments for Church reform:

Update Church doctrine and practice after listening to the advice of independent, competent scholars, pastoral councils, and experienced pastors.

Glossary

apostolic letter – shorter papal document that is mainly pastoral in character

bishops' conference – official assembly of Catholic bishops in a particular territory

catechumen – a person undergoing instruction before Baptism

celibacy – the practice of abstaining from marriage and sex

"churching" – a custom formerly practiced by Catholics in several countries in which women who had recently given birth had to be ritually "purified" (from menstrual stains) before being given Holy Communion. Deemed to be "unclean" and thus prohibited from Communion for 40 days, she would present herself at the church door with a candle in one hand and an offering in the other. She was then blessed by the priest and cleared for Communion.

concelebrating – priests presiding together at the same Eucharistic celebration

Congregation for the Doctrine of the Faith – the Roman department that assesses questions of faith and morals

consecration – the moment at Mass when the priest, in the name of Christ, says "This is my Body," "This is my Blood"

dispensation – releasing a person from obligations incurred by a vow

encyclical – longer papal document that treats a topic in depth

excommunication – declaration that a person no longer belongs to the Church

exegesis – the science of determining the original meaning of an inspired text, especially Scripture

exorcism – the rite of driving the devil out of a person

First Holy Communion – the festive occasion when a person receives the Body of Christ for the first time

General Chapter – assembly by delegates of a religious congregation to elect new superiors and reassess policies

hermeneutics – the science of interpreting the meaning of an inspired text, especially Scripture, for our own time

the Holy Office – previous name for the Congregation for the Doctrine of the Faith (See above)

Holy Orders – the episcopacy, priesthood and diaconate

incardinate – assigning an ordained person to a diocese or religious congregation

licentiate – a degree awarded by an ecclesiastical institute equivalent to a Master's Degree

major seminary – theological college for the education of future priests

minor seminary – high school for the education of future candidates for the priesthood

motu proprio – papal document containing an important declaration

new religious movements – sects mainly from the East invading Europe and North America in the 20th century

Opus Dei – controversial religious order founded by Josemaría Escrivá Balaguer

paten – a small gold-covered plate to hold the host during the Eucharistic celebration

personal prelature – an ecclesiastical structure independent from the jurisdiction of any diocese

pharisee – Jewish religious person dedicated to a strict observance of the law

prelate – an ecclesiastical dignitary

Roman *Index* – list of books forbidden by the Vatican

Second Vatican Council – a gathering of all Catholic bishops from around the world from 1962 to 1965 to lay down instructions on faith, morals and religious practice

sects & cults – another name for the "new religious movements" (See above)

sede vacante – means "while the papal See has no occupant," while the chair is vacant

sensus fidelium – a Latin phrase translated as "sense of the faithful," this means the intuitive grasp of correct Christian doctrine by the faithful. Also, how the faithful together understand and live the faith

stigmata – miraculous wounds on the hands and feet of some visionaries, said to be copies of Jesus' wounds while on the cross

Vatican II – alternative name for the Second Vatican Council (See above)

Vicar General – second in command in a diocese or religious congregation

Appendix 1

Ten Commandments for Church Reform

1. Allow theologians and other scholars unrestricted freedom of research.

2. Recognize that a pastoral leader's first priority is caring for people, not upholding ecclesiastical institutions.

3. Select perceptive administrators in the Roman Curia, not narrow-minded bureaucrats intent on blocking Church reform.

4. Appoint open-minded, pastoral bishops, not hard-line traditionalists.

5. Abandon the misguided repression of sex advocated by St. Augustine.

6. Grant parents total freedom to plan their families responsibly.

7. Give women full access to Holy Orders.

8. Allow priests to benefit from the support of a loving spouse.

9. Respect and promote the adult dignity of every member of the community.

10. Update Church doctrine and practice after listening to the advice of independent, competent scholars, pastoral councils, and experienced pastors.

Appendix 2

Timeline

(The Life and Times of John Wijngaards)

1935 – 1939	Childhood	Surabaya, Indonesia
1940 – 1942	Nursery school	Malang, Indonesia
March 1942 – May 1943	POW Camp Bergenbuurt	Malang, Indonesia
May 1943 – May 1945	POW Camp Mankubhumi	Surakarta, Indonesia
May – Dec. 1945	POW Camp 6	Ambarawa, Indonesia
Dec. 1945 – May 1946	Rehabilitation camp	Tah Muang, Thailand
1946 – 1947	At home	Baarn & Utrecht, the Netherlands
1947 – 1951	Missionary College	Hoorn, the Netherlands
1951 – 1953	Missionary College	Haelen, the Netherlands
July 24, 1953	Passed 'Staatsexamen A' [Dutch University Entrance Exam]	Amersfoort, the Netherlands
1953 – 1955	Studying Philosophy	Roosendaal, the Netherlands
1955 – 1959	Studying Theology	Mill Hill, England
July 12, 1959	Ordained a priest as a Mill Hill Missionary	London, England
1959 – 1963	Higher studies. Obtained the *Licenciate of Sacred Scripture* [MA] at the Pontifical Biblical Institute and the *Doctorate of Divinity* at the Gregorian University.	Rome, Italy

1963 – 1976	Professor at St. John's College, Hyderabad; moderator of the Conference of Religious for Andhra Pradesh; founder of *Jeevan Jyothi* formation college for Sisters and *Amruthavani* media centre; lecturer at the *National Biblical, Catechetical and Liturgical Centre* at Bangalore; secretary of the *Catholic Biblical Association of India*; member of various commissions of the *Catholic Bishops' Conference of India*.	Hyderabad, India
1976 – 1982	*Vicar General* of the Mill Hill Missionaries; *Director of the Home Regions* annual visits to Austria, Belgium, Canada, England, Ireland, Italy, the Netherlands, Scotland, and the USA.	Headquarters in Mill Hill, England
1983 – 1998	Director of *Housetop Communications Centre* and Professor at the *Missionary Institute London*. Five months each year as visiting lecturer to India.	Main location London, England
Sept. 7, 1998	Resignation from the priestly ministry	
Feb. 21, 2000	Decree of 'laicisation' from the Vatican	
May 27, 2000	Married Jackie Clackson in a church wedding	Arnhem, the Netherlands
1998 – now	'Housetop Centre' upgraded to *Wijngaards Institute for Catholic Research*. Director of the Board.	Denham, North London, England

Appendix 3

My resignation from priestly ministry

(Press Statement of September 17, 1998)

I have resigned from the priestly ministry on account of a
conflict of conscience with the supreme authority
of the Catholic Church in Rome.

Over the past decades I have become increasingly uncomfortable with
the official Church's decrees concerning sexual doctrine and ethics. Married
couples are forbidden the use of contraceptives, even if applied with discretion.
Obligatory celibacy remains arbitrarily imposed on clergy of the Latin Rite in
spite of the spiritual anguish thus inflicted on many priests and their flocks.
Homosexual partnerships are discriminated against. And – the last straw, as far
as I am concerned – women are barred from ordination to the priesthood in
spite of there being no proven objections from either Scripture or Tradition.

The official teaching emanating from Rome in these matters has done and
is doing great damage to the Body of the Church. Millions of believers have
stopped attending the Eucharist on account of it, turning for spiritual con-
solation elsewhere. The teaching authority has lost its credibility even among
loyal pastors, who often struggle to limit the damage inflicted by offering their
faithful a more sensitive pastoral guidance than Rome does. Most alarming of
all is the inevitable corruption Rome causes at all levels of responsibility in the
Church by forcing on all a complicity of silence.

- Bishops and Bishops' Conferences fail by not challenging Rome publicly.
- Theologians and theological institutes fail by not standing up for what
  they believe to be the truth.
- Parish priests fail by not reassuring the faithful from the pulpit.
- Religious superiors and seminary professors fail their students by leading
  them into an establishment that will inhibit their autonomy and responsibility.

The question of the ordination of women is the breaking point for me
because I have been personally involved in theological research and pastoral
ministry concerning this issue for the last 20 years.

The ordination of women

When the Congregation for the Doctrine of Faith promulgated its reasons
for rejecting women from the priesthood in 1976, I published counter arguments in "Did Christ Rule Out Women Priests?" The booklet, which carried

the *imprimatur*, was reprinted in a number of languages and countries, the last enlarged UK edition appearing in 1986. It has recently been made available on the Internet. I am a member of various organizations which promote Catholic Women's Ordination: CWO (Catholic Women's Ordination), St. Joan's International Alliance, and the Canon 1024 Mailing List. I have continued writing on the question, in spite of Rome's attempt to suppress theological research or pastoral discussion. See my recent article, "Thérèse and the Question of the Ordination of Women" in *Mount Carmel* (November 1997) and *The Catholic Citizen* (March 1998).

Conflict of conscience

I have always considered it my duty, as a theologian and a priest, to sincerely pursue the truth as I perceive it, after careful study and reflection. Vatican II states that "all the faithful, both clerical and lay, should be accorded a lawful freedom of inquiry, freedom of thought and freedom of expression, tempered by humility and courage in whatever branch of study they have specialized" (*Gaudium et Spes*, No. 62). Since I perceive Rome's ban on women's ordination as not legitimately founded on Scripture or Tradition, not arrived at after proper consultation in the Church, harmful to ecumenism, and highly injurious to the spiritual wellbeing of the faithful, I feel bound in conscience to continue voicing my sincere opposition.

On the other hand, I see that the authorities in Rome pursue a policy of rigorous enforcement of the ban, silencing all theological reflection and discussion. Through the *motu proprio* of Pope John Paul II, *Ad Tuendam Fidem* of 28 May 1998 and the accompanying commentary by Cardinal Ratzinger, Prefect of the Congregation for the Doctrine of the Faith, defence of the ordination of women is presented as tantamount to heresy. Anyone who holds that women can be ordained priests is "no longer in full communion with the Catholic Church," we are told (Statement by Joseph Cardinal Ratzinger, 29 June 1998).

In view of this stand of the official Church, whose ultimate pastoral leadership and teaching authority I have to respect in spite of the mistakes it has committed in the past and may still be committing in the present, I am myself in conscience bound to resign from the priestly ministry. I can no longer represent the official Church while disagreeing with it on such a fundamental matter.

Moreover, I want to stand on the side of those men and women who are so casually and unjustly dismissed by the Vatican. It is only by distancing myself now from the institutional Church that I can extract myself from the guilt of taking part in the conspiracy of silence.

Explaining my position

By resigning from the priestly ministry, I have in no way renounced my right and duty as a theologian to publicly express my opinion. Neither have I stopped being a member of the Church itself. All my life I have been a conscientious and orthodox Catholic and I intend to remain so until I die.

I do not want to betray the trust my family, friends and sponsors have always given me. I hope they will accept my conviction that only by following my conscience can I be truly faithful to my prophetic and missionary calling.

I appreciate the position of Catholic bishops, priests and religious who gallantly continue in their ministry in spite of their disagreement with Rome. I respect their sincerity in acting thus for pastoral reasons. I hope they, in turn, will respect mine.

I am deeply concerned about the various groups I have ministered to, such as my former students in India, readers of my books and articles, and those who follow my faith formation courses worldwide. I reassure them that I have not renounced my Catholic faith, and that I stand by all spiritual and theological matters on which I have written and taught.

Finally, I want to express my appreciation and gratitude to Mill Hill Missionary Society. I salute my Mill Hill comrades and colleagues with whom I have shared so much labour and joy during my forty years of membership. I wish them God's speed, and I promise them a never-ending friendship on my part.

– *John Wijngaards*

Index

Note: Page numbers in bold refer to photographs, maps, illustrations.

Photo and Art Credits

Most photographs in this book are from family albums and personal records. However, I gratefully acknowledge the following outside sources:

Pg. 33 – Prisoners-of-war in Thailand march. From *A Life for Every Sleeper*, by H. V. Clarke, Allen & Unwin, Sydney, 1986, p. 28.

Pp. 35 and 36 – Prisoner-of-war camps in Central Java. From *Geïllustreerde Atlas van de Japanse Kampen in Nederlands-Indië*, 1942-1945, E. Braches et al., Asia Maior, Zierikzee, the Netherlands, 2002, pp. 128 & 132.

Pg. 41 – *Tah Muang* camp. From a collection of photographs of Thailand in 1946 by a Dutch journalist whose name has not been preserved.

Pg. 78 – Cartoon by Fred Marcus, printed in *De Bazuin*, circa 1963.

Pp. 98, 144, 146 and 151 – Photographs by Fr. Josef Klotzner, MHM, for *Mission Archive*, the Vatican, in 1973.

Pg. 109 – Photograph from *Mill Hill Archives*, Herbert House, Freshfield, England.

Pg. 138 – Fresco of St. Augustine. From *Wikimedia*.

Pg. 141 – Tombstone of Lucius and Publicia, preserved in the Walters Art Museum, Baltimore, Maryland, USA.

Pg. 163 – Beach scene from *Holidify* Tourist Agency.

Pg. 179 – Cartoon by Tom Adcock in *How to Make Sense of God*, by John Wijngaards, Sheed & Ward, Kansas City, 1995, pg. 254.

Pg. 192 – Photograph of Peter III. *Wikipedia* under "Palmarian Catholic Church".

Pg. 219 – Drawing by Fr. Christopher Coelho, OFM, based on Isaiah 62,1, circa 1998.

Pg. 237 – Photograph of mosaic taken in Croatia by Dr. P.M.E. Hogervorst-van Kampen, August 1997.

About the Author...

JOHN WIJNGAARDS, DD, LSS, is an internationally renowned theologian and Scripture scholar and is the founder of the Wijngaards Institute for Catholic Research, headquartered in London. His is one of the leading voices in the worldwide movement to include women in the Catholic priesthood.

He was a Mill Hill Missionary priest, and from 1964 to 1976 he was stationed in Hyderabad, India. There he taught Scripture to future priests at St. John's Major Seminary, founded a formation centre for religious sisters, and co-founded the Catholic Biblical Association of India. Later, he served as vicar general of his Congregation, from 1976 to 1982.

In 1998, he resigned from the priestly ministry mainly because of a conflict of conscience over the Church's refusal to ordain women.

In a prolific writing career that has spanned six decades, he has authored over two dozen books related to spirituality and theology, some 20 booklets and pamphlets, and 10 film scripts. His books include *What They Don't Teach You in Catholic College*, *The Ordination of Women in the Catholic Church* (in 5 languages), *Experiencing Jesus* and *Background to the Gospels* (in 7 languages).

In 1982 he founded Housetop International Centre for Faith Formation in London, which produced video courses and films for adult faith formation, such as the award-winning *Journey to the Centre of Love*. The Centre developed into the Wijngaards Institute, which runs 16 educational websites and coordinates research on questions of church reform, such as church governance, artificial contraception in family planning, and the ordination of women as deacons and priests. (See www. wijngaardsinstitute.org.)

He is married to Jackie Clackson, a former art teacher, and they reside in Denham, England, a suburb of London.

Publications
By John Wijngaards

1963   *The Formulas of the Deuteronomic Creed*, Brill, Leiden, the Netherlands.

1965   *Vazal van Jahweh*, Bosch & Keunig, Baarn, the Netherlands.

1969   *The Dramatization of Salvific History in the Deuteronomic Schools*, Brill, Leiden, the Netherlands.

       What we can learn from secular efficiency, St. Paul Publications, New Delhi, India.

1970   *Background to the Gospels*, St. Paul Publications, New Delhi, India.

1971   *God's Word to Israel*, Theological Publications, Ranchi, India.

1973   *Deuteronomium uit de grondtekst vertaald en uitgelegd*, Romen & Zonen, Roermond, the Netherlands.

       Reading God's Word to Others, Asian Trading Corporation, Bangalore, India.

1975   *Christ's Idea of Authority*, Amruthavani, Secunderabad, India.

1976   *Mukti Margamu*, Amruthavani, Secunderabad, India.

1977   *Did Christ rule out women priests?*, McCrimmons, Great Wakering, UK.

1978   *Brathuku Baata*, Amruthavani, Secunderabad, India.

       Communicating the Word of God, McCrimmons, Great Wakering, UK.

1981   *Experiencing Jesus*, Ave Maria Press, Notre Dame, Indiana.

1985   *Inheriting the Master's Cloak*, Ave Maria Press, Notre Dame, Indiana.

1986   *The Gospel of John and his Letters*, Michael Glazier, Wilmington, Del.

1987   *The Spirit in John*, Michael Glazier, Wilmington, Del.

       The Seven Circles of Prayer, McCrimmon, Great Wakering, UK.

       Jesus For Ever: Fact & Faith, Catholic Truth Society, London.

1988   *God within us*, Collins, London.

1990   *My Galilee, My People*, Paulist Press, Mahwah, N.J.

       For the sake of his people, McCrimmons, Great Wakering, UK.

1991   *Together in My Name*, Paulist Press, Mahwah, N.J.

1992   *I have no Favourites*, Paulist Press, Mahwah, N.J.

1995 *How to make sense of God*, Sheed & Ward, Kansas City, Missouri.

1999 *www.womenpriests.org*, online archive on the ordination of women.

2001 *The Ordination of Women in the Catholic Church*, Darton, Longman & Todd, London.

2002 *No Women in Holy Orders? The Ancient Women Deacons*, Canterbury Press, London.

2007 Major expansion of *www.womenpriests.org*.

2011 *Amrutha. What the Pope's man found out about the law of nature*, Author House Publications, Bloomington, Ind.

2012 *www.churchauthority.org*, website on church governance.

2016 *www.thebodyissacred.org*, website on the ethics of sexuality.

2020 *What They Don't Teach You in Catholic College: Women in the priesthood and the mind of Christ*, Acadian House Publishing, Lafayette, Louisiana.

2021 *Ten Commandments for Church Reform: Memoirs of a Catholic Priest*, Acadian House Publishing, Lafayette, Louisiana.

Inspiring Books
from
Acadian House Publishing

Ten Commandments for Church Reform
Memoirs of a Catholic Priest

The 264-page memoir of a Catholic priest and theologian who has spent a lifetime advocating for the reform of out-dated policies and practices of the Church. A prolific writer of Christian literature and film scripts, he was the founder and director of a center for faith formation in London, which continues today as the Wijngaards Institute for Catholic Research. This book reveals his "Ten Commandments" for Church reform – ranging from the inclusion of women in the priesthood to the appointment of open-minded, pastoral bishops rather than hard-line traditionalists. (Author: John Wijngaards, DD, LSS. Hardcover ISBN: 1-7352641-5-6; price $22.95. Softcover ISBN: 1-7352641-6-4; price $16.95)

What They Don't Teach You in Catholic College
Women in the priesthood and the mind of Christ

A 216-page hardcover book that makes the case for women in the Catholic priesthood – even though the hierarchy of the Church has traditionally opposed the idea, based largely on their belief that Christ wanted a male-only priesthood for all time. The author, a renowned theologian, disputes that ultra-conservative viewpoint and explains why it is in the Church's best interest to ordain women. (Author: John Wijngaards, DD, LSS. ISBN: 0-9995884-4-3. Price $16.95, hardcover.)

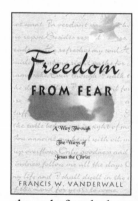

Freedom From Fear
A Way Through The Ways of Jesus The Christ

Everyone at one time or another feels fear, guilt, worry and shame. But when these emotions get out of control they can enslave a person, literally taking over his or her life. In this 142-page softcover book, the author suggests that the way out of this bondage is prayer, meditation and faith in God and His promise of salvation. The author points to the parables in the Gospels as Jesus' antidote to fears of various kinds, citing the parables of the prodigal son, the good Samaritan, and the widow and the judge. Exercises at the end of each chapter help make the book's lessons all the more real and useful. (Author: Francis Vanderwall. ISBN: 0-925417-34-3. Price: $14.95)

Bryan G. Sibley, M.D.

God First
Setting Life's Priorities

A 96-page hardcover book that encourages persons of faith to set priorities, starting with "God first, family second, and everything else third." The book has 10 chapters, with themes that center on gratitude, care for the poor, forgiveness, trusting in God's providence, etc. The chapters are anchored in Scripture and illustrated with inspiring stories from the author's faith journey. (Author: Bryan G. Sibley, M.D. ISBN 0-925417-88-2. Price $14.00)

Dying In God's Hands

A 152-page hardcover book that provides keen insights into the hearts and minds of the dying. It is based on a dozen or more interviews with terminally ill hospice patients, in which they share their hopes, dreams, fears and needs. The majority of the interviews provide evidence that faith in God and belief in the hereafter are the greatest strengths of the dying. Designed to comfort the dying and their loved ones, the book also contains a section of prayers and prose from all major world religions. (Author: Camille Pavy Claibourne. ISBN: 0-925417-64-5. Price: $16.95)

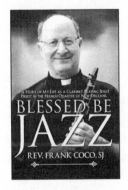

Blessed Be Jazz

The 192-page hardcover autobiography of Rev. Frank Coco, SJ (1920-2006), a Jesuit priest who served for more than 50 years in south Louisiana as a retreat director, high school teacher and jazz musician. Using his clarinet, he performed extensively in New Orleans nightclubs, sitting in with some of the best-known jazz musicians of his time, including Ronnie Kole, Al Hirt and Pete Fountain. (Author: Rev. Frank Coco, SJ. ISBN: 0-925417-89-0. Price: $19.95)

Growing With Eli
Our Journey into Life and Light

Growing With Eli is the third in an inspiring and heart-warming set of books that tell the story of a Lafayette, La., couple and their child, Eli, who was born with a birth defect called *spina bifida*. This volume, published when Eli was 9 years old, tracks the boy's growth from infancy to a healthy, happy youngster. At the same time, on a parallel track, the book chronicles Eli's father's growth in and understanding of his Catholic faith. (Author: Chad Judice. ISBN: 0-9995884-2-7. Price: $17.95, hardcover)

Book 3 of the internationally recognized "Waiting For Eli" trilogy

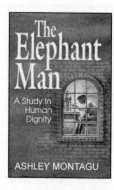

The Elephant Man
A Study in Human Dignity

The Elephant Man is a 138-page softcover book whose first edition inspired the movie and the Tony Award-winning play by the same name. This fascinating story, which has touched the hearts of readers throughout the world for over a century, is now complete with the publication of this, the Third Edition. Illustrated with photos and drawings of The Elephant Man. (Author: Ashley Montagu. ISBN: 0-925417-41-6. Price: $12.95.)

Getting Over the 4 Hurdles of Life

A 160-page hardcover book that shows us ways to get past the obstacles, or hurdles, that block our path to success, happiness and peace of mind. Four of the most common hurdles are "I can't / You can't," past failures or fear of failure, handicaps, and lack of self-knowledge. This inspiring book – by one of the top motivational speakers in the U.S. – is brought to life by intriguing stories of various people who overcame life's hurdles. Introduction by former LSU and NBA star Shaquille O'Neal. (Author: Coach Dale Brown. ISBN: 0-925417-72-6. Price: $17.95)

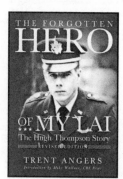

The Forgotten Hero of My Lai
The Hugh Thompson Story (Revised Edition)

The 272-page hardcover book that tells the story of the U.S. Army helicopter pilot who risked his life to rescue South Vietnamese civilians and to put a stop to the My Lai massacre during the Vietnam War in 1968. Revised Edition shows President Nixon initiated the effort to sabotage the My Lai massacre trials so no U.S. soldier would be convicted of a war crime. (Author: Trent Angers. ISBN: 0-925417-90-4. Price: $22.95)

TO ORDER, list the books you wish to purchase along with the corresponding cost of each. For shipping in the U.S., add $4 for the first book, and $1 per book thereafter. For shipping out of the U.S., email us at info@acadianhouse.com for a price quote. Louisiana residents add 9% tax to the cost of the books. Mail your order and check or credit card authorization (VISA/MC/AmEx) to: Acadian House Publishing, P.O. Box 52247, Lafayette, LA 70505. Or call (800) 850-8851. To order online, go to www.acadianhouse.com.